1998

Responsibility Center Budgeting

Responsibility Center Budgeting

An Approach to Decentralized
Management for Institutions
of Higher Education

EDWARD L. WHALEN

INDIANA UNIVERSITY PRESS
Bloomington and Indianapolis

The paper used in this publication meets the minimum requirements of American National Standard for Information Sciences—Permanence of Paper for Printed Library Materials, ANSI Z39.48–1984.

Manufactured in the United States of America

Library of Congress Cataloging-in-Publication Data

Whalen, Edward.
     Responsibility center budgeting : an approach to decentralized management for institutions of higher education / Edward L. Whalen.
p.   cm.
          Includes bibliographical references and index.
       ISBN 0-253-36480-9 (alk. paper)
       1. Universities and colleges—United States—Finance.
     2. Universities and colleges—United States—Accounting.
     3. Universities and colleges—United States—Business management.
     4. Indiana University—Accounting—Case studies. 5. Indiana University—Appropriations and expenditures—Case studies.
       I. Title
       LB2342.W44 1992
       378'.02'0973—dc20   91-14148
1 2 3 4 5   96 95 94 93 92

Contents

List of Tables

Foreword

by Thomas Ehrlich

Expenses rise to exceed revenues. That is an inexorable rule of university administration. It is one of the reasons why responsibility center budgeting makes sound sense for any university.

Ed Whalen tells his story with wit and verve. This book should serve as a guide for any college or university that wants to put its money behind its academic priorities.

Three basic principles underlying this system for the financial management of a college or university can be simply stated: (1) all costs and income attributable to each school and other academic unit should be assigned to that unit; (2) appropriate incentives should exist for each academic unit to increase income and reduce costs to further a clear set of academic priorities; and (3) all costs of other units, such as the library or student counseling, should be allocated to the academic units.

When I came to Indiana University, as Ed indicates, I found a budget system that was virtually impenetrable. It provided no help for deans and other academic administrators trying to set academic priorities. A dean knew the expenses of compensation, supplies, and little else. The costs of space, heat, light, and other utilities, for example, were not part of the school's budget and there was no reason for the dean to reduce those expenses. The income attributable to the school—tuition, state support, grants and contracts—was similarly not part of a dean's budgetary domain. No rewards existed for increasing that income.

The eyes of business people begin to roll at this point. They ask why institutions of higher education stayed with this outmoded budgetary approach—an approach that divorces academic responsibility from budgetary authority. Full-cost and income accounting has, after all, been part of the business scene for many years.

I am not clear why the development of what we call responsibility center budgeting has taken so long. When I went to the University of Pennsylvania in 1981, a similar system had been in place for some years, and it was also in operation at the University of Southern California in somewhat different form. A few other private institutions, I have been told, have also adopted it. My colleagues at Indiana University spent considerable time working with their counterparts at USC, though each institution faces special issues that make its system unique. Insofar as my Indiana University colleagues are aware, however, other public and private colleges and universities have not yet followed suit.

My hope, of course, is that Ed's book will be a best-seller and that many colleges and universities will adopt his insights. At the same time, it may be wise to underscore two key cautions. First, responsibility center budgeting does not: (1) produce any more money for an institution; or (2) set academic priorities for an institution. Indeed, the system should not be followed unless an institution has clear academic priorities and is prepared to follow those priorities with its budget. Second, the system can be misused, like any other system. As an example, it makes no academic sense for a business school to replicate an existing math course in a school of arts and sciences simply to increase its income. Needless duplication of courses would be a misuse of the system and must be proscribed through clearly defined roles and missions of the academic units. Similarly, if a public university enrolls in-state and out-of-state students at different tuitions, those differentials should not become an incentive for schools to compete with each other for out-of-state as opposed to in-state students. Such competition serves no useful purpose from the institution's perspective.

Any financial system of management can, in short, be mismanaged—and the one discussed by Ed Whalen is no exception. But that caution should not lessen enthusiasm for responsibility center budgeting. It provides powerful tools to assist academic leaders in ensuring that their budgets follow—not lead—their academic priorities. Anyone concerned about the quality and costs of higher education should pay attention.

Preface

Like Thucydides, who wrote the history of the war between the Peloponnesians and the Athenians, I began this account of the development of responsibility center budgeting at Indiana University at the moment it began, believing that it would be an important occasion, and more memorable than any that had preceded it. One of Thomas Ehrlich's first acts after he became President of Indiana University was to initiate a move to responsibility center budgeting. From the vantage point of the University Budget Office, I had an opportunity to observe, participate, and even on occasion to direct the ensuing proceedings.

Unlike Thucydides (probably), I wrote parts of this chronicle before events actually occurred. Once writing commenced, its usefulness as a reference in recording how Indiana University undertook and is undertaking its transition from a traditional and centralized system of planning and budgeting was often demonstrated. Anticipating events that were about to happen required only a little imagination and some extra effort. When new approaches were being developed, describing them in writing and explaining how they were to work before and as they were presented to others proved helpful. Harsh realities and the good ideas of others required substantial revisions of the original written material, but the course of events was not entirely unaffected by the writings that preceded it.

Responsibility center budgeting is a system designed to help institutions of higher education accomplish their objectives more effectively. It puts in place incentives that lead deans and other center managers to accomplish their missions in ways that promote institutional objectives. It couples program responsibility with meaningful authority over resources. It gives an institution's central administration leveraged ability to determine overall objectives, set priorities and policies, and coordinate activities among centers. In short, responsibility center budgeting provides a structure for a college or university president to direct an institution's performance in a way that encourages everyone to put forth her or his best effort.

Despite its promise of helping to make complex universities and colleges more manageable, responsibility center budgeting has not been widely utilized. It appears to have been first adopted in the early 1970s, and its use has been confined to leading private institutions of higher education on the East and West Coast.

Indiana University appears to be the only major public institution of higher education embarked on making such a change. And it would not have happened here without dynamic and imaginative leadership. The persistence of existing ways for doing business evidently is very great.

Nevertheless, our activities have been noticed. Expressions of curiosity and questions about our progress from other institutions have been numerous, and what you now are staring at is a response to those inquiries. It is prepared for those of you who are curious and interested about developing a rational and incentive based system of resource management that is responsive to your institution's academic objectives. May it speed your progress.

Responsibility
Center Budgeting

1. When It All Started

Look with favor on a bold beginning.

Virgil, Georgics, I, line 40

"What do you know about responsibility center budgeting?" he asked.

My inquisitor was Thomas Ehrlich, who two months before had come to Indiana as Indiana University's fifteenth president. I had barely met the man, having only attended several receptions for him and stood in long lines waiting for a brief opportunity to press the flesh. Opportunities for discussion had been limited.

Now here was an opportunity. We were flying in a chartered Indiana University Foundation airplane to a two-day meeting of the Indiana Commission for Higher Education which was to be held in the northwestern corner of the state. On Thursday, the commission was meeting on the campus of Indiana University Northwest in Gary; on Friday, at Purdue University's regional campus in Calumet.

When we took off, Tom's first concern was with the commission agenda. After covering items relating to Indiana University and to which a response from him was expected, he began talking about internal university matters. And then, without much preliminary comment, he asked his question.

Although it came literally out of the blue, a question about responsibility center budgeting was not entirely unanticipated. In one sense, I had been waiting for it for a long time. Finally, someone in a leadership position was expressing interest in a resource allocation arrangement that makes major academic and support units responsible for generating their own income and managing their own expenditures!

Some seventeen years before, when first becoming involved in university administration as an associate dean for academic affairs, I had started exploring the arcanum of budgeting processes and procedures. Initially, some of those processes and procedures seemed rather odd.

Once I asked Robert L. Siebenthal, director of the budget office, why student fee income earned from degree credit courses was not attributed to schools which offered them. Sieb looked at me as if I had turned green and had broken out in red spots and replied, "Well, Dean Whalen, that would be against general fund accounting principles."

Being addressed as "Dean Whalen" suggested my question was about as welcome as flatulence at a quiet dinner party. In budgeting, as in matters of religion, when the respondent to a question refers to an authority or some other source of revealed truth, I have found the opportunity for rational discussion to be quite limited. Debate about the advantages and disadvantages of a particular arrangement is set aside. You either are impressed or are not impressed with the authority or the "truth." Suspecting on those counts we were not about to begin a fruitful discussion, I tried to look appropriately impressed and let the matter drop.

Not long afterward, I heard the expression, "Every tub on its own bottom." That sounded reasonable. But what did tubs have to do with higher education? The expression came from Harvard University. It referred to an arrangement in which each academic unit (the tub) generated its own income and was responsible for covering all of its own expenses (the bottom line). Although such a system seemed to decentralize incentives for imaginative and constructive management, probably accountants and budget officers throughout higher education were clucking about the possible violation of general fund accounting principles. In the minds of many, this development may have marked the beginning of the end for Harvard University as a distinguished institution of higher education.

In the late 1970s, I was given an opportunity to attend the Institute for Educational Management held at Harvard University for administrators in higher education. Although the topic was not on the agenda, I hoped to learn more about tubs on their own bottoms. Other participants in the institute had similar interests, but our attempts were frustrated. We were kept busy cramming a four week program into six weeks of intensive effort, and the Harvard folks did not volunteer much about the arrangement. I did come away with the impression that it produced an environment in which the School of Business thrived but which the School of Education found difficult.

My participation on a panel sponsored by the National Association of State Universities and Land Grant Colleges in 1984-85 provided an opportunity to meet Jon Strauss, Senior Vice President for Administration at the University of Southern California. He described a budgeting system at his university called "Revenue Center Management." It appeared to resemble Harvard University's arrangement. Terminology had improved, but concepts were very similar. Apparently the virus of violation of general fund accounting principles had spread from the East Coast to the West Coast.

Closer to home, adherence to general fund accounting principles continued with unabated and mindless enthusiasm. Only a few months before Tom Ehrlich's question, a proposal to reimburse units that turned in unneeded but usable equipment and furniture to central stores for recycling to other units had been set aside because such payments would be in violation of general fund accounting principles. That such principles wreaked havoc with incentives for desirable behavior on the part of unit managers seemed entirely disregarded.

Tom Ehrlich's appointment as president of Indiana University was announced on March 7, 1987. Almost immediately, individuals from Indiana University began making pilgrimages to the University of Pennsylvania, where Tom was provost, among them Edgar G. Williams, Vice President for Finance and Administration and my immediate superior.

Shortly after Williams returned, Tom sent him a copy of a monthly briefing book, "The President's Report." Williams passed the report on to me for review and to see if we could duplicate it. Inspection of the financial section revealed that student fees and other income were associated with each of the academic units. Moreover, each of the units appeared to be charged for facilities and other overhead costs. My heart beat a little faster. Could it be? Were we about to become infected with the general fund accounting principles violation virus? Was Tom Ehrlich a carrier?

When he asked on that eight-passenger plane, "What do you know about responsibility center budgeting?" I knew that he was a carrier and that we were about to become infected.

Although I had waited a long time for the question to be asked, answering it was not easy because of the circumstances. Airplanes have three orientations: pitch, roll, and yawl. Taken individually, they cause no problem. All day long, I could rock back and forth or from side to side or twist to the right and then to the left. However, in an airplane, they can all occur at the same time, and other orientations must exist that do not appear in the rule books.

It was October, and the winds in Indiana can be a bit blustery at that time of year. Shortly after takeoff, I became aware that it was one of those days. First a little uneasiness. Then a familiar queasy feeling. Then a cold sweat. Tom Ehrlich seemed completely oblivious to the fact that the airplane seemed to be going in every direction at once. He would read the commission agenda. Imagine, reading! Then making notes! Writing! Asking questions! Talking without first swallowing hard! I was barely able to communicate while simultaneously coping with thoughts of how my lunch was going to look if I saw it again.

Responsibility center budgeting was a new term. However, I figured I knew what it meant. Given my distractions, I don't remember exactly what I said, but it seemed to satisfy him.

Then he said, "I want your office to take the lead in bringing responsibility center budgeting to Indiana University."

"Boy," I thought. "This would be a terrible time to throw up."

Throwing up would not have been an appropriate response. The swinging and swaying of the airplane, not the question, produced my nausea, but how would he know? The question, however, did produce two other sensations, very different from one another.

The first sensation was one of joy, excitement, exhilaration. A move to responsibility center budgeting was a bold move, an act of the will, evidence of dynamic leadership. Rather than attempting to understand the existing system, the new president was going to sweep it away with a new one.

As Tom Ehrlich was to recall three years after becoming president, when Indiana University's budget was first described to him he was "totally bewildered."[1] The budget seemed designed to conceal rather than reveal what was going on. A defense of such an arrangement, he observed, is that "if no one knows what you are doing, no one can complain." However, in his view, "that consideration is enormously overbalanced by the advantages of clear identification of costs and expenses for each unit."

Who could explain the old system to anyone? We hardly understood it ourselves! For years, we had been following the same old routines. When problems arose, ad hoc policies and procedures were tacked on the old structure. The original motivation for the policies and procedures was forgotten, yet they remained to limit flexibility, stifle initiative, and ensnare the unwary.

Responsibility center budgeting would require a clear statement of organizational principles and objectives. Policies and procedures would be fashioned in accordance with those principles and to contribute to the accomplishment of the objectives. The matter of incentives would be dealt with. Cost effective activities that addressed the institutions' priorities would be rewarded—not by decree but automatically by the system. Units engaged in self serving and inefficient activities would bear the consequences.

Offsetting the positive sensation was a feeling of melancholy, sadness, and weariness. People go on vacations for change. But most of them go as tourists, not as explorers. Explorers blaze trails, move into unknown territory, experience fear, face danger. The outcome is uncertain. Tourists tread broad paths, see new but expected vistas, complain about inconvenience and discomfort, avoid hazards, are confident of returning unscathed, and are liable to sue if injury results from their pursuit of idle curiosity.

Tourists are many; explorers are few. But embarking on responsibility center budgeting was to be an expedition, not a pleasure trip. Many were content with the existing terrain. Many had invested their careers in activities which relied on an institutional orientation toward "free" goods and services—resources which appeared free to users but which were not free to the

---

1. Memorandum from Thomas Ehrlich to John Gallman dated May 14, 1990.

institution. Uncertainty as to the consequences of cost and benefit knowledge would produce fear. Fear would produce resistance, panic, strife, attempts to derail and sabotage the new way of doing business, particularly at the beginning when it was most vulnerable.

The technical challenges of instituting the new system, while formidable, would be manageable. Over the years, the groundwork had been laid in countless little ways. One step in that direction was taken in 1977, when the Bloomington campus was persuaded to move from a flat fee rate to credit hour charges. Now the process of attributing fee income to academic units would be straightforward. The difficult part of the installation would be dealing with people, containing their concerns, addressing their fears, and securing their cooperation in the new venture.

Striking a delicate balance between steady progress toward implementation and developing broad understanding of and confidence in responsibility center budgeting would require great effort and patience. The course would not be an easy one. Doubts and doubters would be many.

Of the two sensations, the positive one prevailed, of course. An essential ingredient for success—a commitment at the highest echelon—was in place. For Tom Ehrlich, "the only question about responsibility center budgeting was not if it was going to be implemented, but when."

A Propitious Situation

If responsibility center budgeting is such a good idea, why is it not a more common arrangement among institutions of higher education? While a few of the leading private institutions have adopted it, public institutions have adhered to what may be called the general fund concept. Among institutions of higher education, Indiana University's situation made it a likely candidate for a conversion to the new arrangement.

For many if not most institutions of higher education, the general fund concept provides an appropriate budgeting arrangement. As shown in the following table, there are slightly over 2,000 institutions of higher education in the United States. Almost 840 of them (42 percent of the total), a majority of them private, have enrollments under 1,000 students. In such institutions, the scale of operation does not appear to require a decentralized system of resource management. Detailed allocations can be made centrally because operations of all units are familiar to the central management. Unit managers can perceive the effect of their actions on the total institution. Everyone can perceive the effect of the direct as well as indirect costs of their action; the benefits of their activities have a perceptible impact on the entire academic community.

TABLE 1.1 NUMBER OF FOUR YEAR PUBLIC AND PRIVATE
INSTITUTIONS OF HIGHER EDUCATION BY ENROLLMENT SIZE

Size of Institution	Public	Private	Total	Percent of Total
under 1,000	38	801	839	42
1,000 to 9,999	333	604	937	47
10,000 to 29,999	169	37	206	10
over 30,000	24	3	27	1

Source: U.S. Department of Education. Office of Educational Research and Improvement, National Center for Education Statistics, "Institutions of Higher Education and Branches, by Type, Control, and Size of Enrollment: United States: Fall 1985," *Digest of Education Statistics 1988,* Thomas D. Snyder, project director (Washington, D.C.: U.S. Government Printing Office, 1988. p. 184.

Only 233 institutions (11 percent of the total) have enrollments over 10,000 students; only 27 (1 percent), over 30,000 students. For institutions at the upper end of the enrollment scale the requirements for a highly centralized system of decision making and resource allocation are liable to be missing. The central management is not intimately familiar with the detailed operations of each academic and support unit. For heads of operating units, identifying the interests of their units with those of the entire institution becomes increasingly difficult. As the pool of resources devoted to indirect costs becomes larger and larger, the effect of one unit's excessive use of such resources becomes virtually impossible to isolate. At some point in the scale of operation, investment in the subtleties and sophistication required for a decentralized system of resource management and decision making becomes worthwhile.

Relative to most other institutions, Indiana University is mammoth. Certainly, with over 89,000 students, eight campuses, nearly 15,000 employees, and a budget of more than $1.3 billion, Indiana University appears to be at a point in the scale of operation where a decentralized system deserves consideration.

A second condition making the setting for a transition to responsibility center budgeting propitious involves the terms under which Indiana University receives its appropriation from the state of Indiana. Indiana University, and the other public institutions of higher education in Indiana, are fortunate in the manner in which they receive state support. The relationship between the university and the state has served well both the institution and the people of the state of Indiana. The basis for that relationship appears in each biennium's appropriation act in two paragraphs following the amounts of state support.

The sums herein appropriated . . . are in addition to all income . . . from all permanent fees and endowments, and from all land grants, fees, earnings and receipts . . . from whatever source derived.

All such income and all such fees, earnings and receipts on hand June 30, 1987, and all such income and fees, earnings and receipts accruing thereafter are hereby appropriated to the trustees . . . and may be expended for any necessary expenses.

The first paragraph provides the university with powerful incentives to supplement the state resources available to it by earning income in whatever manner is appropriate to the institution's mission. No deduction of state support is made for revenue generating institutional initiatives to increase student access, to advance knowledge through contract research and grants, to provide health care and other professional services, and to seek out benefactors who recognize the value of higher education. In part as a consequence, for each dollar the state invests in Indiana University in the form of appropriation, the institution generates two dollars in the form of fees and other income voluntarily paid by individuals, government agencies, businesses, and foundations for services provided.

The second paragraph does two things. First, it establishes the university as a separate financial entity with the right, privilege, and responsibility to manage its own funds. Balances not spent at the end of a fiscal year do not revert to the state's general fund but are retained by the institution. Second, it places management of the institution's resources with the institution, coupling responsibility with authority and establishing a firm basis for incentives to use those resources effectively.

The efficacy of this arrangement is implied by the prestige that not one but two of the state's public institutions—Indiana University and Purdue University—have achieved. The accomplishments of either of the two institutions would be welcome in many other states that have invested more in higher education than has been the case in Indiana. That the state's participation in higher education in terms of baccalaureate degrees granted relative to population is exceeded by only fifteen other states suggests that all of Indiana's public institutions of higher education have responded well to the opportunities and challenges embedded in two obscure paragraphs of the appropriation act.[2]

---

2. References showing Indiana's ranking with respect to baccalaureate degrees relative to population can be obtained from U.S. Department of Labor, Bureau of the Census, "State Population and Household Estimates to 1985, with Age and Components of Change," *Current Population Reports, Population Estimates and Projections* (December 1986), and U.S. Department of Education, Center for Educational Statistics, *Digest of Educational Statistics 1987* and *Bulletin: Bachelor's and Higher Degrees Awarded in 1984–85* (March 1987).

Those two paragraphs define a simple but effective arrangement between state and institution. The arrangement is based on mutual trust, respect for institutional management, and a shared understanding of the purposes of the institution and expectations about its performance. Although the arrangement is a long-standing one, it is renewed each biennium and cannot be taken for granted.

The arrangement antedates the tremendous growth in size, complexity, and diversity of Indiana University. With that growth comes the opportunity for and feasibility of an appropriately decentralized budgeting system aligned with commensurate responsibilities for delivering the university's major teaching, research, and service programs. Should not an arrangement that worked so well for the institution be extended to operating units within the university? For Tom Ehrlich, the answer to that question was affirmative. The state of Indiana was not an impediment to implementing it.

A final favorable condition for a transition to responsibility center budgeting was the happy coincidence of a major change in the university's top management. The senior vice presidents were retiring within a year of the new president's appointment. Two campus chancellors had just been appointed; eight of twenty-three school deans were to be appointed in his first year. An entrenched and conservative old guard was not around for long to impede the progress of the new regime.

2. Principles of Responsibility Center Budgeting

> There is nothing more difficult to take in hand, more perilous to conduct, or more uncertain in its success, than to take the lead in the introduction of a new order of things.
>
> Niccolo Machiavelli, *The Prince*, ch. 6

Among the attractive features of responsibility center budgeting is its logical structure. The organization adopted is derived from basic concepts and postulates or assumptions. Of course development of responsibility center budgeting from those first principles is less rigorous than the process of mathematical deduction by which laws are determined from sets of axioms. However, the steps are similar.

The budgeting arrangement which develops should reflect the concepts and postulates or assumptions. If you don't like the results, change the first principles and begin again. In much the same way, if Euclidean geometry doesn't suit your purposes, adopt the assumptions of non-Euclidean geometry and start over.

Selecting first principles is an art. If you select too many, the system can be overdetermined. No solution satisfies all the conditions. If you select too few, the system becomes indeterminate. Any number of arrangements satisfy the conditions. Ideally, you want a set of conditions for which a consensus is easily obtainable and from which a structure not readily discernible at the outset can be derived.

The axiom-theorem-proof approach to developing the foundations for responsibility center budgeting was developed in the early 1980s by Jon Strauss, then Senior Vice President for Administration at the University of Southern California, and John R. Curry, currently Vice President, Budget and Planning, at that institution. During 1981, they hammered out the principles as they worked with the Budget Incentives Task Force, a representative group of deans and key administrators, in anticipation of a move to a new budgeting and management system. As John modestly observes, the result

> represented a significant step in the advancement of the understanding and practice of decentralized management in higher education: it elucidated the

TABLE 2.1   BASIC CONCEPTS OF RESPONSIBILITY CENTER BUDGETING

Concepts related to Decision Making
Proximity
Proportionality
Knowledge

Concepts related to Motivation
Functionality
Performance Recognition
Stability

Concepts related to Coordination
Community
Leverage
Direction

underlying notions, and it raised the debate from the plain of petty politics to the plateau of principles. Getting faculty and administrators to buy into such a system is enormously facilitated as a consequence.[1]

Indiana University's move to responsibility center budgeting certainly profited from their path-breaking work.

Basic Concepts

For our purposes, we begin with nine concepts, terms relating to a postulate or assumption about behavior or a condition deemed to be reasonable and desirable.[2] As shown in Table 2.1, three of the concepts relate to decision making, three to motivation, and three to coordination. Nothing contrived in that progression, is there?

1. Proximity

The closer the point of an operating decision is to the point of implementation, the better the decision is likely to be. What do we mean by better? For a given amount of resources, decisions that maximize the effectiveness of an

---

1. Letter from John R. Curry to John Gallman dated March 27, 1990.
2. Many of the principles and concepts presented here are taken from the *Financial Report* of the University of Southern California for fiscal years 1982, 1984, and 1985.

activity are better than those that do not. For a specific task, decisions that minimize the resources required for its accomplishment are better than those that do not. In other words, tell people what to do, not how they should do it.

2. Proportionality

The degree of decentralization is positively related to an organization's size and its complexity as well as to the complexity of its environment. In an organization, not everything should be centralized; not everything should be decentralized. When too much is centralized, problems outside the immediate environs of the central office seem remote, do not seem important, do not receive attention, do not get corrected. Opportunities are lost. Communication burdens become excessive. Decentralization can address those problems but imposes its own costs and hazards in the form of duplication of functions, coordination, and loss of control. An efficiency maximizing balance between the two extremes has to be recognized.

3. Knowledge

Correct decisions are more likely to occur in an information-rich environment. Making correct decisions is not easy, and having timely and accurate information does not guarantee they will be made, but the absence of such information substantially lowers the probability of their being made. Whether decisions are centralized or decentralized, information is needed if the decision makers are to arrive at decisions which promote the objectives of the institution they serve. For decision making in a decentralized environment, local managers must know not only how those decisions affect their units but also their impact on the entire institution. Actions should be planned, undertaken, and evaluated in a context of full information on benefits and consequences.

4. Functionality

Authority and command over resources should be commensurate with responsibility for the task assigned, and vice versa. Explicit organizational rules are required to make clear who is responsible for what kinds of decisions. The accounting structure and budgeting procedures should reflect the organizational structure and promote incentives for effective performance.

In a complex organization, one unit's performance may affect others in very important ways. Attempting to strike a balance by assigning responsibility to one and control over resources or authority to another may force communication between units but does not promote responsible behavior and effective performance.

5. Performance Recognition

To make operational the distribution of responsibility and authority, a clear set of rewards and sanctions is required. Managers should be able to operate in an environment characterized by straightforward and easily understood mechanisms designed to automatically recognize and reward effective performance. However, the full costs as well as the full benefits have to be recognized and attributed to local managers to motivate decisions designed to promote the institution's objectives as well as those of a single operating unit.

6. Stability

Good planning and performance are facilitated by stable environments. If motivation of behavior is to be effective, assignment of responsibility, authority, and resources has to be relatively constant, and the rules for performance evaluation and the consequences of alternative outcomes have to be known before a course of action is undertaken. In order for those rules to be effective, there has to be the expectation that they will not change and that they will be enforced.

7. Community

Institutions of higher education are collective human endeavors. That the fate of individual units is bound up in the success of the entire institution must be recognized in the structure and operating procedures of the organization. Just as the property value of a house is limited by the condition of the neighborhood in which it is located, so also recognition of the national and international distinction of any one unit ultimately is limited by the performance of the entire institution. The relationship of the parts to the whole and to one another has to be explicitly reflected in the assignment of responsibility and authority and in the allocation of resources.

8. Leverage

In a decentralized decision making and operating system, the legitimacy of both institutional and local responsibilities has to be recognized. Central management should retain sufficient academic and fiscal leverage to facilitate achievement of institutional goals, maintain an institutional balance among programs, and respond to initiatives and opportunities presented by the environment in which the institution operates. Certain services are needed for the collective benefit of the academic community and are provided as public utilities. In those instances, the central management must determine the level of such services and the resources to be allocated to provide them in accordance with appropriate governance procedures.

9. Direction

The existence of a mutually supportive academic and administrative plan for the institution is assumed. A clear set of objectives for the short and long run must be defined; trade-offs between scope and quality identified; priorities among programs established. A plan is needed to focus decision making. Only in the context of a plan can performance be evaluated.

Decision Making

The first three concepts—proximity, proportionality, and knowledge—relate to decision making. In a large organization, closing the gap between the point of decision and the point of implementation requires that the definition of responsibility centers be configured to correspond with the institution's academic and administrative structure. Academic responsibility centers carry out the institution's primary missions in teaching, research, and public service. Support centers, grouped to reflect the administrative structure, provide services to the primary mission units in the form of academic support, student support, institutional support, and operations and maintenance of physical facilities.

In order to operate effectively, academic and support centers must have access to a flow of comprehensive, consistent, readily manipulatable, and timely information. Within its sphere of influence, a center needs the same range of information available to central management. While information should be designed to serve the needs of a unit, it has to be based on a common standard for comparability across all centers.

Responsibility center budgeting creates a demand for decentralized, up-to-date information. Center managers can be responsible for their programs and accountable for the fiscal integrity of their enterprise only if they act upon accurate and timely information and are able to perform and monitor transactions easily. Moreover, the information available to them must be the same as that used by central administrators to monitor performance if evaluation and accountability are to be conducted according to a common standard. To realize the full potential of responsibility center budgeting, an information system involving budget administration and construction, accounting, payroll, personnel, purchasing, sponsored programs, student records, facilities, gifts, donors, and alumni is required.

Motivation

The second set of three concepts—functionality, performance recognition, and stability—relate to motivation. Responsibility of a dean of a school or head of an academic unit for accreditation, recruitment, appointment, promotion, and tenure of faculty, determination of curriculum and degree requirements, the research program, and generation of outside support should be accompanied by authority to make decisions relating to those issues and by command over resources necessary to execute them. Who knows better than a dean the number of faculty needed to deliver the courses in his or her discipline? where to recruit the best faculty? their performance? the optimum trade-off between graduate student support and equipment expenditures? If someone else is better prepared to make those decisions, that person should be the dean.

As a well-defined entity, an institution enjoys the full benefit of its performance and bears the full consequences of its actions. Such an arrangement is deemed to produce responsible behavior. Under responsibility center budgeting, responsibility centers become microcosms of the university. Like a university, they are charged with academic, service, and management missions. Like a university, they retain the income they earn from their activities. Like a university, they pay for all the costs of their activities—indirect as well as direct. Like a university, they function as separate financial entities retaining their year end balances. Like a university, the heads of centers are expected to manage the resources at their disposal to maximize the effectiveness of their performance. Like a university, academic units receive state support—not directly but through allocations of central management.

Under such an arrangement, all income and costs accrue to the centers whose activities generate them. Center managers make their decisions and carry out their programs in the same context as that of an entire university. While they promote the objectives of their individual units they also serve to promote the objectives of the total institution.

Academic units designated as responsibility centers retain income directly attributable to their departments, programs, and activities. Student and other fee income generated from courses, other earned income, indirect cost recovery from external grants and contracts, designated fund income from continuing education and public service activities, restricted fund income from grants, contracts, and gifts, and income from auxiliary and service units will be credited to the schools and other major primary mission units. In addition, central administration will allocate a portion of a central pool of resources obtained from state appropriated funds or through contributions from all academic units as part of the annual budgetary review process. At that review and through that allocation, each school's role in meeting university objectives can be assessed and adjusted.

Not only will a responsibility center receive the income generated by its activities, but also it will incur all costs, both direct and indirect, associated with them. An academic unit's budget typically consists of planned expenditures for personnel compensation, office and classroom supplies, telephone charges, travel, departmental equipment, and miscellaneous general supplies and expenses. Under responsibility center budgeting, all costs associated with conducting teaching, research, and public service activities are recognized. Academic units are assessed or charged for academic support services, library and computing services, student services, general administration, space and related physical plant costs.

Like academic responsibility centers, major support units designated as responsibility centers receive income attributable to their activities. Some of that income is generated from external sources. Much of it is received in the form of assessments and charges to academic units for academic support, student services, general administration, and facilities operation and maintenance. Like academic responsibility centers, support centers will incur all costs associated with delivering their services.

Heads of responsibility centers develop revenue and expenditure budgets and manage their fiscal operations in a manner consistent with their revenue potentials and university policies. Fiscal accountability extends beyond the general education fund and includes designated and restricted fund groups as well as auxiliary and service enterprises involved in carrying out a center's responsibilities. Just as a center's year end balances are carried forward as funds available, so also will its deficits be carried forward as an obligation against future resources.

Each dean or head of a responsibility center, under such an arrangement, can be expected to manage the resources at the unit's disposal to achieve its goals with the greatest possible effectiveness. Goals established for each center as a result of the university planning process are reviewed annually as a part of the budget process. With integration of responsibility and authority, deans and other managers have an opportunity to balance evolving program objectives with available resources.

The extent to which such an environment influences decisions and performance depends on local managers' understanding of the arrangement and their expectation that the rules will not change. What happens if a unit runs a deficit? It has been said, "There's nothing like watching a hanging in the morning. It keeps your attention all day." Fiscal responsibility will be achieved only if the discipline of retaining year end balances—negative as well as positive—applies without exception. Ad hoc improvisation with the rules of income and expenditure will diminish responsibility center budgeting's effectiveness in motivating responsible behavior.

Coordination

The last three concepts—community, leverage, and direction—relate to coordination. The last concept, direction, is the foundation for all the others. All of the above concepts and the contrivances which derive from them are superfluous if the institution and its components lack a sense of purpose. How can good decisions be distinguished from poor ones if the direction is unclear? How can performance be evaluated except in terms of its contribution to clearly defined objectives whose priorities are established? What balance between academic programs and support services is appropriate except in the context of a mutually supportive academic and administrative plan? The raison d'être of responsibility center budgeting is to help an institution focus its energies and resources on accomplishing its mission. If a sense of purpose and vision is lacking, the mechanism is not needed and can be a prescription for mischief.

In a university, schools vie with schools for additional resources. Support units attempt to increase their share of the total allocation. While such competition is a healthy manifestation of able and ambitious managers trying to advance the capacity of their units, all must recognize that as parts of a single institution they share a common destiny. Someone must preside over the management of that common destiny, and the legitimacy of central university administration's claim to that role has to be reflected in the organizational arrangement.

The central administration coordinates and guides the university's planning efforts for the entire institution and among centers, establishes policies and procedures defining relationships among centers, and allocates a central pool of resources among the primary mission units to achieve the university's overall academic objectives. That pool of resources is generated through the defined participation of each of the academic units or through state general fund operating appropriations, or a combination of both. Through the distribution of those funds to the primary mission responsibility centers, central administration directs resources to the achievement of institutional goals. By determining the assessments of support units to the primary mission responsibility centers and monitoring their charges, central administration strikes a balance between academic and service functions.

Prerequisites

For many institutions of higher education, responsibility center budgeting may appear to offer an attractive alternative to existing arrangements. But however great its potential advantages, it is not for everyone. Certain conditions—necessary, but not sufficient—have to be in place before responsibility center budgeting can operate effectively in a university's environment.

1. Academic Leadership

Academic priorities should lead rather than follow the budget process. Responsibility center budgeting is designed to make the budget process responsive to academic priorities. Strong academic leadership is required to identify those priorities and follow through with the allocation decisions necessary to realize them. Strong implies having moral or intellectual power. We like to think academic leadership in higher education often possesses those qualities. Among the synonyms for strong are tough and tenacious. Those characteristics seem to be less common but are essential. The rules of responsibility center budgeting have to be maintained and enforced. Without strong academic leadership, responsibility center budgeting is an idle exercise.

2. Administrative Support

Academic leadership is the prime mover in responsibility center budgeting. University administration plays the role of a facilitator. High professional standards in financial and personnel management and other service functions are required if the system is to work well. Having a few able individuals in central administration is not adequate. A well trained and able administrative staff has to be dispersed to the operating units and function as part of a team with central administration.

3. Full Disclosure

An information-rich environment means more than lots of numbers that are accurate, easily retrieved, current, and subject to analysis. Under responsibility center budgeting, there are no secrets. And no hidden agendas. The objectives and priorities of the institution have to be common knowledge. The books have to open. No little deals on the side can be cut without everyone's knowledge. Every allocation should have an explanation. The time for allocation comes once a year during the performance evaluation and budget review process. University officers with preferences for secrecy and inscrutable arrangements should avoid responsibility center budgeting.

4. Involvement

Responsibility center budgeting emphasizes the fact that a university is first and foremost an academic enterprise. The deans of schools and the heads of other primary mission units are key players in the enterprise and must be involved in the development of responsibility center budgeting and in its subsequent evolution. With involvement in the system's development comes not only understanding but also a sense of ownership and a commitment to its success. Without the full participation of the academic leadership, installation is fraught with peril. Their continued participation not only helps assure orderly change but also provides a self monitoring mechanism.

Although strong academic leadership, a capable administrative team, full disclosure of objectives, decisions, and allocations, and involvement of the academic leadership do not assure success of responsibility center budgeting, they make its realization highly probable. Such prerequisites should characterize all institutions of higher education where all the programs are strong, all the campuses are good looking, and all the students are above average.

3. Defining Responsibility Centers

De gustibus non disputandum. [There is no
argument about tastes.]

Latin proverb

When viewed over a long distance, mist is palpable. At close range, however,
it seems to disappear. So it is with responsibility centers and the income and
indirect costs we want to assign to them. On a large scale, we have an idea of
what we want. As we approach the detail, the overall vision seems to evapo-
rate. How are individual operating units grouped into responsibility centers?
Specifically, what income does each of them earn? What and how are indirect
costs allocated to them?

Standards for Defining Responsibility Centers

Responsibility centers fall into three general categories: (1) academic responsibility centers charged with carrying out the institution's primary missions of teaching, research, and public service; (2) responsibility centers
providing supporting services to the primary mission units; and (3) executive
management, the collection of units coordinating and guiding the university's
planning efforts among centers, establishing policies and procedures defining
relationships among them, and allocating resources to achieve the overall
objectives of the university's academic plan. The academic centers seem easier
to define than the support centers, since the former correspond to schools,
colleges, or other degree granting units. However, a single set of standards
equally applicable to units in all three general categories is needed to develop
a consistent arrangement of academic and support centers and executive
management. As shown in Table 3.1, at Indiana University we adopted seven
standards to define responsibility centers.

1. Organizational Structure

The existing organizational structure of the university plays a major role in
determining how operating units are grouped into responsibility centers, both
academic and support. At the beginning of the process toward a move from

TABLE 3.1 STANDARDS FOR DEFINING RESPONSIBILITY CENTERS

1. Organizational structure
2. Clear definition of management responsibility
3. Number of centers to reflect size and complexity
4. Approximate parity among units in terms of size and complexity
5. Intracenter decentralization at the discretion of each center
6. Policy issues
7. Inclusion of all fund groups

traditional budgeting techniques to responsibility center budgeting, it clearly dominates all other standards. Unfortunately, as becomes clear when other standards are evaluated, the existing organizational structure does not necessarily provide an optimum configuration for responsibility centers. However, a transition has to begin at some point in time, and attempting to achieve perfection from the outset will delay progress indefinitely. As Voltaire observed, "Le mieux est l'ennemi du bien."[1]

Existing schools and colleges determine most of the academic responsibility centers. Research centers, institutes, and such operations as hospitals are candidates as well. Administrative structure also dictates how support centers providing academic support, student support, institutional support, and physical plant services are defined. Executive management includes an institution's chief executive officer and supporting staff.

2. Clear Definition of Management Responsibility

If a responsibility center is to operate, someone has to be in charge. This second standard is related closely to the first and sometimes conflicts with it. As programs and activities are arranged into what appear to be reasonable groups, aggregations may develop for which no one is clearly responsible. Equally possible are arrangements in which responsibilities of two or more heads of other responsibility centers are involved.

Grouping libraries, museums, galleries, computing, and audiovisual services into a support center may seem reasonable, but it is not plausible unless someone is charged with responsibility for coordinating the activities of those units. Delivering off-campus courses for degree credit presents a different issue. Who is in charge? The unit which identifies demand for the courses, finds facilities, and makes other administrative arrangements, or the academic

---

1. "The best is the enemy of the good." Voltaire, *Dictionnaire Philosophique,* 1764.

units whose courses are being offered? Are research institutes under the purview of a dean for research and graduate development, responsible for coordinating a campus's research effort, or under the academic units whose disciplines are represented in the institutes' activities?

When all units feed from a common trough and are concerned only with their direct expenses, overlapping jurisdictions can be ignored, and coordination of related operations can be more casual. When earned income is to be directed to specific units, and full costs are assigned, clarification of those arrangements becomes essential.

3. Number of Centers to Reflect Size and Complexity

The number of responsibility centers tends to increase with the size and complexity of the environment. Indiana University consists of eight campuses differing widely in size and complexity. At these campuses, fall 1989 enrollments ranged from less than 2,000 headcount students to more than 34,000. Campus expenditures in 1988-89 ranged from less than $7 million to nearly $500 million. The range of services in terms of teaching, research, and public service similarly varies appreciably.

For the two largest campuses, Bloomington and Indianapolis—with enrollments exceeding 34,000 and 26,000, respectively—the initial number of responsibility centers varied between twenty and twenty-five. For the smaller campuses, the number ranged from ten to fifteen.

In terms of enrollment, the largest campus was more than fifteen times larger than the smallest. In terms of expenditure, the largest campus was more than seventy times larger. The number of centers clearly does not rise in proportion with size, suggesting that a greater degree of decentralization was attempted on the smaller campuses than on the larger ones. The absence of proportionality suggests that the results are less than optimum.

As the number of centers rises, the benefits of making improved decisions close to the point of implementation are offset by costs of coordination and communication in a decentralized system. With the operating environment and technology available for coordination and communication similar on all campuses, a greater difference between the number of centers on large and small campuses could be expected.

At this point in our development of responsibility center budgeting, we cannot tell whether an optimum will be found by reducing the number of centers on the smaller campuses or increasing it on the larger campuses. Experience will be required to determine the proper balance and an optimum level of decentralization.

4. Approximate Parity among Units in Terms of Size and Complexity

Given the axiom that the effectiveness of decision making improves as the point of decision approximates the point of implementation, benefits will be maximized if centers are about equal in terms of size and complexity. If one responsibility center is twice as large or complex as all the rest, decision making in that unit is liable to be farther from points of implementation than in the smaller units. With no increase in the number of centers, decision making and implementation can be brought into closer alignment by achieving a more even balance in the size and complexity of centers.

This standard is liable to be violated by adherence to the existing organizational structure when defining responsibility centers. In the case of Indiana University, at any rate, the size and complexity of schools and support units varies enormously. On the Bloomington campus, for example, the largest academic center, the College of Arts and Sciences, is over sixty times larger than the smallest, the School of Library Science. Tradition and considerations other than effectiveness of decision making appear to have played major roles in their development. If decentralization does in fact lead to improved performance and if that performance is recognized appropriately, a tendency toward centers more homogeneous with respect to size and complexity can be expected. In the absence of such demonstration of cause and effect, however, the influence of parity as a standard for defining centers is slight.

5. Intracenter Decentralization at the Discretion of Each Center

Differences in the size and complexity of responsibility centers become less of an issue if decentralization is allowed to occur within responsibility centers. Even for large centers, operating decisions can occur in close proximity to points of implementation if a center's organization parallels the responsibility center budgeting format. With such flexibility, familiar patterns of the existing organizational structure of a campus can be preserved while achieving a relatively homogeneous degree of decentralization.

Initially, no responsibility centers took advantage of this option. Until the heads of responsibility centers had experience with the new arrangement, uncertainties about how it would operate precluded the possibility of further decentralization.

6. Policy Issues

A set of academic or support functions may not be recognized as a separate operating unit in the existing organizational structure. They may not merit center status because of their size and complexity. Nevertheless, because of an institution's priorities, generated internally or imposed externally, they may be grouped together as a responsibility center.

In the case of Indiana University, nursing programs on all campuses provide an example. While not necessarily the most significant academic program on every campus, their centralized funding and supervision by the School of Nursing merited separate status as a responsibility center.

7. Inclusion of All Fund Groups

The sources and uses of funds for a responsibility center involve all fund groups: the general educational fund, designated funds, restricted funds, and auxiliary and service enterprises. Accounting conventions in higher education separate each of those fund groups. Under responsibility center budgeting, center heads are expected to manage and integrate the activities within them as a single unit.

For auxiliary and service enterprises and various designated and restricted fund units, many of the concepts associated with responsibility center budgeting already exist. They generate their own income, manage their expenditures within that income restraint, retain their unspent balances at year end. Under responsibility center budgeting, those concepts are extended to the university's general educational fund.

Some responsibility centers will be concerned exclusively with general educational fund income, allotments, expenditures and assessments. Others may operate exclusively within the auxiliary fund group. However, the operations of a significant number of responsibility centers will involve several and in some cases all fund groups. For heads of such centers, the interaction between activities in different fund groups will become readily apparent.

Identifying the Centers

Using the preceding standards for defining responsibility centers, each campus of Indiana University developed its own list of centers. They were all different! And yet they were similar.

As expected, the criterion of overwhelming importance was the current organizational structure. Academic centers closely followed already existing schools, and lines of demarcation were obvious and predictable. For support centers, organizational lines prevailed as well, but the point at which a collection of administrative units merited center status was less clear. Moreover, administrative centers were less comparable across campuses than academic centers. For example, a responsibility center charged with academic affairs on one campus might include library and computing services found separately on another campus. Student service functions were not necessarily consolidated in a single center but on some campuses were distributed among several.

Local campus preferences held sway. No attempt was undertaken to seek definitions of responsibility centers that were consistent among campuses. Responsibility center budgeting is not prescriptive about tidy or untidy ways of organizing a university.

For illustrative purposes only, a list of responsibility centers for a campus of an institution of higher education is presented in Table 3.2. Twenty responsibility centers are identified: fourteen academic centers and six support

TABLE 3.2 ILLUSTRATIVE LIST OF RESPONSIBILITY CENTERS FOR A CAMPUS OR INSTITUTION OF HIGHER EDUCATION

General Academic
School of Arts and Humanities
School of Physical and Mathematical Sciences
School of Social and Behavioral Sciences

Health Sciences
School of Dentistry
School of Medicine
School of Nursing
School of Optometry

Other Professional Schools
School of Business
School of Education
School of Engineering and Technology
School of Law
School of Music
School of Physical Education
School of Public Affairs

Support Centers
Libraries and Instructional Resources
Academic Computing
Academic Affairs
Student Services
Physical Facilities
Central Administration

---

centers, one of which includes executive management. It attempts to consolidate the best examples from all of Indiana University's campuses into one list. It doesn't correspond to any single campus, but approximates all of them. With responsibility centers defined, a framework is established for arranging a chart of accounts.

Assigning Accounts

Indiana University has thousands of operating accounts. Other institutions of higher education undoubtedly share that distinction of a multiplicity of accounting entities. After defining responsibility centers, our next challenge was arranging those accounts in a format appropriate to responsibility center budgeting.

Because the existing organizational structure prevailed as a criterion for defining responsibility centers, most—say, 90 percent—of the accounts were easily associated with a center. Finding homes for the remaining 10 percent of the accounts consumed about 90 percent of the time and effort devoted to this task.

Nor is the task ever finished. As universities change, their organizational structure changes. And with those changes come shifts in accounts among responsibility centers. Flexibility in allowing for such shifts must be preserved.

When responsibility center budgeting was first announced, naysayers predicted a proliferation of new accounts to handle additional transactions. For twenty responsibility centers, we found introduction of twenty "RCB" accounts was needed—one for each center. Into each of those accounts, as we shall see, income attributions and cost allocations are posted. They could have been posted to an existing account—any account—but isolating responsibility center transactions at least initially seemed prudent.

When the assignment process was completed, each responsibility center had its own chart of accounts. The charts included not only general fund accounts but also accounts for designated and restricted funds, auxiliary enterprises, and service units.

Tables 3.3 and 3.4 display an illustrative chart of accounts for two responsibility centers, one academic and the other support. The academic center selected is the School of Physical and Mathematical Sciences; the support center is student services.

Both tables illustrate the multiplicity of fund groups found within a single responsibility center. General and designated fund accounts are common both to the school and student services. Restricted funds for the school take the form of scholarships and fellowships directed to students in the physical and

TABLE 3.3 ILLUSTRATIVE CHART OF ACCOUNTS FOR
AN ACADEMIC RESPONSIBILITY CENTER: SCHOOL OF
PHYSICAL AND MATHEMATICAL SCIENCES

General Fund
Office of the Dean
Department of Astronomy
Department of Biological Sciences
Department of Chemistry
Department of Computer Science
Department of Geology
Department of Mathematics
Department of Physics

Designated Funds
Chemical Information Center
Quantum Chemistry Program
Mathematics Journal
Faculty Research Incentive Grants

Restricted Funds
XYZ Scholarship Fund
ABC Fellowships Fund
Friends of Science Fund
DOE Grant E-MC2
NIH Grant 96-842
NASA Grant 101-456
PHS Grant EZ-8877

Auxiliary Enterprises
Geologic Field Station

Service Units
Scientific Stores
Liquid Nitrogen Generator
Liquefied Helium

mathematical sciences and of sponsored research grants and contracts. For student services, they include private and government scholarship support whose use is specified but not directed to particular academic programs. Auxiliary enterprise accounts are limited to just one for the school, the Geologic Field Station. Student services' auxiliary enterprise responsibilities include the bookstore, dormitories, and student health center. Only the school maintains a service unit: laboratory stores, which supplies chemicals, glass-

TABLE 3.4 ILLUSTRATIVE CHART OF ACCOUNTS FOR
A SUPPORT RESPONSIBILITY CENTER: STUDENT SERVICES

General Fund
Dean of Students
Activities Office
Career Planning Center
Emergency Student Aid Fund
Statutory Fee Remissions
Student Employment Office
Veteran Affairs Office

Designated Funds
Student Activities
Student Government
Student Legal Services
Lecture Series Program

Restricted Funds
Friends of Student Services
Acme Corporation Scholarship Fund
M. Snerd Memorial Scholarship
Pell Grants
College Work Study

Auxiliary Enterprises
Bookstore
Halls of Residence
Student Health Center

Service Units

ware, and other expendables for laboratory instruction and research for all of its experimental sciences.

Potentially, all fund groups can be represented in a single responsibility center. Total operating costs—indirect as well as direct—are allocated to a center for any and all fund groups. Interaction among fund groups is up to the center manager. Indirect costs associated with sponsored research are charged to the center regardless of whether those projects generate indirect cost recovery income. Dormitory income can be used to cover the cost of fee remissions for residence hall counselors even though fee remissions appear as a general fund expense.

But, before dealing with indirect costs, we have to determine each center's direct costs.

Determining Direct Expenditures of the Centers

With accounts identified for each responsibility center, direct expenditures—both budgeted and actual—can be determined for prior years, and budgeted expenditures can be determined for the current year. Table 3.5 illustrates a display of direct budgeted expenditures for the School of Physical and Mathematical Sciences; Table 3.6 for student services.

Direct expenditures for the School of Physical and Mathematical Sciences total $39.2 million. Nearly 60 percent of the total is accounted for by the general fund. Designated funds—general funds set aside for management purposes—increase that percentage to over 60 percent. Restricted funds are the second largest category, nearly $15 million, and reflect primarily the research activities of the school.

Unlike the School of Physical and Mathematical Sciences, where general fund expenditures dominate, auxiliary enterprises constitute the largest component of student services expenditure. Indeed, halls of residence expenditure, $49.3 million, is larger than the total expenditure of the school. For student services, general and designated fund expenditures comprise the smallest portion of total expenditure, being surpassed in amount not only by auxiliary enterprises but also by restricted funds.

Note that in both tables, expenditures budgeted for the "RCB" account are zero. Income must be attributed to each of the centers and indirect costs must be allocated before the budget is configured to conform the responsibility center budgeting format. At this point in the process, neither of those two steps has been undertaken.

Table 3.7 summarizes direct expenditures by center and by fund group for an entire campus. The centers are listed along the stub; fund groups appear as column headings. The column on the far right displays total direct expenditures for each center across all fund groups.

The fund group expenditures of the School of Physical and Mathematical Sciences and student services are entered in their respective row. Among the support centers, student services is largest in terms of total expenditures; in terms of general fund expenditures it is among the smallest, exceeding only academic affairs in dollar volume. Among the academic centers, the School of Physical and Mathematical Sciences is second largest, but it is a poor second, being only about 18 percent of the size of the School of Medicine.

Column totals, appearing in the bottom row of the table, represent total direct expenditures by fund group across all centers. The hospitals of the School of Medicine and the dormitories of student services contribute signif-

TABLE 3.5 ILLUSTRATIVE DIRECT EXPENDITURES FOR THE
SCHOOL OF PHYSICAL AND MATHEMATICAL SCIENCES

	Amount
General Fund	
RCB: Physical & Mathematical Sciences	$ 0
Office of the Dean	450,000
Department of Astronomy	629,000
Department of Biological Sciences	4,721,000
Department of Chemistry	5,480,000
Department of Computer Science	2,291,000
Department of Geology	1,930,000
Department of Mathematics	3,859,000
Department of Physics	3,500,000
SUBTOTAL	$ 22,860,000
Designated Funds	
Chemical Information Center	$ 24,000
Quantum Chemistry Program	266,000
Mathematics Journal	110,000
Faculty Research Incentive Grants	356,000
SUBTOTAL	$ 756,000
Restricted Funds	
XYZ Scholarship Fund	$ 802,000
ABC Fellowships Fund	1,376,000
Friends of Science Fund	473,000
DOE Grant E-MC2	150,000
NIH Grant 96-842	277,000
NASA Grant 101-456	569,000
NSF Grant IN-1776	7,878,000
PHS Grant EZ-8877	3,397,000
SUBTOTAL	$ 14,922,000
Auxiliary Enterprises	
Geologic Field Station	$ 187,000
Service Units	
Scientific Stores	$ 417,000
Liquid Nitrogen Generator	28,000
Liquefied Helium Operations	13,000
SUBTOTAL	$ 458,000
TOTAL	$ 39,183,000

TABLE 3.6 ILLUSTRATIVE DIRECT EXPENDITURES FOR
STUDENT SERVICES

	Amount
General Fund	
RCB: Student Services	$ 0
Dean of Students	372,000
Activities Office	245,000
Career Planning Center	157,000
Registrar	2,368,000
Student Employment Office	109,000
Veteran Affairs Office	91,000
Student Financial Aid Administration	1,092,000
Emergency Student Aid Fund	28,000
Statutory Fee Remissions	405,000
SUBTOTAL	$ 4,867,000
Designated Funds	
Student Activities	$ 64,000
Student Government	69,000
Student Legal Services	266,000
Lecture Series Program	57,000
SUBTOTAL	$ 456,000
Restricted Funds	
Friends of Student Services	$ 16,000
Acme Corporation Scholarship Fund	438,000
M. Snerd Memorial Scholarship	40,000
Pell Grants	5,199,000
College Work Study	2,078,000
SUBTOTAL	$ 7,771,000
Auxiliary Enterprises	
Bookstore	$ 6,361,000
Halls of Residence	49,349,000
Student Health Center	3,839,000
SUBTOTAL	$ 59,549,000
Service Units	
SUBTOTAL	$ 0
TOTAL	$ 72,643,000

TABLE 3.7 CAMPUS DIRECT EXPENDITURES BY RESPONSIBILITY CENTER AND FUND GROUP

			Fund Groups			
	General	Designated	Restricted	Auxiliaries	Service Units	Total
Arts and Humanities	$ 11,862,000	$ 104,000	$ 1,182,000	$ 0	$ 0	$ 13,148,000
Physicl & Math Sci	22,860,000	756,000	14,922,000	187,000	458,000	39,183,000
Social & Behavrl Sci	25,108,000	211,000	3,870,000	0	0	29,189,000
Dentistry	12,599,000	1,462,000	2,432,000	279,000	462,000	17,234,000
Medicine	59,540,000	15,356,000	38,735,000	190,483,000	3,017,000	307,131,000
Nursing	9,696,000	105,000	659,000	0	0	10,460,000
Optometry	3,291,000	99,000	551,000	0	0	3,941,000
Business	15,535,000	1,925,000	1,064,000	133,000	0	18,657,000
Education	10,215,000	267,000	7,448,000	71,000	0	18,001,000
Engineering & Tech	5,808,000	0	278,000	0	0	6,086,000
Law	4,850,000	49,000	443,000	52,000	0	5,394,000
Music	12,335,000	730,000	183,000	0	0	13,248,000
Physical Education	5,384,000	882,000	1,786,000	809,000	0	8,861,000
Public Affairs	5,687,000	544,000	1,778,000	0	1,059,000	9,068,000
SUBTOTAL: ACADEMIC	$204,770,000	$ 22,490,000	$ 75,331,000	$192,014,000	$ 4,996,000	$499,601,000
Libraries	$ 12,574,000	$ 76,000	$ 747,000	$ 0	$ 0	$ 13,397,000
Academic Computing	6,630,000	0	0	6,761,000	0	13,391,000
Academic Affairs	4,777,000	1,963,000	716,000	0	0	7,456,000
Student Services	4,867,000	456,000	7,771,000	59,549,000	0	72,643,000
Physical Facilities	27,983,000	0	0	0	13,501,000	41,484,000
Centrl Administratn	7,634,000	32,000	0	13,224,000	16,624,000	37,514,000
SUBTOTAL: SUPPORT	$ 64,465,000	$ 2,527,000	$ 9,234,000	$ 79,534,000	$ 30,125,000	$185,885,000
TOTAL	$269,235,000	$ 25,017,000	$ 84,565,000	$271,548,000	$ 35,121,000	$685,486,000

icantly to making auxiliary expenditures the largest fund group. But the position is not uncontested. General fund expenditures are a close second. General and designated funds combined surpass auxiliary fund expenditures.

Total campus direct expenditure, for all centers and fund groups, appears in the lower right hand corner of the matrix, $685 million.

Total general fund expenditures, $269 million, accounts for about 39 percent of total campus expenditure. It is to the general fund that we now turn for the attribution of income and allocation of indirect expenditures to each of the centers. When those steps are completed, the budget will be transformed into the responsibility center budgeting format.

4. Attribution of Income

The laborer is worthy of his hire.

Luke 10:7

Responsibility center budgeting impacts operating units receiving all or part of their support from general funds. For units operating as auxiliary or service enterprises, income sources are defined clearly, and actions required to generate more or less revenue are well known to unit managers. Similarly, directors of research projects receiving sponsored income recognize what they have to do to sustain their programs.

For units operating in the general fund and under traditional budgeting arrangements, the signals relating performance to resource availability often are less clear. Where revenue comes from, the form it takes, how it is produced, its amount, and its disposition are not defined. In order to attribute income to responsibility centers, rules for assigning general fund income to them must be specified.

Income Categories

The most important component of general fund income for most public institutions of higher education is state appropriation. Student tuition and fees constitute the second most important category. For Indiana University, state support accounts for about 60 percent of general fund income; student fees, about 30 percent. The remaining 10 percent is generated from indirect cost recovery on sponsored grants and contracts, interest income earned on invested cash balances, and receipts from sales of service. Each category requires its own method of attribution. Each category and its respective method are summarized in Table 4.1.

1. State Support

As the most important component of general fund income, the method of attributing state support appears to be a very important consideration. It is. But exact rules and formulas for its distribution probably should be avoided.

In a later section, we shall examine how to move from a traditional general

TABLE 4.1   METHODS OF INCOME ATTRIBUTION

Income Category/Components	*Attribution Method*
1. State support	combination: distribute a portion based on central administration decisions; a portion based on specified performance indicators
2. Credit hour fees	attribute to a center according to the courses it teaches
3. Course-related fees	attribute to a center according to the courses it teaches

laboratory fees
   practicum fees
   other special course fees
   auditing
   independent study
   forfeited fees	

4. Other fee income	
noncredit continuing education	attribute to a center offering the educational experience
other special instructional fees	
applications	registrar/admissions
transcript	registrar
late/deferred	bursar
special examination	bursar
late program change	bursar
5. Indirect cost recovery income	attribute to a center according to the projects it manages
6. Title IV administration fee	attribute to student services
7. Interest income	attribute to executive management and general administration
8. Rental income	attribute to center incurring cost of space management
9. Gifts and grants	attribute to center receiving gift or grant
10. Auxiliary service charge	attribute to a center according to the auxiliary enterprises it manages
11. Sales and service income Other income general	attribute to center generating income; when not determinable, to executive management and general administration

fund budgeting and accounting arrangement to a responsibility center budgeting format. Just as income and expenditure must balance for the entire general fund, so also it must balance initially for each responsibility center. That balance is achieved by using state appropriation as a plug or balancing residual—a necessary role if no center is to be penalized or rewarded for the mere implementation of responsibility center budgeting. Meeting that condition, however, automatically allocates all state support in a way which represents the effect of past and current decisions and priorities—and errors of judgment.

To specify a mechanistic approach to future allocations of state support would deny central administration the leverage it needs to respond to the institution's academic plan, set priorities, and exercise judgment regarding the scope and quality of various programs. In other words, specifying exactly how state support is to be distributed is probably a mistake. A compromise between allocation rules and central administration flexibility must be developed.

On average, 60 percent of an academic center's general fund income comes from an allocation of state support. That percentage represents a large dependency on a single source of income. If the entire amount is distributed at the discretion of central administration, the heads of responsibility centers may feel vulnerable and exposed to unexpected shifts in institutional priorities, changes in central management, and capricious decisions.

Furthermore, basing the entire distribution on central administration's judgment precludes reinforcing academic center behavior that promotes institutional objectives. For example, if among those objectives is strengthening sponsored research activities, a portion of state support can be linked as a supplement to indirect cost recovery or some other indicator of research programs activity paid for with outside funding. To emphasize instruction, a portion of state support can be tied to enrollments.

But not all state support should be tied to automated or defined distribution schemes. A portion should be set aside for central administration to influence and coordinate center activities in accordance with an overall academic plan. The size of that discretionary portion is a matter for collective judgment.

The larger the portion set aside for central administration distribution, the greater the role for central direction, the greater the importance of budget negotiations determining that distribution, and the greater the difficulty in achieving full disclosure about the real priorities of the academic plan. If, say, 100 percent of state support is distributed at the discretion of central administration, 60 percent of academic centers' income is—in a sense—outside their control. Decisions of central administration can devastate or enrich a center. In a sense, no center under such circumstances can afford not to be a top priority program in the overall academic plan. With such power to allocate resources concentrated in central administration, every center will frantically court favor. Candor about central administration's objectives will be hard to express.

On the other hand, with limitations on central administration's discretion, a center not marked for favored status in an institution's overall academic plan still can prosper. A forthright announcement of institutional priorities is not a cause for despair among centers whose programs are not a top concern. Nor is it a reason for wild rejoicing among centers whose programs are recognized as major institutional priorities. Central administration's power should be adequate but not excessive for the task of influencing and coordinating.

2. Student Tuition and Fees Related to Instruction

After state support, student tuition and fees account for the second largest source of general fund income. I mention tuition just so people know it's here. From now on, tuition and student fees will be considered synonymous. Under traditional general fund accounting and budgeting arrangements, fee income is pooled with state support and other sources of funds. Allocations for direct expenses then are made from the pool. Under responsibility center budgeting, fee income is attributed to the centers which earn it.

How do academic centers earn fee income? Until one attempts to attribute it, the answer to that question seems obvious. But at least two answers are possible, and probably more exist.

One way of attributing fee income to academic centers is based on enrollments in the courses each of them offers. A student pays so much, say, $150, to enroll in a three credit hour course offered by the School of Business. Attribute that $150 to the School of Business as student fee income.

Alternatively, fee income could be attributed to the centers in which students declare a major. An optometry student pays $1,500 a semester. Attribute that $1,500 to the School of Optometry.

The two attribution methods are likely to elicit very different reactions from the centers. In the first, "as taught" method, centers can be expected to welcome offering low cost, introductory service courses to students majoring in other disciplines. Under the second, "as enrolled" method, providing service courses to nonmajors is liable to be viewed as charity work and not be a welcome assignment. The "as taught" method, however, is not without its hazards. Schools are liable to alter degree requirements to confine their students' enrollments to their discipline. Offering service courses may be viewed as lucrative; offering advanced courses to majors may appear less rewarding. The "as enrolled" method of fee income attribution turns around those perverse incentives.

At Indiana University, we chose the "as taught" method. Determining students' majors is not unequivocal. What to do if a student changes her or his major? In the middle of the semester? Measuring enrollments by course and attributing the resulting income to the center offering it seemed more straight-forward. Nevertheless, possible behavioral reactions deserve to be kept in mind and monitored.

Of course, the mechanics are not so easy. Fortunately, at Indiana University, all student fees are assessed on a credit hour basis—with the exception of professional students in medicine and dentistry. Charging "full-time" stu-dents a flat rate would complicate the attribution process but would not present an insurmountable hurdle.

Even without the complication of a flat rate, details require attention. Students who reside in Indiana pay lower fees than students from outside the state. What should be done with the difference between in-state and out of state fees? We attribute them to the center offering the course in which each student enrolls—as a premium potentially recognizing quality. Graduate students pay different credit hour rates than undergraduate students. We attribute the fees as assessed to the courses in which they were enrolled.

The mechanics of attributing instructional fees to academic responsibility centers is not a trivial exercise. Complications of an institution's fee assessment categories and the number of student records conspire to create a significant electronic data processing project. From a mass of detail a relatively few numbers are produced, but a manageable audit trail is required to assure centers that they are receiving the student fee income produced by enrollment in the courses they offer. Those who have not engaged in such a process may find a review of our approach helpful.

A. STUDENT FEE ASSESSMENT CATEGORIES

Table 4.2 displays an illustrative schedule of fee rates. Each rate represents a fee assessment category. The amount of fee income generated in each category must be computed and attributed to the appropriate responsibility center. To make that determination requires knowledge of both course and student characteristics for each credit hour enrollment in each course.

The center offering a course is a characteristic that definitely must be known. Residency status—in-state resident or out of state resident—is a student characteristic that definitely must be known. If fees are assessed based on course level—undergraduate, graduate, or professional—an additional course characteristic is required. If fees are assessed based on a student's degree objective—baccalaureate, graduate, or professional—an additional student characteristic is required. (At Indiana University Bloomington, fee assessments are based on students' degree objectives; at other campuses, on the course level, so we collect information on both sets of characteristics.)

B. COURSE ENROLLMENT RECORD

The required information is brought together in a course enrollment record which includes both student and course identifiers. One record exists for each enrollment in each course (so a lot of them exist, about five per full time student). The essential elements of information contained in those records is presented in Table 4.3.

The section identifier refers to the specific class offering. It can be used in special instances to handle attribution of fee income to units which incur the costs of offering a class but which are not responsible for its academic content. For example, fee income in an English class ordinarily would be attributed to the School of Arts and Humanities; however, if a particular class is taught off

TABLE 4.2 ILLUSTRATIVE INSTRUCTIONAL CREDIT HOUR FEE SCHEDULE

Degree Objective, Student Residency, School Offering	*Credit Hour Rate (Unless Noted)*
Undergraduate	
Resident	$ 65.00
Nonresident	180.00
Graduate and Professional	
Resident	
Business	90.00
Dentistry*	4,300.00
Law	95.00
Medicine*	4,500.00
Optometry	100.00
Other	85.00
Nonresident	
Business	250.00
Dentistry*	9,000.00
Law	260.00
Medicine*	10,300.00
Optometry	270.00
Other	230.00

*Annual rate

campus and administered as part of an outreach effort in Academic Affairs, the income could be attributed to Academic Affairs.

The final element of information is the amount of the fee income assessed the student for enrollment in a course. At the individual record level, the fee assessment can be calculated unequivocally. As aggregation occurs, the calculation becomes less straightforward. For example, law students taking a course in the School of Music could pay different fee rates than medical students taking the same course.

C. CREDIT HOUR ENROLLMENT BY RESPONSIBILITY CENTER

With the information provided in the Course Enrollment Record, credit hour enrollment and fee income can be assigned to a fee assessment category and attributed to an appropriate responsibility center. For example, a three credit hour enrollment of an undergraduate student, who is classified as an in-state resident, in an undergraduate level biology course offered during the fall semester of the 1990-91 academic year would be included in the sum of credit hours appearing in the first column of Table 4.4 for the Department of Biological Sciences of the School of Physical and Mathematical Sciences.

The twelve columns of the table account for all the fee assessment categories. The first set of four columns contains credit hour enrollments and assessed fees of undergraduate students seeking associate or baccalaureate degrees; the second set of four, enrollments of graduate students who are candidates for master's and doctoral degrees, and the third set, of students seeking professional degrees.

Within each set of four columns, the first two contain credit hour enrollments and fees of students classified as in-state residents. The second two

TABLE 4.3 ESSENTIAL ELEMENTS OF INFORMATION
CONTAINED IN A COURSE ENROLLMENT RECORD

campus
semester and year
course identifier
unit offering
level
section identifier
student identifier
residency status
degree objective
instructional unit (credit hour)
amount of fee assessed

TABLE 4.4 ILLUSTRATIVE SUMMARY OF CREDIT HOUR ENROLLMENTS AND FEE INCOME, SCHOOL OF PHYSICAL AND MATHEMATICAL SCIENCES, FALL SEMESTER

| | Undergraduate | | | | Resident |
| | Resident | | Nonresident | | |
Department	Under-graduate	Grad-uate	Under-graduate	Grad-uate	Under-graduate
Astronomy					
Credit Hours	1,661	0	703	0	3
Fee Income	$ 107,965	0	126,540	0	195
Biological Sciences					
Credit Hours	9,889	19	2,884	6	73
Fee Income	$ 642,785	1,615	519,120	1,380	4,745
Chemistry					
Credit Hours	8,317	0	2,362	9	29
Fee Income	$ 540,605	0	425,160	2,070	1,885
Computer Science					
Credit Hours	2,931	9	1,060	3	97
Fee Income	$ 190,515	765	190,800	690	6,305
Geology					
Credit Hours	2,634	3	885	0	24
Fee Income	$ 171,210	255	159,300	0	1,560
Mathematics					
Credit Hours	17,487	6	6,325	9	133
Fee Income	$1,136,655	510	1,138,500	2,070	8,645
Physics					
Credit Hours	3,538	0	1,051	0	54
Fee Income	$ 229,970	0	189,180	0	3,510
TOTAL CREDIT HOURS	46,457	37	15,270	27	413
TOTAL FEE INCOME	$3,019,705	3,145	2,748,600	6,210	26,845

columns contain enrollments and fees of students whose residence is outside the state.

The first of each pair of columns contains credit hour enrollments and fees of undergraduate level courses. The second of each pair of columns measures credit hour enrollments and fees of graduate level courses.

As the totals of the columns indicate, few undergraduate students take graduate level courses. A higher proportion of graduate students take undergraduate courses. Graduate student enrollments are occasioned by the need to meet prerequisites and by the fact that some advanced undergraduate courses meet graduate degree requirements. Few students seeking profes-

| Graduate | | | Professional | | | | |
| Resident | Nonresident | | Resident | | Nonresident | | |
Grad-uate	Under-graduate	Grad-uate	Under-graduate	Grad-uate	Under-graduate	Grad-uate	Total
40	3	75	0	0	0	0	2,485
3,400	540	17,250	0	0	0	0	$ 255,890
179	67	937	60	5	33	0	14,152
15,215	12,060	215,510	3,900	425	5,940	0	$1,422,695
178	54	1,562	0	81	0	12	12,604
15,130	9,720	359,260	0	6,885	0	2,760	$1,363,475
77	596	337	0	0	0	0	5,110
6,545	107,280	77,510	0	0	0	0	$ 580,410
100	59	302	0	0	0	0	4,007
8,500	10,620	69,460	0	0	0	0	$ 420,905
121	421	670	0	0	3	0	25,175
10,285	75,780	154,100	0	0	540	0	$2,527,085
53	117	628	0	0	0	0	5,441
4,505	21,060	144,440	0	0	0	0	$ 592,665
748	1,317	4,511	60	86	36	12	68,974
63,580	237,060	1,037,530	3,900	7,310	6,480	2,760	$7,163,125

sional degrees (most likely in the health sciences) enroll in courses designed to meet baccalaureate, master's, and doctoral degree requirements.

D. ESTIMATE OF FEE INCOME

To determine the fee income attributable to a responsibility center, a table similar to Table 4.4 must be constructed for each semester. The process of aggregation is illustrated in Table 4.5 for the School of Physical and Mathematical Sciences. Four semesters constitute a fiscal year: summer II—summer session courses offered after the fiscal year begins July 1 and before the fall

TABLE 4.5 ILLUSTRATIVE SUMMARY OF CREDIT HOUR ENROLLMENTS AND FEE INCOME
SCHOOL OF PHYSICAL AND MATHEMATICAL SCIENCES, FISCAL YEAR

| | Undergraduate | | | | Graduate | | | | Professional | | | | Total |
| | Resident | | Nonresident | | Resident | | Nonresident | | Resident | | Nonresident | | |
Semester	Under-graduate	Grad-uate	Under-graduate	Grad-uate	Under-graduate	Grad-uate	Under-graduate	Grad-uate	Under-graduate	Grad-uate	Under-graduate	Grad-uate	Total
Summer II													
Credit Hours	3,285	3	949	2	183	114	565	541	11	22	2	0	5,677
Fee Income	$ 203,670	240	158,483	420	11,346	9,120	94,355	113,610	682	1,760	334	0	$ 594,020
Fall Semester													
Credit Hours	46,457	37	15,270	27	413	748	1,317	4,511	60	86	36	12	68,974
Fee Income	$ 3,019,705	3,145	2,748,600	6,210	26,845	63,580	237,060	1,037,530	3,900	7,310	6,480	2,760	$ 7,163,125
Spring Semester													
Credit Hours	44,710	26	15,291	19	343	639	1,104	4,361	54	199	7	0	66,753
Fee Income	$ 2,906,150	2,210	2,752,380	4,370	22,295	54,315	198,720	1,003,030	3,510	16,915	1,260	0	$ 6,965,155
Summer I													
Credit Hours	3,271	2	1,036	3	92	79	189	419	3	66	0	0	5,160
Fee Income	$ 212,615	170	186,480	690	5,980	6,715	34,020	96,370	195	5,610	0	0	$ 548,845
TOTAL CREDIT HOURS	97,723	68	32,546	51	1,031	1,580	3,175	9,832	128	373	45	12	146,564
TOTAL FEE INCOME	$ 6,342,140	5,765	5,845,943	11,690	66,466	133,730	564,155	2,250,540	8,287	31,595	8,074	2,760	$ 15,271,145

semester begins—the fall semester, the spring semester, and summer I—
courses offered in May and June after the spring semester ends.

For the School of Physical and Mathematical Sciences, we assume fee
assessments are based entirely on course level—undergraduate and graduate—and the residency classification of students. As a result, professional
students pay the same fee rates to enroll in courses offered by the School of
Physical and Mathematical Sciences as do undergraduate and graduate students. In practice, the world is not that simple.

Observe that fall semester undergraduate, graduate, and professional credit
hour enrollments and fee income by residency status and course level appearing in Table 4.4 have been carried forward to Table 4.5. Those who attempt to
check calculations by dividing credit hours into fee income will find that fee
rates for summer II are lower than the ones appearing in Table 4.2. Fee rates
approved by the trustees usually take effect beginning with the fall semester
so summer II assessments are based on the preceding year's rates. Out of habit,
that practice is reflected in Table 4.5.

Credit hour enrollments and fee income are summed in the column on the
right hand side of the table. Fee income attributed to the School of Physical
and Mathematical Sciences year totals $15,271,145.

3. Course Related Fees

Not only credit hour fees but also course related fees are attributed on an
"as taught" basis. Laboratory fees, practicum fees paid by students in education and social work, and other special course fees are attributed to centers
offering the courses for which those fees are charged. If a student audits a
course, the center offering the course gets the fee. The School of Continuing
Studies receives income from fees paid by students enrolled in correspondence courses offered by its Independent Study Division. Students withdraw-
ing from courses after the authorized "drop and add" period forfeit all or a
portion of their fees. Forfeited fees revert to the bursar's office, which incurs
the extra processing cost.

4. Other Fee Income

Not all fees that students pay are related to instruction for degree credit.
Many schools offer continuing education programs, and fees paid by participants in those activities are attributed to them.

In selected disciplines, students pay special instructional fees to reflect costs
uniquely associated with the pedagogy. Students taking courses in telecommunication pay a special fee for use of telecommunication equipment; stu-

dents taking music courses pay a music practice room fee. The list of such fees potentially is endless (certainly, it tends to grow). In each case, an attempt is made to associate the fee with the center whose instructional activity generates the income.

Certain fees paid by students are not related to any instructional program. In such cases, income is attributed to support units in charge of the activity generating it. Application fees are attributed to the admissions office; transcript fees to the registrar; late and deferred charges, special examination fees, and charges for late program changes to the bursar who enforces their collection. Usually, support units do not generate general fund income. Those attributions represent exceptions to the usual pattern.

5. Indirect Cost Recovery Income

Attribution of indirect cost recovery income earned on sponsored research and service grants and contracts is based on their project directors. A center to which a project director is appointed receives the indirect cost recovery income. For most grants and contracts, this method of attribution matches indirect cost recovery income with the indirect costs associated with projects and allocated to centers. Exceptions are addressed on a case by case basis.

6. Title IV Administration Fee

The university is reimbursed in part for costs incurred in administering federal student financial assistance programs: Supplemental Economic Opportunity Grants, Perkins Loans, College Work Study, and Pell Grants. The reimbursement income is attributed to the responsibility center in which the office of student financial assistance administration is located.

7. Interest Income

For the general fund, receipt of income precedes most expenditure. State appropriations are received in monthly installments beginning in July when expenditures are seasonally low. Students pay fees at the beginning of a semester before services are rendered and the cost of providing them is incurred. As a result, the general fund—even when operating on an essentially break-even basis—holds for much of the year a sizeable cash balance available for investment.

The interest income generated from investing cash balances is not attributed easily to any one responsibility center. For the sake of simplicity, it is assigned as an offset to executive management and general administration. As will be seen in the section dealing with allocation of indirect costs, the net assessment for executive management and general administration is distributed broadly and roughly in proportion to the size of a center's operation, so the benefit of the interest income offset appears to be spread appropriately.

8. Rental Income

To a minor extent, space normally used for academic and administrative activities supported by the general fund is rented, sometimes to outside agencies, sometimes to university operations functioning as auxiliaries. Office and meeting room space for professional associations provides an example of the former situation; bookstores, of the latter.

In such instances, the rental income is attributed to the unit incurring the cost of space management. In the case of an academic journal occupying space in a department, the center including that department would receive the income. If a bookstore occupies space normally used for general administration, the support center for general administration receives the income.

9. Gifts and Grants

Gift and grant income is attributed to a unit on whose behalf the university accepts. Most gifts and grants are restricted, and the recipient is designated. In those few instances where gift or grant income is unspecified, executive management and general administration get it. The benefit of the offset to cost of those two functions is widely distributed.

10. Auxiliary Service Charges

Auxiliary enterprises require services from general fund support centers. They take the form of general supervision, accounting, payroll, personnel, general building and grounds maintenance, energy and utilities. In some instances, auxiliaries are charged directly for those services; in other instances, they are not.

As will be seen in the section dealing with indirect cost allocations, all such costs will be assessed the center responsible for managing an auxiliary enterprise. For symmetry, auxiliary service charges, when levied, are attributed to those centers. The choice, then, of whether to levy service charges for their indirect costs is placed with center managers.

11. Miscellaneous Income

Sales and service income and other general fund income are attributed to units generating them. The dental and optometry clinics—general fund operations—generate patient fees which are distributed to their respective schools. When the source of income cannot be associated with an operating unit, it is attributed to executive management and general administration. Collection of bad debts which have been written off provides an example.

Earned Income by Responsibility Center

The results of the process of attribution of income to responsibility centers are illustrated in Table 4.6 for the School of Physical and Mathematical Sciences. An examination of the amounts of income attributed to the unit shows that attribution of credit hour fees is clearly the most important part of the exercise. They account for about $15.3 million of the total $18.1 million in general fund earned income. Next in significance is indirect cost recovery income at nearly $2.1 million.

Table 3.5 in the preceding chapter shows that direct general fund expenditures of the School of Physical and Mathematical Sciences total $22,860,000. Table 4.6 shows that the amount of income attributed to the school is a little over $18.1 million. Why does a difference exist? Our process of developing estimates of total income and and expenditure to responsibility centers is not complete. Only direct expenditures for the school have been determined. Indirect expenses have yet to be allocated. When that step is complete, state support will be determined as the difference between total expenditure and earned income.

One income category shown in Table 4.1 is missing from Table 4.6: state support. Until indirect costs are allocated to the responsibility centers, we do not have sufficient information upon which to base that attribution. As will subsequently be seen, all state support is attributed to primary mission units, responsibility centers providing teaching, research, and public services.

Table 4.7 illustrates general fund earned income attributed to a support unit, student services. The income generated by the activities of student services amounts to $1,073,662.

As shown in Table 3.6, the direct expenditures of student services total nearly $4.9 million, nearly $3.8 million more than earned income. How will the difference be funded?

Support centers have two sources of support: earned income and what we

TABLE 4.6 ILLUSTRATIVE ATTRIBUTION OF GENERAL FUND
INCOME TO THE SCHOOL OF PHYSICAL AND
MATHEMATICAL SCIENCES

Income Category	Amount
Credit hour fees	$ 15,271,145
Course-related fees	
laboratory fees	334,000
practicum fees	
other special course fees	
auditing	11,000
independent study	
forfeited fees	
SUBTOTAL	$ 345,000
Other fee income	
noncredit continuing education	
other special instructional fees	
applications	
transcript	
late/deferred	
special examination	
late program change	
SUBTOTAL	
Indirect cost recovery income	2,067,000
Title IV administration fee	
Interest income	
Rental income	
Gifts and grants	400,000
Auxiliary service charge	
Sales and service income	
Other income general	
TOTAL	$ 18,083,145

call intercenter allocations. Intercenter allocations represent charges and assessments for services rendered by support centers to other units. For the units being served, they appear as indirect cost allocations; for the units providing the service, as income.

Earned income for student services appears in Table 4.7. Its intercenter allocation has yet to be determined in a process that will be described in chapter 6.

TABLE 4.7 ILLUSTRATIVE ATTRIBUTION OF GENERAL FUND INCOME TO STUDENT SERVICES

Income Category	Amount
Credit hour fees	
Course-related fees	
laboratory fees	
practicum fees	
other special course fees	
auditing	
independent study	
forfeited fees	
SUBTOTAL	
Other fee income	
noncredit continuing education	$
other special instructional fees	
applications	205,000
transcript	65,000
late/deferred	
special examination	
late program change	
SUBTOTAL	$ 270,000
Indirect cost recovery income	34,662
Title IV administration fee	160,000
Interest income	
Rental income	
Gifts and grants	
Auxiliary service charge	590,000
Sales and service income	19,000
Other income general	
TOTAL	$ 1,073,662

Extension to All Centers

As a result of the procedures described in this chapter, general fund earned income can be attributed to all responsibility units, both academic and support. In Table 4.8, earned income is displayed for each center. Earned income is divided into three major categories—student fee income, indirect cost recovery income, and other earned income—and totals $129.9 million. Student

TABLE 4.8 EARNED INCOME OF ALL RESPONSIBILITY CENTERS

	Student Fee Income	Indirect Cost Recovery	Other Income	Total Earned Income
Arts and Humanities	$ 11,117,413	$ 278,116	$ 500	$ 11,396,029
Physicl & Math Sci	15,616,145	2,067,000	400,000	18,083,145
Social & Behavrl Sci	19,110,365	910,590	416,327	20,437,282
Dentistry	2,284,720	266,071	1,498,531	4,049,322
Medicine	6,118,652	3,679,181	11,852,636	21,650,469
Nursing	1,957,458	44,144	0	2,001,602
Optometry	1,486,223	86,456	760,000	2,332,679
Business	14,665,290	25,516	18,550	14,709,356
Education	6,582,929	218,776	48,820	6,850,525
Engineering & Tech	2,456,414	30,752	0	2,487,166
Law	3,830,668	1,929	27,262	3,859,859
Music	7,294,751	913	18,000	7,313,664
Physical Education	4,796,731	158,622	139,553	5,094,906
Public Affairs	3,692,501	309,591	3,108	4,005,200
Libraries	0	30,231	171,500	201,731
Academic Computing	0	0	0	0
Academic Affairs	893,467	228,849	74,295	1,196,611
Student Services	270,000	34,662	769,000	1,073,662
Physical Facilities	0	0	37,700	37,700
Centrl Administratn	69,000	0	3,097,000	3,166,000
TOTAL	$102,242,727	$ 8,371,399	$ 19,332,782	$129,946,908

fee income constitutes the largest component, $102.2 million (nearly 77 percent); indirect cost recovery income, $8.4 million; and other income, $19.3 million. Three schools—medicine, social and behavioral sciences, and physical and mathematical sciences—account for over $60 million of total earned income.

5. Allocation of Costs to Responsibility Centers

> Though this be madness, yet there is method in't.
>
> Shakespeare, *Hamlet*, II, ii, 211

Under traditional general fund accounting and budgeting concepts, operating units manage only their direct costs. Direct costs can be narrowly or broadly defined. The narrower the definition, the larger the aggregate amount of indirect costs.

Salaries and wages of a unit's personnel and supplies and expenses used by them constitute a definition of direct costs at the narrow end of the spectrum. Allocating to operating units the fringe benefits associated with total compensation of their personnel represents in dollar terms a significant broadening of the definition.

The extent to which units manage their nonpersonnel costs can vary widely. From only expenditure for direct use of supplies, it can be broadened to include travel, telephone, equipment, and on occasion space rent. However, whether the convention is narrow or broad, traditional accounting and budgeting arrangements do not aspire to assign all of a unit's costs to it.

Full Cost Approach

Under responsibility center budgeting, all of a center's cost is allocated to each responsibility center. With a decentralized approach to decision making, the head of each center must recognize the effect of her or his decisions not only on the center but also on the entire institution. That perspective can be gained when total—not partial—costs of alternative courses of action are readily apparent.

When all costs are allocated, the illusion of free goods and services—goods and services which appear free to operating units but which are not free to the institution—vanishes. Under traditional budgeting arrangements in which rent is seldom if ever charged, space appears free to operating units even though typically more than 10 percent of general fund expenditure must be allocated for operation and maintenance of facilities. When units are not charged for telephones, they appear free. Similarly for library acquisitions and services and for academic computing and audiovisual services. If charges are not levied for such services, alert and aggressive managers will attempt to maximize their unit's performance by securing more "free" inputs. Their clamor will not cease until the additional contribution to their productivity— as they see it—of additional amounts of those "free" inputs diminishes to zero. However, since for an institution those inputs are not free, its overall performance is not optimized. Signals given to unit managers when they are unaware of the total cost of their actions lead to decisions which do not promote the institution's objectives. If they are rational individuals, their actions will appear irrational when viewed as a group.

Cost Allocation Criteria

The distinction between direct and indirect costs is somewhat artificial. In a sense, indirect costs are direct costs that are more difficult to associate with specific activities. Because their association is less obvious, we have to adopt conventions to allocate them. As summarized in Table 5.1, conventions can be seen to vary by type of cost.

To categorize indirect costs, we adopt a modified version of the program classification structure developed by the National Center for Education Management Systems in 1972.[1] The major support categories are academic support, student services, institutional support—which includes executive management and general administration—and physical plant operations and maintenance.

Assessments and Charges

The cost of those support categories can take two forms: (1) assessments and/or (2) charges. Assessments are employed to cover the public goods or public service aspect of support services; charges, to cover the portion of support services which is marketable.

Assessments resemble a tax. They are assigned to responsibility centers

---

1. The classification structure is described in National Center for Education Management Systems, *Program Classification Structure*, Technical Report 27, 1st ed. (Boulder, Colorado: 1972.)

TABLE 5.1   COST ALLOCATION CRITERIA

Cost Category/Components	*Allocation Method*
1. Academic support	
a. Library b. Academic Computing	Costs of academic computing and library services are to be distributed to centers on the basis of a combination of charges and allocations developed by heads of those units

c. Academic Affairs
         Academic administration
         Learning resources
         Personnel development
         Research & Graduate
           Development
	Other academic support is to be distributed in proportion to total direct expense of general, designated, and restricted funds

2. Student Services and Student Financial Assistance	

Student Services
     Student services administration
     Admissions, Registrar
     Counseling and guidance
     Financial aid administration
	Student services costs are to be distributed in proportion to credit hour enrollment

Student Financial Assistance
     Scholarships
     Fellowships
     Fee remissions
	The costs of financial aid programs oriented primarily to academic programs are to be allocated to the appropriate center; the cost of other financial aid programs are to be distributed in proportion to undergraduate and graduate enrollments

3. Physical Plant	Physical plant costs are to be distributed according to space occupied by a center
4. Central Administration	

Executive Management
     Trustees, President
     Community relations
     Alumni relations
     Contingencies
     General administration
     Fiscal operations
     Business office
	The costs of executive management and general administration are to be distributed in proportion to total direct expenses of general, designated, and other restricted funds and some fraction of the direct expenses of auxiliary & service units

according to formula. Once determined, the amounts are fixed, and center managers have little ability to change assessments in the short run and no discretion about paying them. Like a tax, they must be paid.

Charges are payments for services provided by a support center specifically for a user. By forgoing the service, a user can avoid making a payment. When more of a service is desired, the user can obtain more of it through paying more.

1. Academic Support

Academic support includes such operations as deans of faculties and of research and graduate programs, course and program development, libraries, museums, galleries, academic computing, and audiovisual services. A major portion of library, computing, and audiovisual services is user specific. However, another portion reflects the public good nature of their operation. Initially, the public good aspect prevails, and all costs are allocated in the form of an assessment to centers.

A. LIBRARY

Direct expenditures for library operations and acquisitions account for between 4 and 5 percent of total general fund expenditures. Their significance for the academic programs they serve is even greater.

Library services generally are provided without charge to users. Access to and use of the facility is free. Books can be borrowed without charge. When due no fee is levied. A faculty member can place books on reserve for courses she or he teaches without charge to the department. Faculty and graduate student study spaces are provided without charge. Funds for acquisitions of monographs and serials and more recently access to data bases are distributed to disciplines out of total resources allocated to the library.

The absence of charges suggests that library services fall into the category of public goods and services. However, even a casual inspection reveals that the beneficiaries of the services can be identified and that costs can be assigned to the services they receive. People pay to attend theatrical and musical performances and to visit museums. Why not libraries? Tools can be rented. Publishers persuade readers to buy books. Why not rent library books? Academic departments pay for telephones, duplicating services, and equipment. Why should they not pay for book reservation services their faculty require? For study spaces reserved for their faculty and graduate students? For books and periodicals their faculty request?

Librarians typically eschew user charges, cloaking their role in the university community aura of being too valuable to be subjected to a market test.

TABLE 5.2 ALLOCATION PARAMETERS FOR LIBRARY SUPPORT COSTS

| | Full Time Equivalent Faculty | | Full Time Equivalent Students | | | | | | Weighted Total | Percent of Total |
| | | | Undergraduate | | Graduate | | Professional | | | |
	Number	Wt	Number	Wt	Amount	Wt	Amount	Wt		
Arts and Humanities	115	1.00	3,420	0.05	188	0.25	0	0.25	333	8.8
Physical and Math Sci	220	1.00	4,541	0.05	527	0.25	0	0.25	579	15.3
Social & Behavrl Sci	256	1.00	5,449	0.05	753	0.25	0	0.25	717	19.0
Dentistry	103	0.20	115	0.05	65	0.05	129	0.05	36	0.9
Medicine	517	0.20	334	0.05	155	0.05	1,450	0.05	200	5.3
Nursing	128	1.00	610	0.05	197	0.05	0	0.05	168	4.4
Optometry	45	0.50	56	0.05	5	0.25	325	0.25	108	2.8
Business	138	1.00	2,984	0.05	831	0.25	8	0.25	497	13.1
Education	117	1.00	832	0.05	786	0.25	2	0.25	356	9.4
Engineering & Tech	74	1.00	1,266	0.05	51	0.25	0	0.25	150	4.0
Law	43	0.20	0	0.05	5	0.05	594	0.05	39	1.0
Music	131	1.00	1,026	0.05	605	0.25	1	0.25	334	8.8
Physical Education	40	1.00	1,129	0.05	218	0.25	0	0.25	151	4.0
Public Affairs	32	1.00	673	0.05	157	0.25	3	0.25	106	2.8
SUBTOTAL: ACADEMIC	1,959		22,435		4,543		2,512		3,774	99.6
Libraries	21	0.00	0	0.00	0	0.00	0	0.00	0	0.0
Academic Computing	0	0.00	0	0.05	0	0.25	0	0.25	0	0.0
Academic Affairs	16	1.00	0	0.05	0	0.25	0	0.25	16	0.4
Student Services	0	1.00	0	0.05	0	0.25	0	0.25	0	0.0
Physical Facilities	0	1.00	0	0.05	0	0.25	0	0.25	0	0.0
Central Administratn	0	1.00	0	0.05	0	0.25	0	0.25	0	0.0
SUBTOTAL: SUPPORT	37		0		0		0		16	0.4
TOTAL	1,996		22,435		4,543		2,512		3,790	100.0

Their patrons likewise do not seem particularly eager to pay directly for the services they receive. Perhaps librarians are correct. Perhaps their patrons like the appearance of receiving something for nothing.

Attempting to change current conventions, however tempting, postpones indefinitely implementation of responsibility center budgeting. Therefore, to get on with the task, the illusion of a free service for users is not challenged, and all library costs are assigned as an assessment to other responsibility centers. Committees of librarians and faculty members can be counted on to develop needlessly complex assignment arrangements. A workable arrangement which has been adopted without the benefit of their counsel is displayed in Table 5.2.

In Table 5.2, library cost allocations are based on a weighted total of each center's number of full-time equivalent faculty and full-time equivalent student enrollment. The number of full-time equivalent faculty is generated from budget data. Credit hour enrollments in courses taught by each responsibility center are divided by 30 to produce the number of full-time equivalent undergraduate and professional students and by 24 to produce the number of full-time equivalent graduate students. Those divisions require knowledge of which credit hours are taken by undergraduate, graduate, and professional students—information which is obtained in the course of estimating each center's instructional fee income.

Weights range from 1.00 to 0.00. For most centers, faculty are weighted at 1.00; undergraduate students, at 0.05; graduate and professional students, at 0.25. Faculty are weighted twenty times more than undergraduate students and four times more than graduate and professional students. Such weighting is not intended to imply that faculty members use the library twenty times more frequently than undergraduate students. All weights are negotiated numbers intended to achieve a reasonable distribution of library costs among responsibility centers.

Note the exceptions to a 1.00 weight for faculty. Dental, medical, and law faculty are weighted at 0.20; for optometry faculty, at 0.50; for librarians (considered as faculty—no second class citizens among the servants of the servants of scholarship), at 0.00. The reduced weights are not intended to imply that the teachers of future dentists, physicians, optometrists, and lawyers are less scholarly than their academic colleagues—a suspicion in some circles—but rather reflect the fact that those schools operate separate libraries. Separate library facilities provide a rationale for reduced weights for their respective graduate and professional students.

Librarians do use the library (probably). However, their weight is zero because we are allocating all library costs to the other centers. For the same reason, the weights for undergraduate, graduate, and professional students are zero as well, even though the library has no enrollments.

The weighted total is calculated as the sum of the products of the number of full-time equivalent faculty and students and its respective weight. The total for Arts and Humanities, for example, is:

$115 * 1.00 + 3420 * 0.05 + 188 * 0.25 + 0 * .025$

or

$115 + 171 + 47$

or

333

The sum of the weighted totals for all centers is 3,790.

Each of the weighted totals is expressed as a percent of 3,790 in the right column of Table 5.2. Under the allocation arrangement displayed here, fifteen of the twenty responsibility centers share library cost assessments. Nearly 19 percent of the assessment for library services is levied on the School of Social and Behavioral Sciences. With the School of Physical and Mathematical Sciences, the assessments accounted for become slightly over one third of the total. Almost three fourths of the assessment is distributed to six centers. Clearly, not every academic unit has an equal stake in the investment in library services and acquisitions—or is willing to admit to it.

B. ACADEMIC COMPUTING

Computers can keep track of those who use them. Unlike the patrons of libraries, the extent of user use of computer facilities can be precisely determined. However, academic (and administrative) computing center directors are no more eager than their bibliomaniacal counterparts to charge directly for the services they provide. Even in times of exponential growth and budget-balance-bursting demands for additional resources, the once relevant need to increase awareness and use of computers is cited as a reason for hiding the cost of employing them from potential customers.

Not only is the desire to charge for services rendered absent but also the amount to charge is not automatically determined. While the number of central processing units, connect time, pages printed, and other measures of user consumption can be used as a basis for charges, they do not indicate what the services are worth. They must be assigned a value or weighted before charges can be calculated. Determining those weights is not entirely a technical process, and negotiations among users and vendors may be required to reach a consensus. However, since both the measures of user consumption and the cost of providing them fall entirely in the domain of the computer center, vendors are somewhat disadvantaged in the bargaining process.

An arrangement which introduces additional parameters for negotiation purposes is displayed in Table 5.3. In addition to an index of unfunded usage based on weighted measures of user service, the number of student, faculty, and staff full time equivalents are included in the calculation of an allocation parameter for each responsibility center.

Faculty and support staff full time equivalents are weighted at 1.00 for all units except for academic computing itself. Two different weights are assigned to student full time equivalents. Those centers whose students make extensive use of computing are assigned weights of 1.50. They include physical and mathematical sciences, social and behavioral sciences, nursing, business, education, engineering and technology, law, and public affairs. Other disciplines, judged to use computing less extensively, are assigned weights of 1.00.

The index of past unfunded usage is derived from estimated cost of each center's use of academic computing. Each center's cost as calculated by the academic computing center has been multiplied by (32,155/$5,180,000), where 32,155 is the sum of faculty, staff, and student full time equivalents and $5,180,000 is the total estimated unfunded cost for all centers. That arrangement serves to equalize the significance of the computer center's algorithm for allocating costs with outside parameters subject to negotiation. For most users, the index is assigned a weight of 1.00. Three high volume users—physical and mathematical sciences, medicine, and engineering and technology—get a discount and are weighted at 0.75.

As shown in the right hand column, the allocation methodology assesses the School of Physical and Mathematical Sciences 29 percent of the total cost of academic computing center services. Nearly 58 percent falls to three schools: Physical and Mathematical Sciences, Social and Behavioral Sciences, and Medicine. Like the library, academic computing services are concentrated in relatively few centers.

C. ACADEMIC AFFAIRS

Support in the form of academic administration, research and graduate development, and such learning resources activities as course and program development is not user specific. In Indiana University's case, allocating that cost as a fixed assessment to academic units in proportion to total direct expense of general, designated, and restricted funds expenditure was adopted.

Academic administration includes the dean of faculties and faculty records.

TABLE 5.3   ALLOCATION PARAMETERS FOR ACADEMIC COMPUTING COSTS

	Full Time Equivalent Faculty & Staff		Full Time Equivalent Students		Past Unfunded Usage			Weighted Total	Percent of Total
	Number	Wt	Number	Wt	Amount	Index	Wt		
Arts and Humanities	125	1.00	3,608	1.00	$ 64,465	400	1.00	4,133	6.2
Physical and Math Sci	234	1.00	5,068	1.50	2,521,089	15,650	0.75	19,574	29.0
Social & Behavrl Sci	274	1.00	6,202	1.50	42,514	264	1.00	9,841	14.7
Dentistry	124	1.00	309	1.00	135,043	838	1.00	1,271	1.9
Medicine	724	1.00	1,939	1.00	1,389,058	8,623	0.75	9,130	13.6
Nursing	135	1.00	807	1.50	39,179	243	1.00	1,589	2.4
Optometry	54	1.00	386	1.00	278	2	1.00	442	0.7
Business	178	1.00	3,823	1.50	40,291	250	1.00	6,163	9.2
Education	149	1.00	1,620	1.50	7,225	45	1.00	2,624	3.9
Engineering & Tech	76	1.00	1,317	1.50	812,484	5,044	0.75	5,835	8.7
Law	50	1.00	599	1.50	556	3	1.00	952	1.4
Music	154	1.00	1,632	1.00	556	3	1.00	1,789	2.7
Physical Education	44	1.00	1,347	1.00	0	0	1.00	1,391	2.1
Public Affairs	45	1.00	833	1.50	110,869	688	1.00	1,983	3.0
SUBTOTAL: ACADEMIC	2,366		29,490		$ 5,163,607	32,053		66,717	99.5
Libraries	22	1.00	0	1.00	$ 278	2	1.00	24	0.0
Academic Computing	47	0.00	0	0.00	0	0	0.00	0	0.0
Academic Affairs	30	1.00	0	1.00	9,725	60	1.00	90	0.1
Student Services	41	1.00	0	1.00	1,389	9	1.00	50	0.1
Physical Facilities	17	1.00	0	1.00	0	0	1.00	17	0.0
Central Administratn	142	1.00	0	1.00	5,002	31	1.00	173	0.3
SUBTOTAL: SUPPORT	299		0		$ 16,394	102		354	0.5
TOTAL	2,665		29,490		$ 5,180,001	32,155		67,071	100.0

The cost of such functions could be distributed according to the number of faculty, but the level of general and designated fund expenditures correlates well with the number of faculty and encompasses broader academic considerations.

The activities of research and graduate development similarly relate closely with those of academic administration but also extend to the level of research. To capture that feature of research and graduate development operations, restricted fund expenditures are included as one of the bases for allocating costs.

Although audiovisual user data are not obtained as automatically as they are in the case of computing services, a well-run audiovisual operation should be able to provide a basis for allocating the cost of its operations among centers. Inasmuch as those services can be expected to vary among users in proportion to their size, general and designated fund expenditures can be— and are—used as a proxy if the audiovisual unit is unable or unwilling to develop estimates.

Assistance in course and program development likewise appears to be an expense chargeable to units desiring such services. However, the basis for allocating those charges fades upon request. Like their counterparts in libraries and computing centers, learning resources academic entrepreneurs become very nervous when their "essential" and "invaluable" contributions to the academic enterprise are subjected to a market test.

Academic administration, research and graduate development, and learning resources could be shown as separate responsibility centers. For purposes of this illustration, they are combined.

The calculation is illustrated in Table 5.4. Direct general, designated, and restricted fund expenditures for all centers are displayed. All support units receive weights of zero, since academic support is presumed to relate only to those units directly engaged in teaching and research. With the exceptions of dentistry and medicine, the direct expenditures of all the academic units are assigned weights of one. The expenditures of dentistry and medicine receive weights less than one to reflect their practice of providing a portion of academic support services themselves. The School of Medicine, for example, operates its own educational resources unit which also serves dentistry. As a result, its demand on academic support is judged to be somewhat less than its relative size would indicate.

As shown in the last column of Table 5.4, despite reduced weights, 30 percent of academic support costs are allocated to the School of Medicine. Medicine with the Schools of Physical and Mathematical Sciences and of Social and Behavioral Sciences accounts for over 55 percent of the costs.

TABLE 5.4 ALLOCATION PARAMETERS FOR ACADEMIC SUPPORT COSTS

	General Fund		Designated Fund		Restricted Fund		Weighted Total	Percent of Total
	Amount	Wt	Amount	Wt	Amount	Wt		
Arts and Humanities	$ 11,862,000	1.00	$ 104,000	1.00	$ 1,182,000	1.00	$ 13,148,000	4.9
Physical and Math Sci	22,860,000	1.00	756,000	1.00	14,922,000	1.00	38,538,000	14.4
Social & Behavrl Sci	25,108,000	1.00	211,000	1.00	3,870,000	1.00	29,189,000	10.9
Dentistry	12,599,000	0.92	1,462,000	1.00	2,432,000	1.00	15,485,080	5.8
Medicine	59,540,000	0.60	15,356,000	0.90	38,735,000	0.80	80,532,400	29.9
Nursing	9,696,000	1.00	105,000	1.00	659,000	1.00	10,460,000	3.9
Optometry	3,291,000	1.00	99,000	1.00	551,000	1.00	3,941,000	1.5
Business	15,535,000	1.00	1,925,000	1.00	1,064,000	1.00	18,524,000	6.9
Education	10,215,000	1.00	267,000	1.00	7,448,000	1.00	17,930,000	6.7
Engineering & Tech	5,808,000	1.00	0	1.00	278,000	1.00	6,086,000	2.3
Law	4,850,000	1.00	49,000	1.00	443,000	1.00	5,342,000	2.0
Music	12,335,000	1.00	730,000	1.00	183,000	1.00	13,248,000	4.9
Physical Education	5,084,000	1.00	882,000	1.00	1,786,000	1.00	7,752,000	2.9
Public Affairs	5,687,000	1.00	544,000	1.00	1,778,000	1.00	8,009,000	3.0
SUBTOTAL: ACADEMIC	$204,470,000		$ 22,490,000		$ 75,331,000		$ 268,184,480	100.0
Libraries	12,574,000	0.00	76,000	0.00	747,000	0.00	0	0.0
Academic Computing	6,630,000	0.00	0	0.00	0	0.00	0	0.0
Academic Affairs	4,777,000	0.00	1,963,000	0.00	716,000	0.00	0	0.0
Student Services	4,867,000	0.00	456,000	0.00	7,771,000	0.00	0	0.0
Physical Facilities	27,983,000	0.00	0	0.00	0	0.00	0	0.0
Central Administratn	7,634,000	0.00	32,000	0.00	0	0.00	0	0.0
SUBTOTAL: SUPPORT	$ 64,465,000		$ 2,527,000		$ 9,234,000		$ 0	0.0
TOTAL	$268,935,000		$ 25,017,000		$ 84,565,000		$ 268,184,480	100.0

2. *Student Services and Student Financial Assistance*

Student services include such operations as the dean of students, related administrative activities, admissions, registrar, student records, academic advising, career counseling and placement, and student financial assistance administration. As shown in Table 5.5, student credit hour enrollment by center provides a basis for allocating costs associated with those activities to academic centers. But some credit hours are more equal than others! Weighting undergraduate credit hour enrollments more heavily than graduate and professional enrollments reflects a tendency for student services to be directed primarily for the benefit of undergraduate students. For graduate and professional students, many of those services are provided directly by academic units.

Scholarships for undergraduate students, fellowships for graduate students, and fee remissions for both groups constitute the student financial assistance category. Those transfer payments from the institution are distributed to students based on evidence of financial need, demonstration of exceptional academic merit, the program of study selected, or performance of service to the university.

Financial assistance which is program specific—e.g., fee remissions for student participation in music ensembles, fellowship awards to attract graduate students in specific schools—and which is related to performance of services—e.g., fee remissions to student counselors in residence halls—can be budgeted as a direct expense of responsibility centers. Unlike other allocations in the form of assessments, center managers are able to adjust the amount of student financial assistance to the level that they feel maximizes the effectiveness of their operation.

Other forms of financial assistance are less amenable to budgeting as a direct expense. Need based and merit based assistance, particularly for undergraduate students, is liable not to be targeted to specific programs or activities. That portion of financial assistance, therefore, is distributed to academic centers as an assessment based on their undergraduate and graduate credit hour enrollment.

Inasmuch as the parameters for distributing student financial assistance are identical for distributing the cost of student financial services, the weighting can be—and is—incorporated in Table 5.5. Displayed are credit hour enrollments in courses taught by the academic responsibility centers for the fall and spring semesters and summer sessions to undergraduate, graduate, and professional students. Credit hours taught to undergraduates are assigned a weight of one; to graduate students, 0.50; and to professional students, 0.25.

TABLE 5.5 ALLOCATION PARAMETERS FOR STUDENT SERVICES SUPPORT COSTS AND STUDENT FINANCIAL ASSISTANCE

| | Credit Hour Enrollments | | | | | | | |
| | Undergraduate | | Graduate | | Professional | | Weighted Total | Percent of Total |
	Number	Wt	Number	Wt	Number	Wt		
Arts and Humanities	102,600	1.00	4,512	0.50	0	0.25	104,856	14.0
Physical and Math Sci	136,230	1.00	12,648	0.50	0	0.25	142,554	19.1
Social & Behavrl Sci	163,470	1.00	18,072	0.50	0	0.25	172,506	23.1
Dentistry	3,450	1.00	1,560	0.50	3,870	0.25	5,198	0.7
Medicine	10,020	1.00	3,720	0.50	43,500	0.25	22,755	3.0
Nursing	18,300	1.00	4,728	0.50	0	0.25	20,664	2.8
Optometry	1,680	1.00	120	0.50	9,750	0.25	4,178	0.6
Business	89,520	1.00	19,944	0.50	240	0.25	99,552	13.3
Education	24,960	1.00	18,864	0.50	60	0.25	34,407	4.6
Engineering & Tech	37,980	1.00	1,224	0.50	0	0.25	38,592	5.2
Law	0	1.00	120	0.50	17,820	0.25	4,515	0.6
Music	30,780	1.00	14,520	0.50	30	0.25	38,048	5.1
Physical Education	33,870	1.00	5,232	0.50	0	0.25	36,486	4.9
Public Affairs	20,190	1.00	3,768	0.50	90	0.25	22,097	3.0
SUBTOTAL: ACADEMIC	673,050		109,032		75,360		746,408	100.0
Libraries	0	0.00	0	0.00	0	0.00	0	0.0
Academic Computing	0	0.00	0	0.00	0	0.00	0	0.0
Academic Affairs	0	0.00	0	0.00	0	0.00	0	0.0
Student Services	0	0.00	0	0.00	0	0.00	0	0.0
Physical Facilities	0	0.00	0	0.00	0	0.00	0	0.0
Central Administratn	0	0.00	0	0.00	0	0.00	0	0.0
SUBTOTAL: SUPPORT	0		0		0		0	0.0
TOTAL	673,050		109,032		75,360		746,408	100.0

The weighted total column contains the results of summing the products of each of the credit hour categories and their respective weights for each center. As shown in the right hand column, the first three centers—Arts and Humanities, Physical and Mathematical Sciences, and Social and Behavioral Sciences—account for over 55 percent of the cost assessments for student services and student financial assistance. Including the School of Business boosts the percentage to 69 percent.

3. Physical Facilities

As shown in Table 3.7, over 10 percent of the direct costs of all responsibility centers is accounted for by expenditures for physical facilities. The cost of operations and maintenance of the physical plant may include such related functions as security and environmental health and safety. Most, if not all, of such costs lend themselves to allocation to centers according to the space they occupy.

Prorating physical plant cost based on space occupancy can be adjusted for the cost of operating and maintaining different facilities. Not all space is equal with respect to its operating and maintenance cost, nor with respect to its desirability. Moreover, university space is not necessarily the least costly.

At the outset of such allocations, the advantage of adjusting space for its operating and maintenance cost is unclear. If desirable, generally newer, space is less expensive to operate and maintain, centers will be assessed more for inferior space and less for superior space. Supply of and demand for different types of space are liable to become askew. Rates assessed for square footage of space should reflect both supply and demand considerations, not just operating and maintenance cost. The balancing of supply and demand for different types of space through different prices can be achieved only through experience and approximation.

Nevertheless, because of the relative significance of physical facilities among the assessments allocated to responsibility centers, an allocation methodology recognizing costs deserves consideration. Moreover, service rendered by the support center for physical facilities varies markedly among users. Hospitals and dormitories provide their own housekeeping and maintenance; academic and administrative offices, classrooms, and laboratories rely completely on the support center. While a weighting approach can adjust for such differences, without cost data it begs the question. Since hospitals and dormitories occupy a large amount of space, legitimizing the adjustments becomes imperative.

The direct costs of the responsibility center for physical facilities approximate $28 million. The distribution of its expenditures among eight major

TABLE 5.6 DIRECT EXPENDITURE CATEGORIES OF
RESPONSIBILITY CENTER FOR PHYSICAL FACILITIES

Expenditure Category	Expenditure	Expenditure as a Percent of Total
Building Maintenance	$ 4,587,601	16.4
Campus Maintenance	1,226,824	4.4
Building Services	5,547,767	19.8
Prorated Costs	2,309,370	8.3
SUBTOTAL: OPERATIONS	$13,671,562	48.9
Electricity	7,970,507	28.4
Steam	4,351,978	15.6
Gas, Oil, Propane	458,065	1.6
Water and Sewer	1,530,888	5.5
SUBTOTAL: ENERGY AND UTILITIES	$14,311,438	51.1
TOTAL EXPENDITURE	$27,983,000	100.0

categories is shown in Table 5.6. The eight categories are divided into two groups of four each. The first group, operations, is a little less than $14 million; the second group, energy and utilities, is a little more. Energy and utilities represent "pass through" costs which are relatively inflexible. Their prices are largely set by external factors, and the amount used is difficult to change appreciably—at least in the short run.

Of the individual categories, electric power, nearly $8 million (28 percent), is largest. It is followed by building (mainly custodial) services, $5.5 million (20 percent). Virtually all facilities use electric power; building services are less widely distributed, so in selected buildings it frequently constitutes the largest cost per square foot.

Building maintenance at $4.6 million (16 percent) is next in importance and is distributed among the facilities in a fashion similar to building services. Steam for space and water heating is a major consideration for those buildings connected to the central facility, and in terms of dollar magnitude is followed in size by "prorated costs," a euphemism for physical plant overhead costs not assignable on a basis other than gross square footage. Since the buildings connected to the central electric and steam distribution system are not metered, most of those costs are distributed in proportion to gross square feet per building as well.

For each building, a statement of direct costs is prepared based on the eight

TABLE 5.7 STATEMENT OF COST FOR
BUILDING OPERATIONS AND MAINTENANCE

BUILDING: Geology Building   BUILDING NUMBER: 528
SQUARE FEET: GROSS 127,174   ASSIGNABLE: 80,120

Expenditure Category	Expenditure	Expenditure per Assignable Square Foot
Building Maintenance	$ 105,383	$ 1.31
Campus Maintenance	19,213	0.24
Building Services	119,881	1.50
Prorated Costs	32,871	0.41
SUBTOTAL: OPERATIONS	$ 277,348	$ 3.46
Electricity	216,157	2.70
Steam	50,390	0.63
Gas, Oil, Propane	180	0.00
Water and Sewer	11,391	0.14
SUBTOTAL: ENERGY AND UTILITIES	$ 278,118	$ 3.47
TOTAL EXPENDITURE	$ 555,466	$ 6.93

major physical facilities cost categories. An illustration of a statement for the Geology Building is shown in Table 5.7. All eight categories are represented and total to $555,466. Although many physical plant costs relate directly to gross square feet, a cost per assignable square foot of $6.93 is calculated. The latter figure is used to estimate direct physical plant costs to each operating unit occupying space in the Geology Building. Although most of the Geology Building is occupied by the Department of Geology, other units have managed to invade its precincts.

With a direct cost per assignable square foot calculated for each building and with an inventory of space assignments, each responsibility center's share of facilities costs can be estimated. Note the careful wording: "each responsibility center's share of facilities costs." Only the direct costs of the center responsible for physical facilities have been considered. Its indirect costs have not been included. Support centers, like the primary mission centers, incur indirect costs. At this point, we are developing a framework for the allocation of all such costs, and total costs for none of the centers have been determined.

In chapter 3, we used as an example the School of Physical and Mathematical Sciences. Let us return to that example to illustrate how the share of

TABLE 5.8 DEPARTMENTAL SPACE AND COST ASSIGNMENT

RESPONSIBILITY CENTER: School of Physical and Mathematical Sciences
DEPARTMENT: Chemistry

Building Number	Building Name	Cost per Assignable Square Foot	Assigned Area	Assigned Cost
071	Chemistry Building	$ 7.02	141,391	$992,564.82
528	Geology Building	6.93	5,674	39,320.82
608	Cyclotron Facility	6.71	658	4,415.18
703	Owen Hall	4.98	4,633	23,072.34
855	University Warehouse	1.01	5,697	5,753.97
TOTAL			158,053	$1,065,127.13

physical facilities costs can be estimated. One of the departments in the School of Physical and Mathematical Sciences was the Department of Chemistry. Table 5.8 shows how the chemistry department's share of facilities costs are estimated.

The chemistry department occupies space in five separate buildings: the Chemistry Building, the Geology Building, the Cyclotron Facility, a building called Owen Hall, and the University Warehouse, a storage facility. For each building, the square footage assigned to the chemistry department and its cost per assignable square foot is shown. Altogether, 158,053 square feet of space (over 3.6 acres!) is assigned to the department, and its cost per square foot varies from $7.02 in the case of the Chemistry Building to $1.01 for storage space in the University Warehouse. The total direct cost for the chemistry department amounts to $1,065,127.13—to be absurdly precise.

Similar calculations are performed for each of the departments of the School of Physical and Mathematical Sciences. The results are shown in Table 5.9. The space assigned to all the departments of the school totals to 592,409 (13.6 acres!), and the direct costs amount to $3,829,985. Clearly, space is not a free good!

But the figure we are showing does not represent the total cost of operating and maintaining the facilities occupied by the School of Physical and Mathematical Sciences. It represents only an assignment of the direct costs of the center responsible for physical facilities. At this point, we are attempting to determine only what share of the total (unknown) physical facilities costs can

TABLE 5.9 RESPONSIBILITY CENTER SPACE
AND COST ASSIGNMENT

CENTER: School of Physical and Mathematical Sciences

Operating Unit	Assigned Area	Assigned Cost
Office of the Dean	8,185	$ 35,881
Department of Astronomy	11,494	65,605
Department of Biological Sciences	174,093	1,162,927
Department of Chemistry	158,053	1,065,127
Department of Computer Science	15,624	76,762
Department of Geology	57,596	396,936
Department of Mathematics	26,249	111,376
Department of Physics	141,115	915,371
TOTAL	592,409	$ 3,829,985

be allocated to the School of Physical and Mathematical Sciences. To determine its share, we have to conduct similar estimates for each of the other responsibility centers.

The results of that lengthy and tedious process are displayed in Table 5.10. For each center a dollar amount is shown representing the direct costs calculated for the space its departments occupy. Note that the figure for total assigned costs, nearly $26.8 million, differs from the direct expenditures figure of $28 million budgeted for physical facilities in Table 3.7. Assignment of costs is based on a prior year's actual expenditures, not the amounts budgeted for a current year.

With one exception, weights assigned to each center's costs are 1.00 since differences in use are accounted for in developing the direct cost per assignable square foot. The one exception is physical facilities, which receives a weight of 0.00, since we are attempting to distribute all of its costs to the other units. The sum of the entries in the weighted total column differs from the direct costs column by the amount of the direct costs calculated for physical facilities. The percents for all the other units in the "Percent of Total" column are based on the weighted total column sum and are thus made sufficiently larger to total to 100.

What the "Percent of Total" column tells us is that the responsibility center incurring the largest percentage of physical plant costs is the School of Medicine, about 24 percent. Next in order by percentage is student services, around 19 percent. Those two units account for approximately 43 percent of all

TABLE 5.10   ALLOCATION PARAMETERS FOR PHYSICAL COSTS

	Assigned Cost		*Weighted*	*Percent of*
	Amount	*Wt*	*Total*	*Total*
Arts and Humanities	$ 293,525	1.00	$ 293,525	1.1
Physical and Math Sci	3,829,985	1.00	3,829,985	14.5
Social & Behavrl Sci	616,402	1.00	616,402	2.3
Dentistry	1,666,400	1.00	1,666,400	6.3
Medicine	6,321,003	1.00	6,321,003	23.9
Nursing	847,026	1.00	847,026	3.2
Optometry	166,412	1.00	166,412	0.6
Business	385,183	1.00	385,183	1.5
Education	413,265	1.00	413,265	1.6
Engineering & Tech	733,278	1.00	733,278	2.8
Law	410,170	1.00	410,170	1.6
Music	1,019,647	1.00	1,019,647	3.9
Physical Education	750,741	1.00	750,741	2.8
Public Affairs	183,911	1.00	183,911	0.7
SUBTOTAL: ACADEMIC	$17,636,948		$17,636,948	66.8
Libraries	1,808,238	1.00	1,808,238	6.8
Academic Computing	258,574	1.00	258,574	1.0
Academic Affairs	654,434	1.00	654,434	2.5
Student Services	5,080,936	1.00	5,080,936	19.2
Physical Facilities	354,811	0.00	0	0.0
Central Administratn	980,898	1.00	980,898	3.7
SUBTOTAL: SUPPORT	$ 9,137,891		$ 8,783,080	33.2
TOTAL	$26,774,839		$26,420,028	100.0

physical facilities costs because of space occupied by hospitals and dormitories which fall under their respective purviews.

Despite the exacting nature of the calculations required to arrive at those conclusions, they can only be regarded as first approximations. Low cost space may be high quality space, and high cost space may be undesirable. If space managers are allowed to ration space perceived as high quality by increasing its price and enticing users into undesirable space by lowering its price, cost estimates can be expected to be less of a consideration. They are necessary only to insure a balancing of total physical facilities expenditures with income earned through user charges.

4. Central Administration

Central administration includes executive management and general administration. Into the executive management category fall the trustees, the president, chancellors, and their immediate entourage. The trustees serve without compensation, of course, but they require a secretary, and costs are associated with their meetings, correspondence, and other services they provide.

General administration includes accounting, budgeting, bursar, controller, data processing, financial management, governmental relations, legal counsel, liability and property insurance, payroll, personnel, purchasing, real estate, treasurer, and university relations functions. The cost of all institutional activities can be allocated to responsibility centers in proportion to their total direct expenditures of all funds: general and designated and a portion of direct expenditures of restricted funds and auxiliary and service units. The general administrative services provided for a center can vary depending on the extent to which it is prepared to attend to its own management and administrative services and is reflected in the weights assigned to the fund groups for the centers.

That variation is shown in Table 5.11. Direct expenditures for all fund groups are displayed for each responsibility center. Beside each of the expenditure figures appears a weighting factor. Differences in the weight reflect a judgment of the level of institutional support provided centrally to a center.

For most centers, general and designated fund expenditures received weights of 1.00. Among the academic responsibility centers, dentistry and medicine are exceptions to recognize the extent to which they provide many of their own administrative support functions. Academic computing is assigned a zero weight since the general fund expenditure amount is only a transfer to the auxiliary accounts where the center is managed. Physical facilities' weight is reduced to 0.80 since a large portion of its expenditures are energy and utility payments.

Restricted fund expenditures receive weights of 0.50; auxiliary and service units, of 0.20. Auxiliary expenditures for the School of Medicine are weighted at 0.10 because the University Hospital manages directly much of its administrative support. The restricted fund, auxiliary enterprises, and service units balance their expenditure with income and provide a greater measure of administrative support than typical general and designated fund operations. Moreover, much of their costs of supervision are already reflected in general fund expenditures.

TABLE 5.11 ALLOCATION PARAMETERS FOR CENTRAL ADMINISTRATION COSTS

	General Fund		Designated Fund		Restricted Fund		Auxiliaries		Service Units		Weighted Total	Percent of Total
	Amount	Wt	Amount	Wt	Amount	Wt	Amount	Wt	Amount	Wt		
Arts and Humanities	$ 11,862,000	1.00	$ 104,000	1.00	$ 1,182,000	0.50	$ 0	0.20	0	0.20	$ 12,557,000	3.9
Physical and Math Sci	22,860,000	1.00	756,000	1.00	14,922,000	0.50	187,000	0.20	458,000	0.20	31,206,000	9.6
Social & Behavrl Sci	25,108,000	1.00	211,000	1.00	3,870,000	0.50	0	0.20	0	0.20	27,254,000	8.4
Dentistry	12,599,000	0.90	1,462,000	1.00	2,432,000	0.50	279,000	0.20	462,000	0.20	14,165,300	4.3
Medicine	59,540,000	0.60	15,356,000	0.90	38,735,000	0.50	190,483,000	0.10	3,017,000	0.20	88,563,600	27.1
Nursing	9,696,000	1.00	105,000	1.00	659,000	0.50	0	0.20	0	0.20	10,130,500	3.1
Optometry	3,291,000	1.00	99,000	1.00	551,000	0.50	0	0.20	0	0.20	3,665,500	1.1
Business	15,535,000	1.00	1,925,000	1.00	1,064,000	0.50	133,000	0.20	0	0.20	18,018,600	5.5
Education	10,215,000	1.00	267,000	1.00	7,448,000	0.50	71,000	0.20	0	0.20	14,220,200	4.4
Engineering & Tech	5,808,000	1.00	0	1.00	278,000	0.50	0	0.20	0	0.20	5,947,000	1.8
Law	4,850,000	1.00	49,000	1.00	443,000	0.50	52,000	0.20	0	0.20	5,130,900	1.6
Music	12,335,000	1.00	730,000	1.00	183,000	0.50	0	0.20	0	0.20	13,156,500	4.0
Physical Education	5,084,000	1.00	882,000	1.00	1,786,000	0.50	809,000	0.20	0	0.20	7,020,800	2.2
Public Affairs	5,687,000	1.00	544,000	1.00	1,778,000	0.50	0	0.20	1,059,000	0.20	7,331,800	2.2
SUBTOTAL: ACADEMIC	$204,470,000		$ 22,490,000		$ 75,331,000		$192,014,000		$ 4,996,000		$258,367,700	79.2
Libraries	12,574,000	1.00	76,000	1.00	747,000	0.50	0	0.20	0	0.20	13,023,500	4.0
Academic Computing	6,630,000	0.00	0	1.00	0	0.50	6,761,000	0.20	0	0.20	1,352,200	0.4
Academic Affairs	4,777,000	1.00	1,963,000	1.00	716,000	0.50	0	0.20	0	0.20	7,098,000	2.2
Student Services	4,867,000	1.00	456,000	1.00	7,771,000	0.50	59,549,000	0.20	0	0.20	21,118,300	6.5
Physical Facilities	27,983,000	0.80	0	1.00	0	0.50	0	0.20	13,501,000	0.20	25,086,600	7.7
Central Administratn	7,634,000	0.00	32,000	0.00	0	0.00	13,224,000	0.00	16,624,000	0.00	0	0.0
SUBTOTAL: SUPPORT	$ 64,465,000		$ 2,527,000		$ 9,234,000		$ 79,534,000		$ 30,125,000		$ 67,678,600	20.8
TOTAL	$268,935,000		$ 25,017,000		$ 84,565,000		$271,548,000		$ 35,121,000		$326,046,300	100.0

TABLE 5.12   ALLOCATION PARAMETERS FOR
ALL SUPPORT CENTERS

	Librar-ies	Acadmic Cmpting	Acadmic Affairs	Student Service	Physcal Fclties	Central Admnstn
Arts and Humanities	8.8	6.2	4.9	14.0	1.1	3.9
Physical and Math Sci	15.3	29.0	14.4	19.1	14.5	9.6
Social & Behavrl Sci	19.0	14.7	10.9	23.1	2.3	8.4
Dentistry	0.9	1.9	5.8	0.7	6.3	4.3
Medicine	5.3	13.6	29.9	3.0	23.9	27.1
Nursing	4.4	2.4	3.9	2.8	3.2	3.1
Optometry	2.8	0.7	1.5	0.6	0.6	1.1
Business	13.1	9.2	6.9	13.3	1.5	5.5
Education	9.4	3.9	6.7	4.6	1.6	4.4
Engineering & Tech	4.0	8.7	2.3	5.2	2.8	1.8
Law	1.0	1.4	2.0	0.6	1.6	1.6
Music	8.8	2.7	4.9	5.1	3.9	4.0
Physical Education	4.0	2.1	2.9	4.9	2.8	2.2
Public Affairs	2.8	3.0	3.0	3.0	0.7	2.2
SUBTOTAL: ACADEMIC	99.6	99.5	100.0	100.0	66.8	79.2
Libraries	0.0	0.0	0.0	0.0	6.8	4.0
Academic Computing	0.0	0.0	0.0	0.0	1.0	0.4
Academic Affairs	0.4	0.1	0.0	0.0	2.5	2.2
Student Services	0.0	0.1	0.0	0.0	19.2	6.5
Physical Facilities	0.0	0.0	0.0	0.0	0.0	7.7
Central Administratn	0.0	0.3	0.0	0.0	3.7	0.0
SUBTOTAL: SUPPORT	0.4	0.5	0.0	0.0	33.2	20.8
TOTAL	100.0	100.0	100.0	100.0	100.0	100.0

Despite the reduced weights, about 27 percent of central administration costs are allocated to the School of Medicine. The remaining 73 percent is distributed broadly among the other centers.

Summary

Allocation parameters for six support responsibility centers have been determined: libraries, academic computing, academic affairs, student services, physical facilities, and central administration. Those allocation parameters are the percentages appearing in the right hand columns of Tables 5.2, 5.3, 5.4, 5.5, 5.10, and 5.11. They are summarized in Table 5.12.

A survey of Table 5.12 shows that the percentage distributions, while similar, are different. Centers with large percentages in one column tend to have large percentages in others. But a center with the largest percentage in one column is not the largest in another. The variations are important. If the columns of percentages were identical, they could be combined into one distribution. Their differences indicate that the additional calculations required to produce them provide a better basis for allocating support center costs.

Selection of the number of sets of percentages for distributing support center costs is a judgment call. If too few are selected, important differences in allocating costs will be ignored. Beyond a certain point, however, the sets of percentages become redundant. One distribution becomes nearly identical to another, and little information is gained for the effort.

What do those percentages mean? They represent the portion of a support center's total net cost which is to be allocated to another center. For example, the first entry in the first column, 8.8, indicates that 8.8 percent of the total net cost of the libraries is to be allocated to the School of Arts and Humanities. And what is total net cost? Total net cost is the total cost of a support center's operation less earned income attributed to it. In chapter 4, we discussed how earned income is attributed to responsibility centers. But how is total cost determined? The answer to that question is addressed in chapter 6.

6. Determining Total Costs

Men must endure what the gods give
And lightly bear our share of good and bad. . . .

Theognis, Elegies [591-2]

Universities are communities. Rarely does an opportunity present itself to express the relationships constituting a university as a community with mathematical precision and elegance. Determining total costs for responsibility centers provides such an opportunity.

Up to this point, we have dealt only with the direct costs of responsibility centers. Our objective, however, is to determine their total costs—not only direct costs but also indirect or overhead costs for services they receive from other centers.

In the preceding chapter, we developed allocation parameters in the form of percentages that can be used to assign a support center's cost to other centers receiving its services. The exercise seems straightforward until we try to begin. What are the support centers' costs we are to allocate? Their direct cost? Their total cost? Or their total cost net of earned income? The correct answer to this multiple choice question is neither all of the above nor none of the above, but the third alternative: total cost net of earned income.

An illustration of earned income for all responsibility centers was presented in Table 4.8. So, if we know total cost for the support centers, we should be able to determine total net costs. But we don't know total cost because that's what we're trying to establish for all centers—academic and support.

Our problem would be simplified if support centers provided services only for academic centers. Then their direct costs would be equal to their total costs. But as our work in the previous chapter indicates, relationships are not that simple. Physical facilities provides services for all centers. Central administration provides services for all centers, including physical facilities. Support centers' direct costs are clearly not equal to their total costs. How can we begin?

Three ways of proceeding are available. We shall adopt the third, which is most elegant and has a more meaningful virtue of providing a better representation of the distribution of indirect costs among the centers. But all three are mentioned in case some prefer one of the other alternatives. The three options are:

1. Allocate support center costs only to academic centers,
2. Allocate support center costs sequentially, or
3. Allocate support center costs simultaneously.

An advantage of the first two options is their apparent simplicity. Until the advent of electronic computing, option three was not feasible. Until the advent of desktop computing, option three was not convenient.

Allocating Support Center Costs Only to Academic Centers

One way to proceed is to ignore services that support centers provide to support centers. With that simplifying assumption, each support center's direct cost—less earned income—can be distributed to academic responsibility centers in proportion to their percentages.

As illustrated in Table 5.12, such an approach is entirely appropriate for academic affairs and student services. All of their services are directed to academic units. It is less appropriate for libraries and academic computing, but the extent of the distortion appears to be insignificant. For physical facilities and central administration, however, support center to support center services are substantial.

Only 66.8 percent of physical facilities costs are assigned to academic responsibility centers. The procedures under the first option require that 100 percent of physical facilities costs are assigned to that 66.8 percent. The School of Arts and Humanities, for example, instead of being allocated 1.1 percent of physical facilities costs, will be allocated 1.6 percent. Similar adjustments in the academic centers' percentages will be required so that all the physical facilities costs are distributed.

Similarly, direct costs of central administration will be allocated only to academic centers. The fact that administrative computing, which is included among central administration's functions, provides services for the library, academic support, and student services is simply disregarded. With such an arrangement in place, a move toward an expensive library automation system will appear to academic users as an increase in central administration's assessments rather than in the library's if administrative computing provides support for the system. Of course, the reason for the increase can be explained to the deans who head academic responsibility centers. To the extent that they are rational and understanding individuals, they will appreciate that the distortion is merely a product of the limitations of the approach and accept a possible windfall or extra burden without emotion or complaint.

Allocating Support Center Costs Sequentially

With adoption of an artificial convention, support center services to support centers can be recognized. All we have to do is agree on the sequence of allocating support center costs. Unfortunately, the sequence adopted affects the cost allocations. But as long as the heads of both academic and support centers can be counted on to put the university's welfare ahead of their own self interest and the welfare of their respective units, securing agreement should present no problem.

Let's assume we have agreed to the following allocation sequence: central administration, physical facilities, academic computing, libraries, academic affairs, and student services. For central administration, only its direct costs less any earned income is distributed. For physical facilities, direct costs plus its allocation for central administration less any earned income is distributed. For academic computing, its direct cost plus its allocations for central administration and physical facilities less any earned income are distributed. And so on until we get to student services.

Although high-minded deans do not engage in such picayune business, some readers may be curious what effect a different sequence has on indirect cost allocations. The effect of allocating central administration costs first and physical facilities second for the School of Medicine is exhibited in Table 6.1.

TABLE 6.1 PHYSICAL FACILITIES AND CENTRAL ADMINISTRATION ASSESSMENTS TO THE SCHOOL OF MEDICINE WITH CENTRAL ADMINISTRATION ALLOCATED FIRST

	Physical Facilities	Central Administratn
Direct costs	$27,983,000	$ 7,634,000
Less: Earned Income	- 37,700	- 3,166,000
Net Direct Costs	$27,945,300	$ 4,468,000
Allocated Central Administration Costs (7.7%)	344,036	
Total Net Costs	$28,289,336	$ 4,468,000
Allocation Percentages for the School of Medicine	23.9%	27.1%
Allocations to the School of Medicine	$ 6,761,151	$ 1,210,828
TOTAL ASSESSMENT		$ 7,971,979

TABLE 6.2 PHYSICAL FACILITIES AND CENTRAL
ADMINISTRATION ASSESSMENTS TO THE SCHOOL OF
MEDICINE WITH CENTRAL ADMINISTRATION ALLOCATED FIRST

	Physical Facilities	*Central Administratn*
Direct costs	$27,983,000	$ 7,634,000
Less: Earned Income	- 37,700	- 3,166,000
Net Direct Costs	$27,945,300	$ 4,468,000
Allocated Physical Facilities Costs (3.7%)		1,033,976
Total Net Costs	$27,945,300	$ 5,501,976
Allocation Percentages for the School of Medicine	23.9%	27.1%
Allocations to the School of Medicine	$ 6,678,927	$ 1,491,962
TOTAL ASSESSMENT		$ 8,169,962

For both support centers, earned income is subtracted from their respective direct costs. Then central administration's net direct costs are distributed: 27.1 percent to the School of Medicine; 7.7 percent to physical facilities. Physical facilities total net costs are distributed: 23.9 percent to the School of Medicine. As a result of those calculations, the School of Medicine is assessed $6,761,151 for physical facilities and $1,210,828 for central administration—a total assessment of $7,971,979.

Suppose—realizing, of course, that no one would be so gauche as to actually perform the calculations—that we had allocated physical facilities costs first. Table 6.2 shows the results of that sequence of events. As before, for both support centers, earned income is subtracted from their respective direct costs. Then physical facilities' net direct costs are distributed: 23.9 percent to the School of Medicine; 3.7 percent to central administration. Central administration total net costs are distributed: 27.1 percent to the School of Medicine. As a result of those calculations, the School of Medicine is assessed $6,678,927 for physical facilities and $1,491,035 for central administration—a total assessment of $8,169,962. This sequence produces an assessment to the School of Medicine which is nearly $200,000 more than the former. While the former sequence will be preferred by the School of Medicine, all indirect costs have to be allocated. Other units will have to pick up that $200,000. Fortunately, complaints in this instance will be few since all people recognize the importance of the School of Medicine for the public's (and their own) health and agree that every benefit should be extended to that particular responsibility center.

If a university community were not inhabited by women and men of good will, allocating indirect costs based on an arbitrary sequence could be a cause of endless controversy. The third option avoids testing that assumption.

Allocating Support Center Costs Simultaneously

By expressing responsibility centers' direct and indirect costs as a set of linear equations and solving them simultaneously, we can recognize interdependence among support centers realistically and avoid protocols which are subject to challenge.[1] Moreover, nine deans in ten will be mystified but impressed by the technique and unwilling to admit they do not understand what is going on.[2]

The mathematical calculations for this chapter have been relegated to the Appendix. Although I bitterly resisted their assignment to the obscurity usually associated with that part of the anatomy of a book, publishers and reviewers have their ways of molding outcomes to their preferences. That hundreds of thousands of general readers may find satisfactory the arrangement that has been adopted is a comforting thought. However, those charged with managing the administration of responsibility center budgeting are advised to read the Appendix.

The concepts are relatively straightforward. Each center's total cost is equal to its direct cost plus allocated indirect costs. In the case of our example, the total cost (net of earned income) of the College of Arts and Humanities for example is equal to:

$465,971		direct costs of $11,862,000 (from Table 3.7) less earned income of $11,396,029 (from Table 4.8)
+	8.8	percent of libraries' total cost net of earned income

---

1. A general but succinct and complete presentation of the approach can be found in Charles T. Horngren, *Cost Accounting: A Managerial Emphasis,* 5th ed. (Englewood Cliffs, New Jersey: Prentice Hall, Inc. 1982), pp. 475–489.

2. John R. Curry observes that while the simultaneous approach is "sequence neutral (sorry for the jargon) and thus obviates a lot of decanal fussing, it also is too complex to grasp conceptually by most deans (they're smart enough, they just don't have the time and patience)." As a result, he thinks it's a bad idea. His experience "suggests that the more complex the rules, the less they're understood, and the more they become the subject of lore and thus, the more they're viewed as dissentives to perform: the rules become the fall guy when you want to hold the guy in charge responsible for the outcome." Letter from John R. Curry to John Gallman dated March 27, 1990.

At Indiana University, our experience has been a bit different. No one objected to the simultaneous equation approach. The general idea is not complicated, and the problems associated with the other approaches are pretty clear. Most deans probably don't have the time and patience to immerse themselves in the complicated arithmetic of a less sophisticated approach. As described in chapter 9, special pains must be taken to insure the neutrality of allocation mechanism adjustments with respect to resource allocation decisions. That attention to detail seems to produce confidence among the participants that nothing strange is happening at the rounding level.

TABLE 6.3   TOTAL COST BY RESPONSIBILITY CENTER
FROM ALLOCATED AND DIRECT COSTS

| | | | *Allocated Costs* | |
| | | *Academic* | *Academic* | *Student* |
	Libraries	*Computing*	*Affairs*	*Services*
Arts and Humanities	$ 1,278,032	$ 430,024	$ 219,351	$ 1,345,072
Physical and Math Sci	2,222,033	2,011,403	644,625	1,835,063
Social & Behavrl Sci	2,759,387	1,019,573	487,945	2,219,370
Dentistry	130,708	131,782	259,640	67,254
Medicine	769,724	943,279	1,338,491	288,230
Nursing	639,016	166,461	174,586	269,014
Optometry	406,647	48,551	67,148	57,646
Business	1,902,525	638,100	308,883	1,277,819
Education	1,365,171	270,499	299,930	441,952
Engineering & Tech	580,924	603,421	102,961	499,598
Law	145,231	97,102	89,531	57,646
Music	1,278,032	187,269	219,351	489,991
Physical Education	580,924	145,653	129,820	470,775
Public Affairs	406,647	208,076	134,297	288,230
SUBTOTAL: ACADEMIC	$ 14,464,999	$ 6,901,193	$ 4,476,560	$ 9,607,660
Libraries	0	0	0	0
Academic Computing	0	0	0	0
Academic Affairs	58,092	6,936	0	0
Student Services	0	6,936	0	0
Physical Facilities	0	0	0	0
Central Administratn	0	20,808	0	0
SUBTOTAL: SUPPORT	$ 58,092	$ 34,679	$ 0	$ 0
TOTAL	$ 14,523,092	$ 6,935,872	$ 4,476,560	$ 9,607,660

+	6.2	percent of academic computing total cost net of earned income
+	4.9	percent of academic affairs total cost net of earned income
+	14.0	percent of student services total cost net of earned income
+	1.1	percent of physical facilities total cost net of earned income
+	3.9	percent of central administration total cost net of earned income.

Similar equations can be developed for each of the other nineteen centers in our example.

Physical Facilities	Central Administratn	Total Allocated Costs	General Fund Direct Expenditures	Total Cost
$ 312,089	$ 216,004	$ 3,800,573	$ 11,862,000	$ 15,662,573
4,113,907	531,702	11,358,732	22,860,000	34,218,732
652,551	465,239	7,604,065	25,108,000	32,712,065
1,787,421	238,158	2,614,963	12,599,000	15,213,963
6,780,853	1,500,951	11,621,527	59,540,000	71,161,527
907,897	171,695	2,328,669	9,696,000	12,024,669
170,231	60,924	811,147	3,291,000	4,102,147
425,577	304,621	4,857,524	15,535,000	20,392,524
453,948	243,697	3,075,197	10,215,000	13,290,197
794,410	99,694	2,681,007	5,808,000	8,489,007
453,948	88,617	932,076	4,850,000	5,782,076
1,106,499	221,543	3,502,684	12,335,000	15,837,684
794,410	121,848	2,243,430	5,384,000	7,627,430
198,602	121,848	1,357,700	5,687,000	7,044,700
$ 18,952,342	$ 4,386,542	$ 58,789,296	$ 204,770,000	$ 263,559,296
1,929,280	221,543	2,150,823	12,574,000	14,724,823
283,718	22,154	305,872	6,630,000	6,935,872
709,294	121,848	896,171	4,777,000	5,673,171
5,447,380	360,007	5,814,322	4,867,000	10,681,322
0	426,469	426,469	27,983,000	28,409,469
1,049,755	0	1,070,563	7,634,000	8,704,563
$ 9,419,427	$ 1,152,021	$ 10,664,220	$ 64,465,000	$ 75,129,220
$ 28,371,769	$ 5,538,563	$ 69,453,516	$ 269,235,000	$ 338,688,516

From Table 3.7, we know the centers' direct costs. From Table 5.12, we know the percentages of total cost net of earned income that is to be allocated to them. From Table 4.8, we know their earned income. What we don't know is each center's total cost.

Determining each center's total cost involves solving all of the centers' equations simultaneously. Such a solution may seem like a major undertaking, and before the advent of electronic computing this approach had little practical significance. Now, however, it almost can be easier done than said. The calculations can be performed quickly at your desk (if a microcomputer sits on it).

Table 6.3 displays the end product of all those calculations. The far right column shows each center's total cost. Proceeding from right to left, the total cost for each center is categorized into direct expenditure and allocated cost. The next six columns show by support center the constituent parts of that allocated cost. For the curious reader, a detailed explanation of how the costs are determined is given in the appendix.

At the bottom of each support center's column appears its total allocated cost. From the standpoint of a support center, that figure is the amount of income it receives from assessments. Note that 8.8 percent of the total allocated cost/assessment income for libraries equals $1,278,032, the amount that is allocated to the College of Arts and Humanities. Similarly, 6.2 percent of academic computing's total allocated cost/assessment income of $6,935,872 equals $430,024, the College's share of that cost.

Alert readers will notice that with one exception, support centers' total allocated costs/assessment income are not equal to their total costs. The one exception is academic computing; both its total allocated cost/assessment income and total cost equal $6,935,872. For the others, allocated costs are less than total costs. What's the difference? If you subtract each support center's total allocated cost/assessment income from its total cost you will find the difference to be the earned income figure appearing in Table 4.8.

That coincidence is not coincidental! Moreover, it's one of a kind. The solution is unique. It's the only arrangement that the support centers' total allocated cost/assessment income and earned income balance to their respective total costs.

Our quest for the total costs of responsibility centers is now complete. Let's see what happens when we bring expenditure and income together.

7. Bringing Income and Expenditure Together

Annual income twenty pounds, annual
expenditure nineteen nineteen six, result
happiness. Annual income twenty pounds,
annual expenditure twenty pounds ought
and six, result misery.

Micawber's equation

In chapter 3, we identified academic and support responsibility centers and
displayed their direct expenditures. In chapter 4, based on attribution criteria,
earned income for each center was identified. In chapter 6, using allocation
parameters developed in chapter 5, indirect costs were allocated to the centers
and their total expenditures determined. Now we are ready to bring total
income and total expenditure together and present a budget developed under
traditional methods in a responsibility center budgeting format.

Announcement of our intention to move to responsibility center budgeting
produced early speculation that existing allocations of resources to operating
units would be changed. Despite assurances that implementation of responsibility center budgeting was neutral with respect to the existing distribution of
funds, concerns persisted, and a need to demonstrate its neutrality was clear.

The Campus Perspective

A neat table forming the focal point of this section of the chapter provides
an overall demonstration of the neutrality of implementation of responsibility
center budgeting. It shows total general fund income and expenditure for all
of the responsibility centers on a single page. When the table appeared to the
disciples of the new budget approach, few Doubting Thomases remained
among them. Seeing is believing; some, of course, refused to look.

General Fund Income and Expenditure by Responsibility Center

Both general fund income and expenditure are displayed in Table 7.1. We
have seen most of the numbers in that table before. Indeed, the only new
numbers calculated for the first time are those dealing with state appropria-

TABLE 7.1 GENERAL FUND INCOME AND EXPENDITURE
BY RESPONSIBILITY CENTER

| | | | Income | |
	Student Fee Income	Indirect Cost Recovery	Earned Income	Subtotal
Arts and Humanities	$ 11,117,413	$ 278,116	$ 500	$ 11,396,029
Physical and Math Sci	15,616,145	2,067,000	400,000	18,083,145
Social & Behavrl Sci	19,110,365	910,590	416,327	20,437,282
Dentistry	2,284,720	266,071	1,498,531	4,049,322
Medicine	6,118,652	3,679,181	11,852,636	21,650,469
Nursing	1,957,458	44,144	0	2,001,602
Optometry	1,486,223	86,456	760,000	2,332,679
Business	14,665,290	25,516	18,550	14,709,356
Education	6,582,929	218,776	48,820	6,850,525
Engineering & Tech	2,456,414	30,752	0	2,487,166
Law	3,830,668	1,929	27,262	3,859,859
Music	7,294,751	913	18,000	7,313,664
Physical Education	4,796,731	158,622	139,553	5,094,906
Public Affairs	3,692,501	309,591	3,108	4,005,200
SUBTOTAL: ACADEMIC	101,010,260	8,077,657	15,183,287	124,271,204
Libraries	0	30,231	171,500	201,731
Academic Computing	0	0	0	0
Academic Affairs	893,467	228,849	74,295	1,196,611
Student Services	270,000	34,662	769,000	1,073,662
Physical Facilities	0	0	37,700	37,700
Central Administratn	69,000	0	3,097,000	3,166,000
SUBTOTAL: SUPPORT	$ 1,232,467	$ 293,742	$ 4,149,495	$ 5,675,704
TOTAL	$ 102,242,727	$ 8,371,399	$ 19,332,782	$ 129,946,908

tion. Student fee income, indirect cost recovery, other income, and the total of
those three categories—earned income—appeared previously in Table 4.8.
Assessments for each of the support centers, appearing in the Assessment
Income column, were taken from the bottom line of the first six columns of
Table 6.3. Direct expenditure, allocated assessments, and their total, now
appearing under the column heading Total Income/Expenditure, also were
taken from Table 6.3.

State appropriation is calculated as a residual—Total Income/Expenditure
less earned income and less assessment income. Since, in our situation, no
school provides intercenter support services, no school receives assessment
income. Therefore, state appropriation is equal to total expenditure less earned

Appropriatn Allocation	Assessment Income	Total Income/ Expenditure	Expenditure	
			Direct Expenditures	Assessment Expenditures
$ 4,266,544	$ 0	$ 15,662,573	$ 11,862,000	$ 3,800,573
16,135,587	0	34,218,732	22,860,000	11,358,732
12,274,783	0	32,712,065	25,108,000	7,604,065
11,164,641	0	15,213,963	12,599,000	2,614,963
49,511,058	0	71,161,527	59,540,000	11,621,527
10,023,067	0	12,024,669	9,696,000	2,328,669
1,769,468	0	4,102,147	3,291,000	811,147
5,683,168	0	20,392,524	15,535,000	4,857,524
6,439,672	0	13,290,197	10,215,000	3,075,197
6,001,841	0	8,489,007	5,808,000	2,681,007
1,922,217	0	5,782,076	4,850,000	932,076
8,524,020	0	15,837,684	12,335,000	3,502,684
2,532,524	0	7,627,430	5,384,000	2,243,430
3,039,500	0	7,044,700	5,687,000	1,357,700
139,288,090	0	263,559,294	204,770,000	58,789,294
0	14,523,092	14,724,823	12,574,000	2,150,823
0	6,935,872	6,935,872	6,630,000	305,872
0	4,476,560	5,673,171	4,777,000	896,171
0	9,607,660	10,681,322	4,867,000	5,814,322
0	28,371,769	28,409,469	27,983,000	426,469
0	5,538,563	8,704,563	7,634,000	1,070,563
$ 0	$ 69,453,516	$ 75,129,220	$ 64,465,000	$ 10,664,220
$ 139,288,090	$ 69,453,516	$ 338,688,514	$ 269,235,000	$ 69,453,514

income for each of those units. Since support centers do not engage in primary mission activities—teaching, research, public service—their expenditures are entirely covered by earned income and assessment income, and they receive no state support.

The dichotomy of state support being received exclusively by academic centers and assessment income being received only by support centers is not intrinsic to responsibility center budgeting. It is peculiar only to the illustration we have adopted. If a school were to provide support services to other centers, assessment income would be appropriate. If a support center were to provide teaching, research, and public services funded all or in part through state support, appropriation would be attributed to it.

Relationship to the Traditional Budget

According to Table 7.1, Total Income/Expenditure under responsibility center budgeting is $338.7 million. Under traditional budgeting arrangements, the total budget is equal only to direct expenditure, $269.2 million—which is matched by $139.3 million of state appropriation and $129.9 million of general fund income earned by the institution. The difference in aggregates between the two approaches, $69.5 million, is assessment income on the revenue side and allocated assessments on the expenditure side.

How do the $69.5 million in assessments relate to $64.5 million in support centers' direct expenditures? Assessments are $5.0 million greater than direct expenditures! Who's the culprit? Is the whole process only designed to cream off $5 million for central administration?

Support centers' direct expenditures of $64.5 million are offset by their earned income of $5.7 million, leaving net direct expenditures of $58.8 million. That amount is precisely the allocated assessment to the academic centers. Intercenter assessments among the support centers total $10.7 million which, when added to $58.8 million in assessments to academic centers, sum to $69.5 million.

As already observed, under traditional budgeting practices, direct expenditure of $269.2 million is matched by state support and earned income. In Table 7.1, $269.2 million is also equal to $263.5 million in total income/expenditure of academic responsibility centers plus $5.7 million in support center's earned income. The use of general fund resources, therefore, can be expressed entirely in terms of primary mission units under responsibility center budgeting.

Comparisons Involving State Appropriation

Table 7.1 is a source of basic information about the distribution of direct and indirect expenditures and of earned income and state appropriation. It also can provide a basis for much idle speculation about justice and injustice in resource allocation among centers, about efficiencies and wastefulness, and about the institution's priorities.

Much interest centers on state appropriation and its distribution among the academic centers, which—as the table shows—are budgeted to spend $263.5 million. Fifty-three percent ($139.3 million) of that $263.5 million comes from state appropriation; the rest, from student fees, indirect cost recovery, and other forms of earned income. That 53 percent of academic centers' expenditure covered by state appropriation applies only in the aggregate. The percentage varies significantly among centers. Among the health sciences—dentistry, medicine, and nursing—the percentage is 70 percent or more. The School of Engineering and Technology shares that dubious distinction. On the other hand, state appropriation provides 33 percent or less of the support for the total expenditures of the Schools of Arts and Humanities, Business, Law, and Physical Education.

The School of Medicine receives the largest share of state support, 36 percent. With the Schools of Dentistry and of Nursing, the health sciences account for 51 percent. Including Physical and Mathematical Sciences and Social and Behavioral Sciences pushes the percentage to 72 percent. The remaining 28 percent is distributed among the nine other schools.

Comparisons Involving Earned Income

Little controversy surrounds earned income. Its attribution was determined according to mutually agreed upon criteria. But state appropriation at least appears to be something new. However, it is not. State appropriation is determined in this initial construction as the difference between total expenditure and earned income. Total expenditure has two components: direct expenditures, which are taken as given in the existing budget, and allocated assessments, which are determined by allocation parameters that have been negotiated and accepted. State appropriation is only a residual, and how it is distributed should generate no surprise. But it does.

About the distribution of state appropriation, some who aspire to righteousness may overlook an an obvious fact: all units receive it. All are on the dole. All receive state support to maintain them in the manner to which they have become accustomed. None of them generate sufficient earned income to cover their expenditures.

Moreover, the academic centers' dependency on state succor is not a product (fortunately) of indirect cost allocation mechanisms of responsibility center budgeting. Their direct expenditures are greater than their earned income, both in the aggregate and by center. Total earned income of the academic centers—$124.3 million—is 61 percent of total direct expenditures—$204.8 million. Among the centers, earned income as a percentage of direct expenditures varies from a low of 21 percent for the School of Nursing to a high of 96 percent for the School of Arts and Humanities. Two other schools show earned income in excess of 90 percent of direct expenditures: the School of Business and the School of Physical Education. Do high percentages suggest particular industriousness, productivity, or abilities to generate earned income? Not necessarily. They are as likely to be the result of charging all undergraduate students the same credit hour fee rates and offering a large number of service courses whose instructional costs are relatively low.

Comparisons Involving Allocated Assessments

Allocated assessments of $58.8 million account for 22 percent of academic centers' total expenditure of $263.5 million. For many centers, allocated assessments as a percentage of total expenditure vary widely from the aggregate. For the Schools of Medicine and of Law, allocated assessments account for only 16 percent of total expenditure. The highest percentages belong to the Schools of Physical and Mathematical Sciences and of Engineering and Technology with 33 percent and 32 percent, respectively. As with earned income, the differences in relative importance of allocated assessments generate little controversy.

One reason for the acceptance of the differences stems from prior agreement on the allocation parameters. The fact that total expenditure is matched with an equal amount of income and state support lessens possible concerns. Moreover, deans don't know how to play the game. Should allocated costs be made as small as possible so a school's efficiency can be argued? Should allocated costs be inflated so that subsequently they can be reduced and the savings used for higher priority objectives? Neither question should be relevant.

The Center Perspective

Tables 3.5 and 3.6 displayed an illustrative chart of accounts for two responsibility centers, the School of Physical and Mathematical Sciences and student services. Each contained an RCB account whose expenditure amount appeared as zero. At that stage in our development, only direct expenditures of the responsibility centers had been determined. Income had not been attributed to the centers; indirect expenditures had not been allocated. Now we are ready to take a closer look at those accounts and see how they are used.

Anatomy of an RCB Account

When the move to responsibility center budgeting was first proposed, skeptics predicted that hundreds if not thousands of accounts would be created to handle the additional transactions. Not so. All that is required is one account for each responsibility center. In other words, in terms of our illustration, twenty additional accounts are required. Those accounts are used to record attributed income and allocated indirect cost.

The addition of even one account per responsibility center could be avoided if one were willing to record income attributions and indirect cost allocations in an existing account. However, to us, keeping responsibility center transactions clearly separate from other accounts seemed best. The fact that little trouble has been encountered suggests that the arrangement of establishing a separate RCB account for each center was a good choice.

All income attributed to a responsibility center appears in an RCB account. It includes state support, student fee income, receipts from sales and services, indirect cost recovery from grants and contracts, rent, interest received from invested cash balances, balances forward, and intercenter assessment income. Within each of those categories, income is classified in finer detail. Student fee income, for example, is recorded by fall, spring, and summer sessions, by student residency status, and by course level: undergraduate, graduate, and professional. Other income classes distinguish incidental student fee income, e.g., laboratory fees, auditing fees, contact hour fees, and education field experience fees.

On the expenditure side of an RCB account appear allocated indirect costs, i.e., the payments a center makes to other centers providing services to it. Those payments take two forms: assessments and charges. Initially, all the payments take the form of assessments, which are computed according to allocation parameters and over which the paying unit has no discretion. Over time, charges can be expected to evolve. A center desiring additional services from a support unit can purchase them for a negotiated amount. The amount of such services and their accompanying charges are subject to negotiation between the receiving and providing centers and can be changed.

Income and Expenditure by Center

With an RCB account included in the chart of accounts of each responsibility center and with posting of attributed income and allocated costs to those accounts, total income and expenditure for each center can be summarized in a routine manner. Those summaries provide each dean of a school or head of a support center with a status report on income and expenditure budgeted for the year. Only when center managers see numbers relating to their operations expressed in a responsibility center budgeting format do they seem to begin really to understand the process. Appreciation comes later.

TABLE 7.2   ILLUSTRATIVE SUMMARY OF INCOME
AND EXPENDITURE, SCHOOL OF PHYSICAL
AND MATHEMATICAL SCIENCES

Income and Expenditure Class	*Amount*
INCOME	
Allocated Appropriation	$16,135,587
Instructional Fees	15,271,145
Other Fees	345,000
Indirect Cost Recovery	2,067,000
Other Income	400,000
SUBTOTAL: DIRECT INCOME	$34,218,732
TOTAL INCOME	$34,218,732
EXPENDITURE	
Faculty Salaries	$12,133,619
Other Academic Salaries	1,634,945
Administrative Staff Salaries	400,942
Clerical & Service Staff	1,129,595
Wages	232,893
Group Insurance Benefits	929,168
Retirement Contributions	3,324,883
SUBTOTAL: PERSONNEL COMPENSATION	$19,786,045
Student Financial Assistance	280,960
General Supplies and Expense	1,471,497
Travel	59,356
Equipment	1,198,948
Repairs and Maintenance	63,194
SUBTOTAL: NONPERSONNEL EXPENSES	$ 3,073,955
SUBTOTAL: DIRECT EXPENDITURES	$22,860,000
Assessment: Libraries	$ 2,222,033
Assessment: Academic Computing	2,011,403
Assessment: Academic Affairs	644,625
Assessment: Student Services	1,835,063
Assessment: Physical Facilities	4,113,906
Assessment: Central Administration	531,702
Charges	0
SUBTOTAL: INDIRECT EXPENDITURES	$11,358,732
TOTAL EXPENDITURES	$34,218,732

SCHOOL OF PHYSICAL AND MATHEMATICAL SCIENCES

Tables 7.2 and 7.3 display general fund income and expenditure summaries for the School of Physical and Mathematical Sciences and for student services. For the School of Physical and Mathematical Sciences, budgeted income of $34.2 million for 1990-91 equals budgeted expenditure. The largest single source of income is state appropriation, $16.1 million (47 percent of total income). Next in importance—and a close second—is student instructional fees, $15.3 million. Other fees, indirect cost recovery, and other income contribute the rest.

Direct expenditures account for $22.9 million of the school's total expenditure of $34.2 million. Their distribution among expense classes is standard for an academic unit. Faculty salaries constitute the largest expenditure category, $12.1 million—53 percent of direct expenditures and 35 percent of total expenditures. Personnel compensation for all of the school's employees, $19.8 million, accounts for all but $3.1 million of direct expenditure and for two thirds of total expenditure.

People clearly are a major input in the process of teaching, research, and public service—at least as technology is currently applied. "What technology?" some may ask.

Following personnel compensation, the largest single expense is an assessment for physical facilities, $4.1 million. A look behind that figure indicates that energy and utility costs account for about half of the total expenditure of physical facilities. Library services, academic computing, and student service assessments—$2.2 million, $2.0 million, and $1.8 million—amount to another $6.0 million in costs. Services that formerly appeared to be free now show up as a major input for the school.

The amount for charges is zero. However, a line appears on the table in anticipation of an evolution from a complete reliance on assessments to a greater reliance on negotiated transactions between support centers and the centers using their services.

STUDENT SERVICES

In Table 7.3, the summary of general fund income and expenditure for the responsibility center for student services is similar to the one for the School of Physical and Mathematical Sciences. But certain differences are noteworthy.

As a support center, student services does not receive an allocation of state appropriation. Since it teaches no courses, income from instructional fees is zero. Other fees, indirect cost recovery on grants and contracts, and miscellaneous income generate less than $1.1 million of its total income of $10.7

TABLE 7.3 ILLUSTRATIVE SUMMARY OF INCOME
AND EXPENDITURE, STUDENT SERVICES

Income and Expenditure Class		Amount
INCOME		
Allocated Appropriation	$	0
Instructional Fees		0
Other Fees		270,000
Indirect Cost Recovery		34,662
Other Income		769,000
SUBTOTAL: DIRECT INCOME	$	1,073,662
RCB: Arts and Humanities	$	1,345,072
RCB: Physicl & Mathematicl Sciences		1,835,063
RCB: Social and Behavioral Sciences		2,219,370
RCB: Dentistry		67,254
RCB: Medicine		288,230
RCB: Nursing		269,014
RCB: Optometry		57,646
RCB: Business		1,277,819
RCB: Education		441,952
RCB: Engineering & Technology		499,598
RCB: Law		57,646
RCB: Music		489,991
RCB: Physical Education		470,775
RCB: Public Affairs		288,230
SUBTOTAL: ASSESSMENTS & CHARGES	$	9,607,660
TOTAL INCOME	$	10,681,322
EXPENDITURE		
Faculty Salaries	$	0
Other Academic Salaries		4,042
Administrative Staff Salaries		1,316,058
Clerical & Service Staff		806,194
Wages		130,769
Group Insurance Benefits		145,935
Retirement Contributions		429,221
SUBTOTAL: PERSONNEL COMPENSATION	$	2,832,219
Student Financial Assistance		1,337,469
General Supplies and Expense		634,918
Travel		43,979
Equipment		13,426
Repairs and Maintenance		4,989
SUBTOTAL: NONPERSONNEL EXPENSES	$	2,034,781
SUBTOTAL: DIRECT EXPENDITURES	$	4,867,000
Assessment: Academic Computing	$	6,936
Assessment: Physical Facilities		5,447,380
Assessment: Central Administration		360,007
Charges		0
SUBTOTAL: INDIRECT EXPENDITURES	$	5,814,322
TOTAL EXPENDITURES	$	10,681,322

million. Most of student services' income, $9.6 million, comes from assessments of the academic units.

All the schools are assessed for student services. However, assessments vary widely. The Schools of Optometry and of Law assessments amount to less than $60,000 each. Four schools are assessed over $1 million: Arts and Humanities, Physical and Mathematical Sciences, Social and Behavioral Sciences, and Business. Collectively, those four schools account for $6.7 million (nearly 70%) of student services' total assessment income. The head of student services should be able to figure out who his/her most important customers are.

Expenditures for student services are unusual in that assessments account for a larger share of total expenditure than direct expenditure. The cause of that phenomenon centers on assessments for physical facilities. The halls of residence and the student health center are assigned to student services. An anachronism in the halls of residence bond indentures precludes charging energy and utility costs to dormitories. Nevertheless, the costs are incurred and have to be allocated. Given the reporting line, they are lodged with student services.

No bond indenture protects the student health center from incurring its cost of physical plant operations and maintenance. But it is such a sick cat financially and such a sacred cow to those espousing socialized medicine for students, the costs have not been charged. We allocated them, therefore, to student services. If the head of student services can shift those costs to the student health center, she or he will realize a net benefit to the general fund part of the operation.

Personnel compensation, at $2.8 million, follows physical plant assessments as the most important expenditure category of student services. Among the personnel compensation categories, administrative staff salaries are the largest component. Not unexpectedly, faculty salaries are zero. In student services, faculty do not meet with students to discuss their academic programs, need for financial assistance, living conditions, and participation in cultural and extracurricular activities.

One other expenditure category deserves mention: student financial assistance, $1.3 million. Only a small portion of total student financial assistance comes from general fund sources administered by student services. It is used mainly to cover fee remissions that the university is required to grant by state statute to children of disabled veterans.

Use of the Summaries

The Summary of Income and Expenditure for each responsibility center and the overall display of general fund income and expenditure for the campus shown in Table 7.1 were used in discussions with each of the responsibility center heads. Both tables proved helpful. The summaries helped deans and heads of support units put the direct expenditures, which were familiar to them, in a responsibility center budgeting context. They could see that the resources for direct expenditures available to them under the former budgeting approach remained intact. Assessments for services received did not appear threatening since appropriation allocations or assessments to other centers supplemented the earned income attributed to them to fully cover total expenditures.

Summaries for all centers were made available to each dean. Their attention centered on their own unit. Making all information available seemed to promote a feeling of trust and openness. Occasionally, constructive comparisons among units contributed to improved allocation algorithms.

The overview of general fund income and expenditure for the campus served as a vehicle for putting all centers in a larger context. In addition to center heads, its audience included interested faculty groups, members of the Board of Trustees, and—eventually—state reviewing agencies.

8. Implementation

Haste in every business brings failures.

Herodotus, *The Histories of Herodotus*, VII, 10.

Virtually all of the preceding commentary deals with the mechanics of responsibility center budgeting. Mechanics are important. A close approximation to flawlessness is necessary if the transition to and operation of responsibility center budgeting are to proceed smoothly. Imperfections are inexcusable and not likely to be forgiven—as U.S. automobile manufacturers discovered after foreign cars invaded their domestic markets.

However, while perfect mechanical arrangements and operating systems are essential, they are not sufficient for successful implementation of responsibility center budgeting. The essential and sufficient ingredient for successful implementation, in my opinion, is people: people who understand responsibility center budgeting and who want to make it work. Even less than perfect systems can be made to work if the people involved are informed and united in their purpose.

As we suspected from the very first instant that responsibility center budgeting became a possibility for Indiana University, the challenge in implementation involves not mechanics but people. Colleges and universities are people oriented institutions. They educate people, and the major input in that service is people—educators and those who support them.

Educators and their supporting staff, in performing their teaching function, deal with students—persons with open minds and amenable to being transformed by the learning process. That characteristic of students does not necessarily characterize their mentors. Fortunately, in making a move to responsibility center budgeting, educating every faculty member and every administrator is not required. Key players in the process—the executive, academic, and financial officers of a campus, the deans and their academic and financial assistants—must understand. For the others, an intensive course of study in responsibility center budgeting can be an elective.

Of course, when responsibility center budgeting is first announced, every campus busybody feels threatened—probably appropriately under any system—and is sure that she or he must understand it to maintain "academic quality" and protect "academic freedom." Keeping such nosy and usually noisy people under control is a dean's responsibility, so making sure deans understand and appreciate responsibility center budgeting is imperative. Moreover, an able dean will insure that her or his faculty—at least the best faculty—are provided a working environment conducive to their effective performance under any budgeting arrangement.

In academe, there are no secrets. Attempting to implement responsibility center budgeting in secret in such an environment is impossible and indeed inappropriate given the approach's commitment to full disclosure. Announcing the intention to move to a new system is the only viable approach. Temptation to anything less than complete openness should be rejected. Discretion in this instance might not be sinful, but it definitely appears to be unwise.

However, the course of wisdom presents its own challenges. Those teaching and those learning know that education is a long and difficult process. The announcement unleashes concern and conversation—never a scarce item among faculty and university administrators. Rumors abound. Lack of information does not inhibit authoritative statements. Keeping those forces under control while those with legitimate leadership roles learn about and participate in the development of responsibility center budgeting requires attention.

How any university's leadership deals with making a transition to responsibility center budgeting depends on local circumstances and personal style. Nevertheless, Indiana University's experience may prove instructive.

Getting Organized

Tom Ehrlich announced his intentions to introduce responsibility center budgeting to the University Faculty Council in October 1987 and to the University Budget Committee the following month. The University Faculty Council is the faculty governing group composed of faculty members from each of Indiana University's eight campuses. The University Budget Committee consists of the chief executive officers of each campus, the executive vice president, the vice president for finance and administration, who serves as chairman, the treasurer, and several of the other vice presidents. With announcements to those two groups, the word spread rapidly. In addition and in advance, he discussed responsibility center budgeting with each dean individually.

On December 1, the Responsibility Center Budgeting Advisory Group was formed. It consisted of the university budget director, who chaired the group, the treasurer, to whom accounting reported, and the business officers from the Bloomington campus, from the Indianapolis campus, and from two of the six regional campuses. Its membership included as well two faculty members, one from Bloomington who chaired the Budgetary Affairs Committee of the Bloomington Faculty Council and the other who occupied a similar position from Indianapolis.

The group was charged with developing statements of objectives and policies, criteria defining responsibility centers, and methods for attributing income and for allocating expenses to them. Despite the impending holiday season, the group met several times in December and made rapid progress on its assignment. The work benefited substantially from the insights provided in the 1981-82 financial report of the University of Southern California, which documented their operating principles and described how revenue center management was being designed at that institution.

By January a summary of organizational principles, operating policies, standards for defining responsibility centers, and criteria for attributing income and for allocating expenses to responsibility centers were ready to recommend to the University Budget Committee. With few modifications, the recommendations were adopted.

Responsibility Center Budgeting Format

The next several months were spent casting the 1987-88 operating budget in a responsibility center budgeting format. First, centers were identified. Second, accounts were associated with each of the centers. Third, income was attributed to each center. Fourth, parameters for allocating indirect expenses to each center were developed and then used to allocate those expenses to them. Work proceeded rapidly, and by March 1988 the operating budget was in a responsibility center budgeting format.

Then progress stopped!

By March, preparation of the 1988-89 operating budget was under way. Responsibility center budgeting activities were set aside so attention could be devoted to the imperative of getting next year's budget constructed. No one was sufficiently familiar with the new system to use it effectively in budget construction, so traditional allocation methods prevailed. As a result, the 1988-89 operating budget was developed on a business as usual basis.

After preparation was completed, we moved quickly to place the budget in a responsibility center budgeting format. Each center had an RCB account which included budgeted fee income, recovery of indirect costs on grants and contracts, and other earned income. It also contained assessments for support center services. Budget administration and accounting were poised to make budget changes in a manner recognizing the fiscal integrity of each center and to report financial condition by responsibility center. Mechanisms were in place by June 30 to implement responsibility center budgeting, along with all the opportunities and hazards appertaining thereto.

But it was not implemented.

Cause for a Pause

People did not feel comfortable moving so quickly. They wanted to take another look at the cost allocation criteria. The distribution formulas adopted were rather simple, and some felt fine tuning would be desirable. Because of time constraints produced by budget construction, deans had not participated in developing the student fee income projections for their schools. If actual fee income fell short of budget, a dean could complain legitimately that her or his school should not be liable for the shortfall. A second look at the responsibility centers produced second thoughts about how they should be identified.

So in the summer of 1988 we decided to postpone implementation of responsibility center budgeting for a year, until July 1, 1989. Budget administration and accounting would perform as if responsibility center budgeting were in place so campus and center administrators could familiarize themselves with the additional information and reports that were being provided. The fall semester was scheduled for any desired or required revisions to responsibility centers and for modification of indirect cost allocation parameters. An adjusted base budget incorporating those changes was to be developed early in calendar year 1989 so that the 1989-90 operating budget could be constructed in a responsibility center budgeting mode.

On September 1, 1989, John T. Hackett arrived on the Indiana University scene as the vice president for finance and administration. Certain chancellors and deans wasted no time confiding to John their concerns about moving to responsibility center budgeting. At the first University Budget Committee meeting over which he presided, one chancellor seemed hopelessly confused about the workings of responsibility center budgeting. If the apparent confusion was a delaying tactic, it worked. As a newcomer and not having had an opportunity to view developments that already had transpired, John responded in two ways. First, he hired a consultant, George Kaludis of George Kaludis Associates, who had experience in budgeting schemes akin to responsibility center budgeting. Over the next six months, George provided me with advice and counsel. His experience and professional approach were helpful but not intrusive. He apparently sized up the situation, evidently found it to be under control, and did not get in the way of our proceeding on schedule.

Concentrating the Effort

Second, John told me to slow down and recommended that we proceed with implementing responsibility center budgeting on only one or two campuses in 1989-90. Hugh L. Thompson, the Kokomo campus chancellor, was willing, but his campus seemed to be too small to fully test a new approach. Blooming-ton and Indianapolis were the two campuses sufficiently large and complex to provide a representative training ground.

Of the two, the Indianapolis campus seemed the better choice. The campus has enjoyed rapid growth and development in both size and academic pro-grams over the past twenty years. It started as the site for the School of Medicine, and soon was joined by dentistry and nursing. Along with the development of other professional schools, a tradition of strong deans has persisted. Although not generously funded, the campus's fiscal condition was excellent. In a dynamic and improving environment, the first reaction to change was not fear and automatic resistance. The leadership style was open and welcomed assistance and involvement of the President's Office in campus affairs.

I called the chancellor, Gerald L. Bepko, and asked him if he would be willing to have his campus take the lead in implementing responsibility center budgeting at Indiana University. Without hesitation, he accepted the invita-tion. Based on subsequent events, I suspect his acceptance was largely an act of trust. He really didn't know much about the details of responsibility center budgeting, having left them up to his budget officer, David L. Robbins. Whatever his reasons, his decision got us moving again.

Pilgrims' Progress

Another outcome of John's initial reservations was encouragement to visit other institutions where responsibility center budgeting was in operation. A year before, Tom Ehrlich suggested I visit the University of Pennsylvania where he himself had experienced the virtues of that approach to allocating and managing resources. Off I went on a pilgrimage to Philadelphia where I met Glen R. Stine, the budget officer, and was instructed about Penn's operation.

At the University of Pennsylvania, responsibility center budgeting had been in place since the early 1970s. The transition from traditional to new budgeting methods occurred before Glen's time. His situation was typical. After fifteen years, hardly anyone was left who had participated in the change in budgeting techniques. (After fifteen years, probably anyone who had participated in the change would have remembered a lot of things that did not happen.) We needed advice from someone who had experienced a recent shift in budget approaches.

The University of Southern California adopted revenue center management in 1982-83. In October 1988, I called Dennis F. Dougherty, the vice president for finance, and he put me in contact with John R. Curry, the vice president for budget and planning, who became for us the philosopher king of the new approach to budgeting. By November 16, six of us—two from the University Budget Office, two from the Bloomington campus, and two from the Indianapolis campus—were on our way to Los Angeles for what turned out to be a most informative and insightful two days at the University of Southern California.

Our visit included meetings with school deans, the heads of support units, and key administrators who had participated in the move to revenue center management. Over all the proceedings, John Curry presided and was from the first moment to the last a perfect host.

Most of the University of Southern California's general fund revenue takes the form of student fee income and recovery of indirect costs on grants and contracts. Both forms of income are attributable to schools. In order to garner resources for central direction, each school is taxed 20 percent of its student fee and indirect cost recovery income—a levy euphemistically called "participation." (How could higher education possibly be managed without euphemisms!) Central administration combines those receipts with its own sources of revenue (e.g., interest on invested bank balances which could be—but is not—attributed to the schools) and distributes the entire amount back to the schools in accordance with university priorities and its long term plans for development. The subsidy is referred to politely as "subvention."

"Why a tax of 20 percent?" we wondered. Our philosopher king and his colleagues had an answer. Twenty percent was judged to be the amount required by central administration to accomplish its long term objectives of redistributing resources among schools in order to maximize the institution's overall academic quality. Less ambitious long range plans might call for a smaller percentage, but 20 percent was not considered so oppressive that revenue generating incentives for the schools would be inhibited. As John Curry explained, "We wanted the tax to be large enough that every revenue center needed something back (in the form of subvention) to balance its budget. The argument for subvention requires that the individual school makes its case *in the context of University-wide goals and priorities*. (We imaged a decentralized system integrated by the common need for subvention.)"[1]

---

1. Letter from John R. Curry to John Gallman dated March 27, 1990.

Long range planning provided an important role in central administration's distribution of subvention. Planning was based on a ten year time horizon: five years back and five forward. The preceding four years of actual experience were used to assess how the school had been performing. The current year provided information on current performance. The next year's subvention was based on specific goals, but they were seen in a context for longer term objectives over the following four years. Based on those longer term objectives for a school, a dean could expect that her or his share of subvention would be increasing or decreasing.

Interviews with three deans during our visit stand out: Scott H. Bice, of the Law Center; Leonard M. Silverman, of the School of Engineering; and Alan C. Kreditor, of the School of Urban and Regional Planning. Under the university's long range plan, an increasing share of subvention went to law and engineering. Not unexpectedly, the deans of those two schools were supportive of the system. However, they understood their favored status would not last indefinitely and recognized that when the objectives for their schools had been attained emphasis appropriately would shift elsewhere.

Alan Kreditor's school was not an academic priority for the university. His share of subvention was declining. Nevertheless, he was very enthusiastic about revenue center management. In that environment and under his direction, the School of Urban and Regional Planning had blossomed. Enrollments had risen, grants and contracts had grown, and gifts from donors had increased. He was getting ready to finance construction of a new building for the school! And yet he was not an institutional priority. The system gave him sufficient discretion to exercise his entrepreneurship and the talents of his faculty to make decisive progress and advance the program. Alan said something that went like this, "I know I'm a small school and not all that important. And yet, when I telephone the provost's office, my call goes through. They know I've usually got good news."

Such conversations revealed the many facets of responsibility center budgeting and revenue center management. The budgeting system has to be tailored to an institution, its leadership, and academic objectives. Deans and heads of responsibility centers need to know what they can expect in terms of central administration's resource allocations both in the long and the short run. Central administration's power to allocate resources must be sufficient but also constrained so that initiative at the responsibility center level is not stifled.

Overall, what we found was an exceedingly well managed institution of higher education. The University of Southern California is a private institution that offers distinguished academic programs and manages to compete successfully in a state populated with high quality public universities, well supported, readily accessible, and available at low cost to students. "How do you do it?" we asked. "Aggressive management," was the answer. And revenue center management was one manifestation of that aggressive management.

Seeing such a performance was an inspiration far exceeding our expectations. The experience was a reassurance that we had been traveling along the right path. Responsibility center budgeting at Indiana University would be different from revenue center management at the University of Southern California in certain details but not in essence. Their structure and operating environments are different, but they are both institutions of higher education.

We imposed on our cordial California hosts twice more. In February 1989 Jerry Bepko led a delegation of his key administrators on the Indianapolis campus to the University of Southern California to see what we had seen. Once again, we were dazzled. Even before the first day of our two day visit was completed, Jerry confided to me, "This is great. Even if we had to leave right now, the trip would be worthwhile."

Anticipating implementation of responsibility center budgeting on the Bloomington campus with the beginning of the 1990-91 fiscal year, Kenneth R. R. Gros Louis, chancellor of the Bloomington campus, and his entourage went to California in October 1989 to be welcomed and informed by our indefatigable host, John Curry, and his colleagues. The third visit confirmed our first and second impressions, and the number of believers in responsibility center budgeting at Indiana University grew day by day.

Involving the Deans

The time between our first visit in November and our second in February was spent meeting with each of the Indianapolis deans and members of their immediate staff, describing what we had seen, and discussing their concerns. The experience at the University of Southern California taught us that involvement of the deans at an early stage in the development of responsibility center budgeting was important. They were the ones to be most affected by the change, and we encouraged them to contact their counterparts at USC. Many of them did so and found that support for the arrangement there was widespread. Such reassurances from their colleagues really helped assuage local nervousness that the new system would work to their detriment.

To further familiarize the Indianapolis deans with responsibility center budgeting, Jerry Bepko invited Cornelius J. Pings, the Provost and Senior Vice President, Academic Affairs, at the University of Southern California to come to Indiana to address them. Provost Pings did an impressive job describing revenue center management and answering their questions. Dave Robbins and I were gratified that his message was the same as the one we had been telling them. But they believed him! Prophets are without honor in their own place, especially when that place is a nonprofit institution.

Business as Usual

As the time for preparing the 1989-90 operating budget for Indianapolis approached, Dave and I hoped that planning and allocation decisions would be made as if responsibility center budgeting were in place. We imagined a situation in which the level of support center operations would be determined. Their earned income then would be netted against their total expenditure with the difference being allocated among the primary mission units as assessments, which would be covered by state support. The remaining state support would be distributed to recognize allowances for inflation, enrollment change, and any special funding considerations addressed by the legislature, and to reflect campus academic programs and priorities.

That hope was not fulfilled. Budget reviews with the deans proceeded in the usual fashion. Long lists of personnel position needs, supplies and expense shortfalls, and equipment deficiencies were presented. Sympathy was extended, but no promises were made. Budget construction concentrated in a traditional fashion on direct expenses and dealt with expense class categories. Responsibility center budgeting concepts were still too new for the chancellor and his deans to change from former approaches.

After Jerry Bepko first agreed that Indianapolis would be the first campus to implement responsibility center budgeting, he referred to the new approach as an "experiment" when talking to deans and faculty groups. For some reason, they seemed to find comfort in the idea that we were embarked on a learning experience. To my way of thinking, the experiment was akin to the kind of things that biology students do to frogs. Neither the students nor the frogs emerge from the experience quite the same as when they began. Some students but no frogs ever recover.

Projecting Enrollment and Income

However, we did make some progress. The deans of the schools developed their own projections of next year's enrollment. To assist in the process, we provided them with four years of historic data plus a mechanistically deter-

TABLE 8.1 SCHOOL OF PHYSICAL AND MATHEMATICAL SCIENCES
CREDIT HOUR ENROLLMENT PROJECTION

| | Undergraduate | | | | Graduate | |
| | Resident | | Nonresident | | Resident | |
	Under-graduate	Graduate	Under-graduate	Graduate	Under-graduate	Graduate
Summer II						
1985	3,550	5	927	3	205	161
1986	3,397	9	965	13	203	136
1987	3,456	7	888	7	210	115
1988	3,285	2	950	2	183	114
1989*	3,826	2	961	2	185	115
Projctn	——	——	——	——	——	——
Fall						
1985	43,808	46	13,975	29	517	830
1986	43,040	37	14,279	28	497	694
1987	44,767	30	15,186	35	417	737
1988	46,112	36	15,010	26	400	727
1989*	46,641	36	15,182	26	405	735
Projctn	——	——	——	——	——	——
Spring						
1986	39,579	60	12,943	31	465	718
1987	39,730	54	13,466	42	401	690
1988	41,341	56	14,484	42	403	677
1989	42,525	46	14,308	39	343	653
1990*	43,013	46	14,472	39	347	660
Projctn	——	——	——	——	——	——
Summer I						
1986	2,809	2	991	2	104	74
1987	2,905	2	915	1	92	67
1988	3,208	2	1,016	3	98	78
1989	3,271	2	1,036	3	92	79
1990*	3,308	2	1,048	3	101	80
Projctn	——	——	——	——	——	——

* Preliminary projection.

| Graduate | | Professional | | | | |
| Nonresident | | Resident | | Nonresident | | |
Under-graduate	Graduate	Under-graduate	Graduate	Under-graduate	Graduate	Total
406	612	18	40	2	0	5,929
524	521	3	58	4	0	5,833
528	495	8	53	0	4	5,771
565	541	11	22	2	0	5,677
571	547	11	22	2	0	6,244
1,227	4,442	85	745	83	7	65,794
1,222	4,376	97	634	42	16	64,962
1,261	4,067	62	523	23	24	67,132
1,276	4,371	58	84	35	12	68,147
1,291	4,421	59	84	35	12	68,927
1,059	4,055	8	545	6	13	59,482
1,086	4,026	19	505	6	8	60,033
1,069	3,910	13	421	6	12	62,434
1,104	4,096	3	199	7	0	63,323
1,117	4,143	3	203	7	0	64,050
151	428	0	31	4	0	4,596
186	423	3	35	0	0	4,629
186	411	3	66	0	0	5,071
189	419	3	66	0	0	5,160
191	424	3	66	0	0	5,226

mined preliminary projection for next year as a base line reference. Table 8.1 shows the arrangement. Five years of credit hour enrollments are displayed by semester or summer session by fee assessment category for each school. Except for the first summer session, four years of actual data are presented. Following our preliminary projection appears a space for their best guess.

The forms went out. The forms came back completed without protest or resistance. Not surprisingly, deans had been keeping track of and anticipating enrollments in the courses their schools offer for years. Now that the exercise had relevance and was part of a larger scheme it did not appear to pose a threat.

All units, support centers as well as schools, submitted projections of income from other sources. Under the former budgeting arrangement we had solicited such information, so that part of the process was not new.

Another step toward a responsibility center budgeting approach to budget construction was taken in the case of student fee income for selected professional schools. For all schools, fee rates were expected to increase by about six percent. A combination of the prestige of some schools, student demand, and comparisons with peer institutions made larger increases for MBA students in business and professional students in law, medicine, and dentistry appear plausible. With the expectation that the fee income would accrue to the schools, the deans were interested in exploiting this opportunity for additional income. If the income had disappeared into the general fund pool, they would have resisted.

The Moment of Truth

As soon as the direct expenses of all of the units were determined and approved, we once again configured the budget in a responsibility center budgeting format and distributed it to the campuses and the centers. For all campuses except Indianapolis, the additional budget data were for information only. For Indianapolis, with the implementation of responsibility center budgeting on July 1, 1989, the numbers began to lead lives of their own.

July 1 came and went. No upheaval. Then August. Then September. With the completion of the first three months of the year, the time had come for what we call the first quarter fiscal analysis. Year to date income and expenditure experience is compared with last year's experience and used as one of the bases for anticipating year end income and expenditure. Formerly, we had performed the analysis for each campus. Now the exercise was extended to the responsibility centers of the Indianapolis campus.

Monitoring Performance

Table 8.2 provides an illustration of the first quarter reports for the School of Physical and Mathematical Sciences. Similar reports were prepared for the other schools and the support centers. With respect to expenditures, the reports are equally interesting for both schools and support centers. When income is considered, the schools receive greater attention because fee income and indirect cost recovery can vary significantly and account for a substantial part of their income.

How a fiscal performance report is arranged is largely a matter of taste, but certain features of the arrangement presented in Table 8.2 deserve comment. The first two columns place actual income and expenditure activity during the first three months of the prior year beside income and expenditure activity for the first three months of the current year. At risk of cluttering up the form, columns for amount and percent change for the three month periods could be added, but placing the data for the two years side by side obviates those additions. A glance down the columns indicates, for example, that indirect cost recovery income is up substantially and that other income is down. Other expenses are down from a year ago this time, and a major contributing factor is a reduction in expenditures for general supplies and expense. Those observations can lead to further inquiry.

For the first three months of the current year, income exceeded expenditure by almost $4.9 million! An encouraging sign? In the first quarter of the prior year, income exceeded expenditure by $3.9 million, but as the bottom line of the prior year column shows the school incurred an operating deficit of nearly $1.1 million by year end. The financial condition in the first three months looks rosy because about 50 percent of student fee income has been received, but only about 25 percent of the annual costs have been incurred.

For ease of comparison, actual income and expenditure for the entire prior year are placed next to the column for the current year's budgeted income and expenditure. The arrangement makes it easier to spot situations in which the prior year's experience exceeds the current year's expectations. Other income, other academic salaries, wages, student financial assistance, general supplies and expenses, and repairs and maintenance expenditures are such instances. They tend to raise questions.

To the extent that income and expenditure patterns are fixed from one year to the next, the first quarter experience can be used as a basis for estimating financial condition at year end. As indicated by the column showing the codes for year end estimates, the prior year's actual income and expenditure can be increased or decreased in proportion to increases or decreases in income and

TABLE 8.2 ILLUSTRATIVE FIRST QUARTER FISCAL PERFORMANCE
REPORT, SCHOOL OF PHYSICAL AND MATHEMATICAL SCIENCES

Income & Expense Class	*Prior Year*	*Current Year*	*Code*
		YEAR TO DATE	
INCOME			
Allocated Appropriation	$ 3,805,934	4,033,897	B
Instructional Fees	7,181,308	8,045,297	A
Other Fees	126,875	153,622	A
Indirect Cost Recovery	440,467	573,158	C
Other Income	133,786	113,448	A
RCB: Assessments	0	0	
RCB: Charges	0	0	
TOTAL INCOME	$11,688,370	12,919,422	
EXPENDITURE			
Faculty Salaries	$ 2,540,508	2,729,336	A
Other Academic Salaries	384,333	406,120	A
Admin Staff Salaries	85,989	97,092	A
Clericl & Service Staff	220,831	230,098	A
Wages	49,828	54,427	A
Group Insurnce Benefits	187,250	211,059	A
Retiremnt Contributions	614,715	680,770	A
SUBTOTAL: COMPENSATION	$ 4,083,454	4,408,902	
Stdnt Financl Assistnce	$ 151,423	152,381	A
Gnrl Supplies & Expense	452,891	380,382	A
Travel	11,473	12,381	A
Equipment	238,197	252,000	C
Repairs and Maintenance	20,256	20,236	A
SUBTOTAL: OTHR EXPENSES	$ 874,240	817,380	
RCB: Assessments	$ 2,828,963	2,839,683	B
RCB: Charges	0	0	
SUBTOTAL: RCB EXPENSES	$ 2,828,963	2,839,683	
TOTAL EXPENDITURES	$ 7,786,657	8,065,965	
INCOME LESS EXPENDITURE	$ 3,901,713	4,853,457	

Codes:
A Automatic: (Prior Year Actual)∗(Year-to-Date Current Year)/(Year-to-Date Prior
   Year)
B Budgeted Amount
C Center Estimate

| Prior Year Actual | CURRENT YEAR | | Estimated Amount | Budgted Prcnt |
	Budgeted	Estimated		
15,223,737	16,135,587	16,135,587	0	0
14,164,961	15,271,145	15,869,159	598,014	4
287,464	345,000	348,065	3,065	1
1,544,992	2,067,000	2,010,422	(56,578)	(3)
490,687	400,000	416,093	16,093	4
0	0	0	0	0
0	0	0	0	0
31,711,841	34,218,732	34,779,326	560,594	2
11,038,525	12,133,619	11,858,984	(274,635)	(2)
1,674,741	1,634,945	1,769,678	134,733	8
354,416	400,942	400,179	(763)	0
1,040,989	1,129,595	1,084,673	(44,922)	(4)
265,124	232,893	289,594	56,701	24
817,687	929,168	921,657	(7,511)	(1)
2,908,696	3,324,883	3,221,254	(103,629)	(3)
18,100,178	19,786,045	19,546,019	(240,026)	(1)
291,620	280,960	293,465	12,505	4
1,819,103	1,471,497	1,527,860	56,363	4
53,745	59,356	57,999	(1,357)	(2)
1,146,295	1,198,948	1,200,000	1,052	0
66,867	63,194	66,801	3,607	6
3,377,630	3,073,955	3,146,125	72,170	2
11,315,876	11,358,732	11,358,732	0	0
0	0	0	0	0
11,315,876	11,358,732	11,358,732	0	0
32,793,684	34,218,732	34,050,876	(167,856)	0
(1,081,843)	0	728,450	728,450	

expenditure for the first three months of the current year relative to income and expenditure for the comparable period a year ago. The calculation is the most prevalent approach to making the year end estimates. Budgeted amounts are used for year end estimates when they have a high probability of being realized—as in the case of the appropriation allocation or responsibility center assessments. In other cases, the center can override mechanically generated estimates when it controls the expenditure level—as is the case for equipment expenditures in the illustration on Table 8.2.

The year end estimates for the School of Physical and Mathematical Sciences indicate an excess of income over expenditure of about $730,000. The column showing the difference between budgeted and estimated income and expenditure shows that income is about $560,000 over budget and that expenditure is about $170,000 under budget.

For this illustration, budgeted current income is equal to budgeted current expenditure. Such equality is not inevitable. If the school had chosen to draw on its reserves to augment expenditure, a deficit would have been budgeted. If it were attempting to increase its reserves or cover a prior year deficit, a surplus would have been budgeted.

Meetings were held with the center business officers as soon as the first quarter fiscal performance reports became available. Adjustments were made in the projections as a result of those discussions and greater understanding by both the campus and the centers about the meaning of the numbers. As soon as technical issues were resolved, Jerry Bepko and his staff met with each of the deans to get their reactions to the new system and to agree on whatever corrective actions appeared necessary.

Fortunately for the Indianapolis campus, enrollments were higher than expected, and most of the schools enjoyed an excess of student fee income over budget. With a new budget regime in place, they managed their expenditures cautiously, so their year end prognosis was favorable. The encouraging news tended to ease the transition.

A similar process was followed in January after the second quarter fiscal performance reports were available. With the year half over, those reports are judged to be more reliable indicators of fiscal performance. Sufficient time in a year remains for corrective action although with the beginning of the spring semester options are rapidly diminishing.

The third quarter fiscal performance reports become available in April. Although the estimates are usually very close to actual year end income and expenditure, opportunities for corrective action are limited. Only the first summer session remains. Although the same pattern of reviews and meetings is followed, it serves mainly as an early warning of year end problems and—on a happier note—as a way of identifying opportunities to obligate anticipated year end balances when constructing next year's budget.

Implementation of responsibility center budgeting caused monitoring fiscal performance of schools and support centers to become more formalized. The additional communication seemed to be welcomed both by the centers and the campus. Fortunately, we were able to extend the monitoring system formerly used to monitor campus performance by the President's Office to the centers. Campus reviews of fiscal performance were enhanced and made more meaningful by the additional level of detail.

Both at the time and in retrospect, the transition to responsibility center budgeting on the Indianapolis campus seemed to go smoothly. The situation did not appear to be out of control, nor was acceptance of the new approach in doubt. Campus leadership, good staff support, hard work, enthusiasm, and dedication all played important roles. But those factors were in place and were not subject to change. What assisted their effectiveness was the fact that we proceeded slowly.

The mechanisms for responsibility center budgeting were in place a year before Indianapolis adopted the new approach. However, few people understood how they would work. Time is required for people to become accustomed to a new idea, to appreciate a new approach to transacting university affairs, and to participate in the development process.

Our experience with implementation of responsibility center budgeting suggests the following advice: Go slowly, but don't falter.

9. Budget Construction under Responsibility Center Budgeting

> It is possible to fail in many ways . . . while to
> succeed is possible only in one way (for which
> reason also one is easy and the other difficult—
> to miss the mark easy, to hit it difficult).
>
> Aristotle, *Nichomachean Ethics*, II, 6

Implementing responsibility center budgeting can be likened to piloting an airplane at takeoff. Budget construction is like landing one, where a successful landing can be defined as one that leaves an airplane (and its passengers) able (and willing) to take off again. In the same way, budget construction has to be conducted so that the mechanism remains intact and the participants feel that responsibility center budgeting continues to provide them with a trustworthy vehicle to get them where they want to go.

After responsibility center budgeting is established, allocations of state appropriated funds assume a fundamental role in budget construction. Prior to implementing responsibility center budgeting, when the budget was merely configured in an RCB format, state appropriation was distributed among centers as a balancing entry to equate income and expenditure. It was determined only after all other income and expenditure considerations were in place.

Once responsibility center budgeting is under way, state appropriation no longer plays a passive role. It becomes the device through which campus, university, and state priorities are reflected in resource allocations among programs. Rather than being the last variable to be determined in the budget construction process, it is among the first, and is set independently—in part, at least—of other sources of income and existing expenditure patterns.

Steps in the Construction Process

Budget construction under both traditional and responsibility center budgeting involves a series of steps. We found that all of the steps for constructing budgets under the traditional arrangement continue to be relevant under responsibility center budgeting. Responsibility center budgeting requires modifying some of the steps and adds another.

Construction under Traditional Budgeting

Before the advent of responsibility center budgeting, budget construction was a nine step process.
Current year's approved base budget
Budget adjustments
Adjusted (Planning) base budget
Next year's income estimates
Allocations to units
Development of detail
Summarization and review
Approval of next year's budget
Dissemination
Budgets are (or should be) representations of underlying plans. Plans change. So budgets do too.

We begin each fiscal year July 1 with a base budget that has been approved in June, sometimes earlier. Because of the time lapse, the approved budget is slightly out of date when July 1 arrives, and budget changes begin immediately and occur constantly thereafter. Some changes are only temporary; others are permanent. New operating units are established (occasionally); old ones are abolished (rarely). Existing units assume new functions; functions (and resources) are transferred from one unit to another (often with difficulty). In response to such structural changes, new accounts are created; existing ones, consolidated. Along with institutional realities, accounting and budgeting practices change—like responsibility center budgeting.

Such developments impact the budget base and must be represented in the base used to plan and construct next year's budget. To keep track of allocation decisions, structural changes anticipated for next year should be built into a modified version of this year's budget base. Failure to adjust this year's budget base as a reference point for building next year's budget obscures planning intentions because base shifts and allocation decisions occur simultaneously.

Two separate steps are vastly superior to one giant step combining base adjustments and allocation decisions. Understanding and explaining adjustments to the approved budget base is a task sufficiently formidable to deserve separate treatment. When base adjustments and allocation decisions occur

together, describing what is happening is liable to become hopelessly complicated.

After—usually as—the current year's adjusted base budget is established
for planning purposes, estimates of next year's available income are developed. How that income pool is to be allocated in accordance with the
institution's overall plan and strategic objectives constitutes the next step.
Along with guidelines and instructions, major operating units receive their
expenditure targets. Instructions and targets are passed along to lower eche-
lons, and development of detailed budgets commences. Thanks to a set of
decentralized (stand alone work station based) budget construction programs,
each echelon can summarize and review detailed budgets to determine if
guidelines and expenditure targets have been met. Aggregations at the university, campus, and school level provide a basis for action by the governing
board.

Dissemination involves not only distributing copies of the approved budget
to operating units—itself a substantial undertaking—but also informing interested parties within and outside the institution about major features of the
budget plan. Resource availability, level and quality of services to be provided,
shifts in allocations and new directions, problems addressed, and objectives
to be accomplished are among the topics presented in the dissemination step.
At the concluding stage in the budget construction process, words become as
important as numbers.

Construction under Responsibility Center Budgeting

Constructing a budget under responsibility center budgeting requires—by
our reckoning—ten steps.

    Current year's approved base budget
    Budget adjustments
    Allocation parameter adjustments
    Adjusted (Planning) base budget
    Next year's income estimates
    Allocations to centers
    Development of detail
    Summarization and review
    Approval of next year's budget
    Dissemination

Allocation parameter adjustments constitute the added step in the sequence.
In addition, responsibility center budgeting affects in ways significant enough
to deserve mention the steps concerned with budget adjustments, the adjusted
(planning) base budget, and allocations to centers.

Budget Adjustments

Making budget adjustments is a step in the budget construction process that is common to both traditional and responsibility center budgeting approaches. However, in the case of responsibility center budgeting, changes in sources as well as in uses of funds must be recognized for intercenter transactions.

Assume, for example, that responsibility for offering a group of mathematics courses is transferred from the School of Engineering and Technology to the School of Physical and Mathematical Sciences. If costs associated with offering those courses total $300,000, expenditures of the School of Physical and Mathematical Sciences increase by $300,000, and expenditures of the School of Engineering and Technology decrease by a like amount. Under traditional budgeting approaches, recognition of the adjustment would be completed with the two offsetting expenditure entries.

Under responsibility center budgeting, income attribution effects also must be recognized. Student fee income and state appropriation allocations shift with the transfer of teaching responsibility.

A complete set of entries is illustrated in Table 9.1. The direct expenditure increase in the School of Physical and Mathematical Sciences is accompanied by corresponding increases of $100,000 in student fee income and $200,000 in state appropriation. The $100,000 in fee income is generated by student enrollments in the courses that are being transferred. State appropriation balances income with expenditure for the School of Physical and Mathematical Sciences.

For the School of Engineering and Technology, the $300,000 expenditure reduction associated with teaching the courses is accompanied by a $100,000 loss of fee income and a $200,000 reduction in state appropriation. Reduced

TABLE 9.1 ILLUSTRATIVE BUDGET ADJUSTMENT TRANSACTIONS
Program Shift: Academic Centers

School of Physical and Mathematical Sciences	
Direct expenditure	$ 300,000
Student fee income	100,000
State appropriation	200,000
School of Engineering and Technology	
Direct expenditure	$ (300,000)
Student fee income	(100,000)
State appropriation	(200,000)

TABLE 9.2 ILLUSTRATIVE BUDGET ADJUSTMENT TRANSACTIONS
Program Shift: Support Centers

Student Services	
Direct expenditure	$ 400,000
Assessment income	400,000
Central Administration	
Direct expenditure	$ (400,000)
Assessment income	(400,000)

command over resources attends reduced responsibility—but in a balanced manner that does not impinge on other programs and activities.

Among support centers, shifts in functions require similar recognition of income as well as of expenditure adjustments. Assume, for example, that an activity formerly handled by central administration is transferred to student services. If the cost of providing that activity amounts to $400,000, student services' expenditure increases and central administration's decreases by $400,000. Under traditional budgeting methods, just changing expenditures would complete the transaction. However, under responsibility center budgeting, we have to allow for changes in income available to each of the centers.

Table 9.2 illustrates the budget adjustment transaction for a shift in functions between the two support centers. Student services' $400,000 expenditure increase is accompanied by an increase of like amount in assessment income. Central administration's $400,000 expenditure decrease is accompanied by an equal decrease in assessment income.

Alert readers will observe that assessments for central administration are distributed differently among centers than are assessments for student services. For the moment, assessments against other centers for central administration and student services activities are unchanged. The change in assessment income is handled as a bilateral transaction between student services and central administration. A complete set of adjustments—neutral with respect to allocation decisions—will be undertaken when the adjusted budget base is developed.

A final example deals with an adjustment peculiar to responsibility center budgeting. Initially, all intercenter payments to support centers take the form of assessments. Over time, greater reliance on charges can be expected to develop.

Of all the services support centers provide, operations and maintenance costs for use of space in buildings and other facilities appear most amenable to a charge basis. Although a shift from assessments to charges initially makes no difference in costs and revenues, it changes the terms on which space is made available. Centers are in a position to negotiate the amount of space they occupy and the quality of the custodial and maintenance services associated with it—up or down to general limits set by university policy. As centers expand or contract, space use can be adjusted with physical facilities acting as a broker or through bilateral negotiations between centers. In a responsibility center budgeting environment, subleasing at a profit (or loss) is permissible.

Table 9.3 shows the entries required to shift intercenter payments from assessments to charges. For physical facilities, aggregate revenue remains the same, but assessment income declines by $26.5 million, and earned income in the form of charges rises by a like amount. For each of the other centers, a reduction in allocated assessments is matched by an increase in direct expenditures in the form of rent or lease payments to physical facilities.

Even with a shift to charges for space use, assessments for certain physical facilities functions continue. Such functions include grounds and infrastructure (utility distribution systems, streets, sidewalks, for example) maintenance and general administration. They are not closely related to space use, and their costs are appropriately covered through assessments.

Summary of Budget Adjustment Transactions

The first budget adjustment example dealt with shifts in functions between schools; the second, with shifts between support centers. The third deals with transactions between a support center and all other centers. The first two changes are typical transactions that are routinely made as part of the budget construction process under a traditional budgeting arrangement. Although transactions now have to recognize revenue considerations to keep centers in balance, they are familiar.

The effects of the three examples on the overall distribution of general fund income and expenditure among responsibility centers are presented in Table 9.4. In the aggregate, total income and expenditure remain unchanged. For selected centers, income and expenditure and their composition may change. For the School of Physical and Mathematical Sciences, direct expenditures increase by $4.1 million. That increase reflects the effect of two transactions, $300,000 for a shift of courses to the school and $3.8 million in space charges paid to physical facilities. Changes in direct expenditures for the School of Engineering and Technology, student services, and central administration similarly are a composite of several adjustment transactions.

Table 9.5 shows how general fund income and expenditure by responsibility center is distributed after accounting for the structural changes illustrated by three examples. It is determined by superimposing Table 9.4 on Table 7.1 but does not provide an adjusted base from which to construct next year's

TABLE 9.3　ILLUSTRATIVE BUDGET ADJUSTMENT TRANSACTIONS
Shift from Assessments to Charges

Physical Facilities	
Earned income	$　26,500,000
Assessment income	(26,500,000)
School of Arts and Humanities	
Direct expenditures	300,000
Allocated assessments	(300,000)
School of Physical & Mathematical Sciences	
Direct expenditures	3,800,000
Allocated assessments	(3,800,000)
School of Social and Behavioral Sciences	
Direct expenditures	600,000
Allocated assessments	(600,000)
School of Dentistry	
Direct expenditures	1,700,000
Allocated assessments	(1,700,000)
School of Medicine	
Direct expenditures	6,300,000
Allocated assessments	(6,300,000)
School of Nursing	
Direct expenditures	800,000
Allocated assessments	(800,000)
School of Optometry	
Direct expenditures	200,000
Allocated assessments	(200,000)
School of Business	
Direct expenditures	400,000
Allocated assessments	(400,000)
School of Education	
Direct expenditures	400,000
Allocated assessments	(400,000)
School of Engineering and Technology	
Direct expenditures	700,000
Allocated assessments	(700,000)
School of Law	
Direct expenditures	400,000
Allocated assessments	(400,000)
School of Music	
Direct expenditures	1,000,000
Allocated assessments	(1,000,000)
School of Physical Education	
Direct expenditures	800,000
Allocated assessments	(800,000)
School of Public Affairs	
Direct expenditures	200,000
Allocated assessments	(200,000)
Libraries	
Direct expenditures	1,800,000
Allocated assessments	(1,800,000)
Academic Computing	
Direct expenditures	300,000
Allocated assessments	(300,000)
Academic Affairs	
Direct expenditures	700,000
Allocated assessments	(700,000)
Student Services	
Direct expenditures	5,100,000
Allocated assessments	(5,100,000)
Central Administration	
Direct expenditures	1,000,000
Allocated assessments	(1,000,000)

budget. Allocation parameters have to be applied to net direct expenditures derivable from the display of income and expenditure found in Table 9.5 before an adjusted base budget is established.

Allocation Parameter Adjustments

To configure the operating budget in a responsibility center budgeting mode, assessments for library acquisition and operating costs were allocated to centers based on weighted totals of their prior year's full time equivalent faculty and student enrollments. Academic computing assessments were allocated according to weighted totals of the prior year's full time equivalent faculty, staff, and student enrollments, and unfunded usage. Academic support assessments were distributed according to weighted totals of the prior year's general, designated, and restricted fund expenditures. Centers were assessed for student support costs according to weighted totals of prior credit hour enrollments of undergraduate, graduate, and professional students. Actual space use expenditures served as a basis for assessing physical facilities costs. Assessments for central administration were allocated in proportion to weighted totals of prior year fund group expenditures.

Time passes. Parameters used to allocate assessments for support center costs become outdated. Student enrollment and staffing patterns change. Computing usage and space occupied by centers expand or contract at different rates. Expenditure patterns shift. As more time passes, a given set of parameters is liable to become less and less representative of an institution's structure and operations and less and less acceptable as a basis for assessing support center costs.

Usually, deterioration is gradual. One possible course of action is to ignore institutional changes and continue to use the original parameters. After all, we recognized at the outset that the way many indirect costs are allocated is pretty arbitrary.

Such a course of action—or lack of it—is not one that augurs well for responsibility center budgeting in the long term. Even in a relatively stable situation, distortions become increasingly great. And future stability is not a condition we should count on. What do we do if a new responsibility center is added? Reorganizations are bound to occur, and when they do modifying the original parameters based on historic data becomes more difficult as time passes and distortions accumulate.

Clever readers already may have thought of an alternative approach: update allocation parameters annually. Brilliant! With annual updates of alloca-

TABLE 9.4 REVISIONS TO GENERAL FUND INCOME AND
EXPENDITURE BY RESPONSIBILITY CENTER

	Student Fee Income	Indirect Cost Recovery	Income Other Earned Income	Subtotal
Arts and Humanities	$	$	$	$ 0
Physical and Math Sci	100,000			100,000
Social & Behavrl Sci				0
Dentistry				0
Medicine				0
Nursing				0
Optometry				0
Business				0
Education				0
Engineering & Tech	(100,000)			(100,000)
Law				0
Music				0
Physical Education				0
Public Affairs				0
SUBTOTAL: ACADEMIC	0	0	0	0
Libraries				0
Academic Computing				0
Academic Affairs				0
Student Services				0
Physical Facilities			26,500,000	26,500,000
Central Administratn				0
SUBTOTAL: SUPPORT	$ 0	$ 0	$ 26,500,000	$ 26,500,000
TOTAL	$ 0	$ 0	$ 26,500,000	$ 26,500,000

tion parameters, assessments will continue to approximate through time a fair assignment of indirect costs among centers.

An illustrative set of updated allocation parameters is exhibited in Table 9.6, which shows the percentage distribution of each support center's cost to other responsibility centers. Table 9.6 compares closely to Table 5.12. The formats are the same. The process of constructing them is similar. Only the numbers are different. Or at least many of them are different. Changes are not dramatic but nonetheless are perceptible—even over a year's time. For example, from Table 5.12, we see that 14.0 percent of student services costs are allocated to the School of Arts and Humanities. In Table 9.6, that percentage appears as 14.7 percent. What difference does seven tenths of one percent make? Given a net cost for student services of $9.6 million, seven tenths of one percent

Appropriatn Allocation	Assessment Income	Total Income/ Expenditure	Direct Expenditures	Assessment Expenditures
$	$	$ 0	$ 300,000	$ (300,000)
200,000		300,000	4,100,000	(3,800,000)
		0	600,000	(600,000)
		0	1,700,000	(1,700,000)
		0	6,300,000	(6,300,000)
		0	800,000	(800,000)
		0	200,000	(200,000)
		0	400,000	(400,000)
		0	400,000	(400,000)
(200,000)		(300,000)	400,000	(700,000)
		0	400,000	(400,000)
		0	1,000,000	(1,000,000)
		0	800,000	(800,000)
		0	200,000	(200,000)
0	0	0	17,600,000	(17,600,000)
		0	1,800,000	(1,800,000)
		0	300,000	(300,000)
		0	700,000	(700,000)
	400,000	400,000	5,500,000	(5,100,000)
	(26,500,000)	0		
	(400,000)	(400,000)	600,000	(1,000,000)
$ 0	$(26,500,000)	$ 0	$ 8,900,000	$ (8,900,000)
$ 0	$(26,500,000)	$ 0	$ 26,500,000	$(26,500,000)

translates into an increased assessment of over $67,000 for the school. Given student services' net cost of $9.6 million, the $67,000 assessment increase for the School of Arts and Humanities means that some other center or centers enjoy a $67,000 reduction in assessments.

Timing Allocation Parameter Adjustments

Comes now a great philosophical question. Should centers bear a burden (or enjoy a windfall) from periodic updating of allocation parameters? Should appropriation allocations be adjusted for parameter changes so that increases and decreases in assessments are matched in equal amounts with changes in

TABLE 9.5   REVISED GENERAL FUND INCOME AND
EXPENDITURE BY RESPONSIBILITY CENTER

	Student Fee Income	Indirect Cost Recovery	Income Other Earned Income	Subtotal
Arts and Humanities	$ 11,117,413	$ 278,116	$ 500	$ 11,396,029
Physical and Math Sci	15,716,145	2,067,000	400,000	18,183,145
Social & Behavrl Sci	19,110,365	910,590	416,327	20,437,282
Dentistry	2,284,720	266,071	1,498,531	4,049,322
Medicine	6,118,652	3,679,181	11,852,636	21,650,469
Nursing	1,957,458	44,144	0	2,001,602
Optometry	1,486,223	86,456	760,000	2,332,679
Business	14,665,290	25,516	18,550	14,709,356
Education	6,582,929	218,776	48,820	6,850,525
Engineering & Tech	2,356,414	30,752	0	2,387,166
Law	3,830,668	1,929	27,262	3,859,859
Music	7,294,751	913	18,000	7,313,664
Physical Education	4,796,731	158,622	139,553	5,094,906
Public Affairs	3,692,501	309,591	3,108	4,005,200
SUBTOTAL: ACADEMIC	101,010,260	8,077,657	15,183,287	124,271,204
Libraries	0	30,231	171,500	201,731
Academic Computing	0	0	0	0
Academic Affairs	893,467	228,849	74,295	1,196,611
Student Services	270,000	34,662	769,000	1,073,662
Physical Facilities	0	0	26,537,700	26,537,700
Central Administratn	69,000	0	3,097,000	3,166,000
SUBTOTAL: SUPPORT	$ 1,232,467	$ 293,742	$ 30,649,495	$ 32,175,704
TOTAL	$ 102,242,727	$ 8,371,399	$ 45,832,782	$ 156,446,908

state funds? Stated in terms of our example, should the School of Arts and Humanities have to adjust its internal expenditure patterns to find $67,000 to pay its increased student services assessment? Or should its appropriation allocation be adjusted to cover the increase?

A strong case can be made for having the School of Arts and Humanities pay for its increased assessment from internal resources. Its allocation parameter increase from 14.0 percent to 14.7 percent presumably reflects a growth in the school's enrollment relative to other academic centers. As a result, it "enjoys" a greater share of the benefits student services provides. The school receives automatically the marginal benefit of increased enrollment in the form of extra student fee income; it should incur as well marginal costs, which include paying for a greater share of the cost of student services.

Appropriatn Allocation	Assessment Income	Total Income/ Expenditure	Expenditure	
			Direct Expenditures	Assessment Expenditures
$ 4,266,544	$ 0	$ 15,662,573	$ 12,162,000	$ 3,500,573
16,335,587	0	34,518,732	26,960,000	7,558,732
12,274,783	0	32,712,065	25,708,000	7,004,065
11,164,641	0	15,213,963	14,299,000	914,963
49,511,058	0	71,161,527	65,840,000	5,321,527
10,023,067	0	12,024,669	10,496,000	1,528,669
1,769,468	0	4,102,147	3,491,000	611,147
5,683,168	0	20,392,524	15,935,000	4,457,524
6,439,672	0	13,290,197	10,615,000	2,675,197
5,801,841	0	8,189,007	6,208,000	1,981,007
1,922,217	0	5,782,076	5,250,000	532,076
8,524,020	0	15,837,684	13,335,000	2,502,684
2,532,524	0	7,627,430	6,184,000	1,443,430
3,039,500	0	7,044,700	5,887,000	1,157,700
139,288,090	0	263,559,294	222,370,000	41,189,294
0	14,523,092	14,724,823	14,374,000	350,823
0	6,935,872	6,935,872	6,930,000	5,872
0	4,476,560	5,673,171	5,477,000	196,171
0	10,007,660	11,081,322	10,367,000	714,322
0	1,871,769	28,409,469	27,983,000	426,469
0	5,138,563	8,304,563	8,234,000	70,563
$ 0	$ 42,953,516	$ 75,129,220	$ 73,365,000	$ 1,764,220
$ 139,288,090	$ 42,953,516	$ 338,688,514	$ 295,735,000	$ 42,953,514

Alternatively, we can argue that no center should bear an additional burden or receive a windfall as a result of allocation parameter updating. Support center costs are allocated to other centers in the form of assessments rather than charges in part—for some, large part; for others, not so large—because the services they provide are in essence public goods. The services are enjoyed collectively by the entire university community, not separately by each of the centers. Assignment of those costs according to the relative size of allocation parameters is a useful accounting convention, but it is only a convention, and changes in the convention should not penalize or reward operating units.

Among the basic principles of responsibility center budgeting is that responsibility should be coupled with authority. Center managers should operate in an environment that makes them fully cognizant of their actions. But

TABLE 9.6   UPDATED ALLOCATION PARAMETERS
FOR ALL SUPPORT CENTERS

	Librar- ies	Acadmic Cmpting	Acadmic Affairs	Student Service	Physcal Fclties	Central Admnstn
Arts and Humanities	8.6	6.3	5.0	14.7	1.1	4.0
Physical and Math Sci	15.9	29.8	15.0	19.6	14.2	9.7
Social & Behavrl Sci	19.4	14.9	11.0	23.5	2.3	8.5
Dentistry	1.9	1.9	5.8	0.7	6.2	4.2
Medicine	5.2	12.9	29.0	2.9	24.4	26.9
Nursing	4.3	2.4	3.9	2.5	3.1	3.1
Optometry	2.7	0.7	1.5	0.6	0.6	1.1
Business	11.7	9.1	6.8	12.7	1.5	5.5
Education	9.6	4.0	6.9	4.7	1.6	4.4
Engineering & Tech	3.8	8.4	2.2	4.8	3.4	1.8
Law	1.0	1.4	2.0	0.6	1.6	1.6
Music	8.8	2.6	4.9	5.0	3.8	4.0
Physical Education	3.9	2.1	2.9	4.8	2.8	2.2
Public Affairs	2.7	3.0	3.1	2.9	0.7	2.2
SUBTOTAL: ACADEMIC	99.5	99.5	100.0	100.0	67.3	79.2
Libraries	0.0	0.0	0.0	0.0	6.7	3.9
Academic Computing	0.0	0.0	0.0	0.0	1.0	0.4
Academic Affairs	0.5	0.1	0.0	0.0	2.5	2.2
Student Services	0.0	0.1	0.0	0.0	18.9	6.5
Physical Facilities	0.0	0.0	0.0	0.0	0.0	7.8
Central Administratn	0.0	0.3	0.0	0.0	3.6	0.0
SUBTOTAL: SUPPORT	0.5	0.5	0.0	0.0	32.7	20.8
TOTAL	100.0	100.0	100.0	100.0	100.0	100.0

they should not be responsible for the actions of others. In terms of our example, the seven tenths of one percent increase in the portion of student service costs allocated to the School of Arts and Humanities is as much a result of the failure of other schools' enrollment to grow as rapidly. On the other hand, some will argue, the actions of others are as much a part of the interdependent environment in which we live as our own actions. Is a university community intrinsically any different?

The question of how allocation parameter updating should affect center operations can be debated endlessly. Additional arguments for one side or the other—more eloquently stated than those here—can be conjured up by disputatious individuals. However, no matter how artful or crafty, no argument will be sufficiently convincing to conceal the reality that the course of action adopted is largely a matter of taste.

More than debate, center managers need a clear answer to the question, one way or the other. Once a decision is in place, resourceful managers will adapt.

The decision can take two forms: (a) resource neutral or (b) resource active. A resource neutral decision infers that in the adjusted budget base used to construct next year's budget, appropriation allocations to centers will be adjusted up or down to compensate for changes in assessments resulting from allocation parameter updates. For the resource active decision, compensating changes in center appropriations for allocation parameter updates are not incorporated into the adjusted budget base. Each decision entails a different set of steps in the budget construction process that deserve explanation.

Resource Neutral Alternative

If a resource neutral alternative decision is selected, our objective becomes developing an adjusted base budget that incorporates the effects of updated allocation parameters (which, in terms of our illustration, are the percentages appearing in Table 9.6). To accomplish the objective, we follow the procedures described in the Appendix, with which I trust my readers are by now thoroughly familiar.

From Table 9.5, we generate revised net direct expenditures for all centers by subtracting general fund earned income from general fund direct expenditure. The result of the subtraction is shown in Table 9.7. General fund direct expenditures appear in the first column of numbers; earned income, in the second. The third column contains revised net direct expenditures, the difference between the first and second columns. It corresponds to the third column of Table A.1, and its numbers are represented by the column vector [K] shown in the formulas presented in the Appendix.

Next we substitute the values in Table 9.6 for the values in Table 5.12 to construct a matrix of allocation coefficients like the one found in Table A.2. The inverse of the revised allocation coefficient matrix is multiplied by the column vector of net direct expenditures to produce total net expenditure for each center. Total net expenditure for each center plus earned income produces earned income for each center. Armed with that information, we can construct Table 9.8a, the adjusted base budget of general fund income and expenditure by responsibility center which incorporates updated allocation parameters.

A comparison of Table 9.8a with Table 9.5 indicates that our calculations have affected appropriation allocations, assessment income, assessment expenditures, and total income/expenditure. Total appropriation remains the same, but its distribution among the centers is altered. The increase in assess-

TABLE 9.7 REVISED NET DIRECT EXPENDITURES

	Direct Expenditures	Total Earned Income	Net Direct Expenditures [K]
Arts and Humanities	$ 12,162,000	$ 11,396,029	$ 765,971
Physical and Math Sci	26,960,000	18,183,145	8,776,855
Social & Behavrl Sci	25,708,000	20,437,282	5,270,718
Dentistry	14,299,000	4,049,322	10,249,678
Medicine	65,840,000	21,650,469	44,189,531
Nursing	10,496,000	2,001,602	8,494,398
Optometry	3,491,000	2,332,679	1,158,321
Business	15,935,000	14,709,356	1,225,644
Education	10,615,000	6,850,525	3,764,475
Engineering & Tech	6,208,000	2,387,166	3,820,834
Law	5,250,000	3,859,859	1,390,141
Music	13,335,000	7,313,664	6,021,336
Physical Education	6,184,000	5,094,906	1,089,094
Public Affairs	5,887,000	4,005,200	1,881,800
SUBTOTAL: ACADEMIC	$222,370,000	$124,271,204	$ 98,098,796
Libraries	14,374,000	201,731	14,172,269
Academic Computing	6,930,000	0	6,930,000
Academic Affairs	5,477,000	1,196,611	4,280,389
Student Services	10,367,000	1,073,662	9,293,338
Physical Facilities	27,983,000	26,537,700	1,445,300
Central Administratn	8,234,000	3,166,000	5,068,000
SUBTOTAL: SUPPORT	$ 73,365,000	$ 32,175,704	$ 41,189,296
TOTAL	$295,735,000	$156,446,908	$139,288,092

ment income from $42,953,516 in Table 9.5 to $42,973,060 in Table 9.8a corresponds to the increase in assessment expenditures among support centers from $1,764,220 to $1,783,764. Note that total assessment expenditures of the schools remains constant at $41,189,294 although its distribution is changed.

Resource Active Alternative

If a resource active alternative is selected, our objective becomes developing an adjusted base budget that uses the current year's allocation parameters (the percentages appearing in Table 5.12). In that case, we multiply the inverse of the current year's allocation coefficient matrix (Table A.3) by the column vector of net direct expenditures found in Table 9.7. The resulting total net expenditures for each responsibility center can be added to their respective earned income to produce total income. With that information, we can proceed to construct Table 9.8b, the adjusted base budget of general fund income and expenditure by responsibility center using the current year's allocation parameters. In Table 9.8b, earned income, appropriation allocations, assessment income, direct expenditure, and allocated assessments reflect structural changes that have occurred since the beginning of the fiscal year but do not include allowances for shifts in the updated allocation parameters used to construct next year's budget.

Adjusted (Planning) Base Budget

Now we have not one but two adjusted base budgets from which to plan next year's operating budget. Table 9.8a includes shifts in updated assessment allocation parameters to develop the adjusted base budget to be used to construct next year's budget. Table 9.8b ignores them. What difference does recognizing or ignoring parameter shifts make to the centers?

A comparison of Table 9.8a and Table 9.8b shows that earned income and direct expenditures are identical. Both tables reflect structural changes affecting those income and expenditure components. Appropriation allocations, assessment income, and assessment allocations differ. Those differences are summarized in total income/expenditure.

Table 9.9 places side by side each center's total income/expenditure found in the two tables and displays a column showing their differences. Total income/expenditure is $6,556 more when updated parameters are used than when current parameters are used. The entire difference is concentrated among the support centers. Total income/expenditure for the academic centers remains at $263,559,294 under both sets of parameters; however, the distribution among them is altered, in some cases, significantly. Total reductions amounting to $592,230 are offset by an equal amount of reductions. Total income/expenditure for the School of Physical and Mathematical Sciences shows the largest reduction, $220,143, and the School of Business the largest increase, $274,866, both caused by comparable changes in assessment expenditures. What do the differences mean?

If the adjusted based budget is constructed from current parameters, the School of Physical and Mathematical Sciences will have to cover $220,143 in

TABLE 9.8A ADJUSTED GENERAL FUND INCOME AND
EXPENDITURE BY RESPONSIBILITY CENTER
USING UPDATED ALLOCATION PARAMETERS

	Student Fee Income	Indirect Cost Recovery	Income Other Earned Income	Subtotal
Arts and Humanities	$ 11,117,413	$ 278,116	$ 500	$ 11,396,029
Physical and Math Sci	15,716,145	2,067,000	400,000	18,183,145
Social & Behavrl Sci	19,110,365	910,590	416,327	20,437,282
Dentistry	2,284,720	266,071	1,498,531	4,049,322
Medicine	6,118,652	3,679,181	11,852,636	21,650,469
Nursing	1,957,458	44,144	0	2,001,602
Optometry	1,486,223	86,456	760,000	2,332,679
Business	14,665,290	25,516	18,550	14,709,356
Education	6,582,929	218,776	48,820	6,850,525
Engineering & Tech	2,356,414	30,752	0	2,387,166
Law	3,830,668	1,929	27,262	3,859,859
Music	7,294,751	913	18,000	7,313,664
Physical Education	4,796,731	158,622	139,553	5,094,906
Public Affairs	3,692,501	309,591	3,108	4,005,200
SUBTOTAL: ACADEMIC	101,010,260	8,077,657	15,183,287	124,271,204
Libraries	0	30,231	171,500	201,731
Academic Computing	0	0	0	0
Academic Affairs	893,467	228,849	74,295	1,196,611
Student Services	270,000	34,662	769,000	1,073,662
Physical Facilities	0	0	26,537,700	26,537,700
Central Administratn	69,000	0	3,097,000	3,166,000
SUBTOTAL: SUPPORT	$ 1,232,467	$ 293,742	$ 30,649,495	$ 32,175,704
TOTAL	$ 102,242,727	$ 8,371,399	$ 45,832,782	$ 156,446,908

additional assessment expenditures from whatever additional income is available to it in next year's budget. If updated parameters are used to calculate the adjusted base budget, the increase in assessments is offset by increases in its base appropriation allocation. Assessment increases caused by allocation parameter shifts will not constitute a claim against additional income in next year's budget. For the School of Business, an adjusted base budget using current parameters results in a $274,866 release of next year's funds required for assessment expenditures. An adjusted base budget using updated parameters anticipates the reduction in next year's assessment expenditures and lowers the base appropriation accordingly.

| Appropriatn Allocation | Assessment Income | Total Income/ Expenditure | Expenditure | |
			Direct Expenditures	Assessment Expenditures
$ 4,372,018	$ 0	$ 15,768,047	$ 12,162,000	$ 3,606,047
16,555,988	0	34,739,133	26,960,000	7,779,133
12,445,766	0	32,883,048	25,708,000	7,175,048
11,320,623	0	15,369,945	14,299,000	1,070,945
49,280,164	0	70,930,633	65,840,000	5,090,633
9,927,992	0	11,929,594	10,496,000	1,433,594
1,794,021	0	4,126,700	3,491,000	635,700
5,442,616	0	20,151,972	15,935,000	4,216,972
6,472,475	0	13,323,000	10,615,000	2,708,000
5,691,424	0	8,078,590	6,208,000	1,870,590
1,895,021	0	5,754,880	5,250,000	504,880
8,475,378	0	15,789,042	13,335,000	2,454,042
2,576,302	0	7,671,208	6,184,000	1,487,208
3,038,302	0	7,043,502	5,887,000	1,156,502
139,288,090	0	263,559,294	222,370,000	41,189,294
0	14,497,107	14,698,838	14,374,000	324,838
0	6,969,096	6,969,096	6,930,000	39,096
0	4,519,449	5,716,060	5,477,000	239,060
0	9,984,572	11,058,234	10,367,000	691,234
0	1,847,422	28,385,122	27,983,000	402,122
0	5,155,414	8,321,414	8,234,000	87,414
$ 0	$ 42,973,060	$ 75,148,764	$ 73,365,000	$ 1,783,764
$ 139,288,090	$ 42,973,060	$ 338,708,058	$ 295,735,000	$ 42,973,058

Allocations to Centers

To build a budget under traditional budgeting approaches, a manager has to know how much his or her operating unit will be permitted to spend. Oftentimes (unfortunately), budget instructions include additional prescriptions about how existing and additional resources will be spent. But the extra detail merely obscures the essential element of information, the bottom line. Heads of operating units want to know, "How much can I spend?" That's all the information they really need—assuming, of course, that plans, perfor-

TABLE 9.8B ADJUSTED GENERAL FUND INCOME AND
EXPENDITURE BY RESPONSIBILITY CENTER
USING CURRENT ALLOCATION PARAMETERS

	Student Fee Income	Indirect Cost Recovery	Income Other Earned Income	Subtotal
Arts and Humanities	$ 11,117,413	$ 278,116	$ 500	$ 11,396,029
Physical and Math Sci	15,716,145	2,067,000	400,000	18,183,145
Social & Behavrl Sci	19,110,365	910,590	416,327	20,437,282
Dentistry	2,284,720	266,071	1,498,531	4,049,322
Medicine	6,118,652	3,679,181	11,852,636	21,650,469
Nursing	1,957,458	44,144	0	2,001,602
Optometry	1,486,223	86,456	760,000	2,332,679
Business	14,665,290	25,516	18,550	14,709,356
Education	6,582,929	218,776	48,820	6,850,525
Engineering & Tech	2,356,414	30,752	0	2,387,166
Law	3,830,668	1,929	27,262	3,859,859
Music	7,294,751	913	18,000	7,313,664
Physical Education	4,796,731	158,622	139,553	5,094,906
Public Affairs	3,692,501	309,591	3,108	4,005,200
SUBTOTAL: ACADEMIC	101,010,260	8,077,657	15,183,287	124,271,204
Libraries	0	30,231	171,500	201,731
Academic Computing	0	0	0	0
Academic Affairs	893,467	228,849	74,295	1,196,611
Student Services	270,000	34,662	769,000	1,073,662
Physical Facilities	0	0	26,537,700	26,537,700
Central Administratn	69,000	0	3,097,000	3,166,000
SUBTOTAL: SUPPORT	$ 1,232,467	$ 293,742	$ 30,649,495	$ 32,175,704
TOTAL	$ 102,242,727	$ 8,371,399	$ 45,832,782	$ 156,446,908

mance objectives, and criteria for subsequently evaluating that performance are already in place.

Under responsibility center budgeting, knowledge of a center's total income/expenditure level is not enough. Decentralized decision making in an informed environment requires that interconnections among centers as part of the total university community be made explicit. Those connections are revealed through assessment income and assessment expenditures. To build their budgets, center managers have to know not only their total income/expenditure but also their assessment allocations.

| Appropriatn Allocation | Assessment Income | Total Income/ Expenditure | Expenditure | |
			Direct Expenditures	Assessment Expenditures
$ 4,315,017	$ 0	$ 15,711,046	$ 12,162,000	$ 3,549,046
16,335,845	0	34,518,990	26,960,000	7,558,990
12,325,018	0	32,762,300	25,708,000	7,054,300
11,181,659	0	15,230,981	14,299,000	931,981
49,390,565	0	71,041,034	65,840,000	5,201,034
9,974,040	0	11,975,642	10,496,000	1,479,642
1,808,502	0	4,141,181	3,491,000	650,181
5,717,482	0	20,426,838	15,935,000	4,491,838
6,417,351	0	13,267,876	10,615,000	2,652,876
5,774,762	0	8,161,928	6,208,000	1,953,928
1,894,771	0	5,754,630	5,250,000	504,630
8,494,165	0	15,807,829	13,335,000	2,472,829
2,600,756	0	7,695,662	6,184,000	1,511,662
3,058,157	0	7,063,357	5,887,000	1,176,357
139,288,090	0	263,559,294	222,370,000	41,189,294
0	14,503,835	14,705,566	14,374,000	331,566
0	6,969,052	6,969,052	6,930,000	39,052
0	4,504,889	5,701,500	5,477,000	224,500
0	9,989,257	11,062,919	10,367,000	695,919
0	1,842,395	28,380,095	27,983,000	397,095
0	5,157,076	8,323,076	8,234,000	89,076
$ 0	$ 42,966,504	$ 75,142,208	$ 73,365,000	$ 1,777,208
$ 139,288,090	$ 42,966,504	$ 338,701,502	$ 295,735,000	$ 42,966,502

Assessment Allocations

Assessment income and assessment expenditures are determined simultaneously, but fortunately that characteristic does not require us to do everything at once. First, central administration must determine next year's funding level for support units. What do we mean by "funding level"? Total income/expenditure? Direct expenditures? Net direct expenditures? Ultimately, net direct expenditures represent the amounts that have to be covered

TABLE 9.9 COMPARISON OF TOTAL INCOME/EXPENDITURE
FOR ADJUSTED BASE BUDGET ALTERNATIVES

	Total Income/Expenditure		
	Current *Parameters*	*Updated* *Parameters*	*Difference*
Arts and Humanities	$ 15,711,046	$ 15,768,047	$ (57,001)
Physical and Math Sci	34,518,990	34,739,133	(220,143)
Social & Behavrl Sci	32,762,300	32,883,048	(120,748)
Dentistry	15,230,981	15,369,945	(138,964)
Medicine	71,041,034	70,930,633	110,401
Nursing	11,975,642	11,929,594	46,048
Optometry	4,141,181	4,126,700	14,481
Business	20,426,838	20,151,972	274,866
Education	13,267,876	13,323,000	(55,124)
Engineering & Tech	8,161,928	8,078,590	83,338
Law	5,754,630	5,754,880	(250)
Music	15,807,829	15,789,042	18,787
Physical Education	7,695,662	7,671,208	24,454
Public Affairs	7,063,357	7,043,502	19,855
SUBTOTAL: ACADEMIC	$263,559,294	$263,559,294	$ 0
Libraries	14,705,566	14,698,838	6,728
Academic Computing	6,969,052	6,969,096	(44)
Academic Affairs	5,701,500	5,716,060	(14,560)
Student Services	11,062,919	11,058,234	4,685
Physical Facilities	28,380,095	28,385,122	(5,027)
Central Administratn	8,323,076	8,321,414	1,662
SUBTOTAL: SUPPORT	$ 75,142,208	$ 75,148,764	$ (6,556)
TOTAL	$338,701,502	$338,708,058	$ (6,556)

through assessment income and allocations among centers. Central administration may choose to focus on direct expenditures and determine net direct expenditure as a residual after deducting whatever earned income support units manage to generate. Or it can focus on net direct expenditures. Support center managers have greater responsibility for and greater incentives to generate earned income under the latter approach.

Whichever approach is adopted, we end up with next year's net direct expenditures for support centers. They are illustrated in the first column of Table 9.10. (Very alert readers—real number gnomes—will note that the net direct expenditure amounts appearing in Table 9.7 have been increased by 8 percent for libraries and academic computing and by 5 percent for all other

TABLE 9.10 NEXT YEAR'S NET DIRECT EXPENDITURES FOR
SUPPORT CENTERS AND ASSESSMENT INCOME AND
ASSESSMENT EXPENDITURE

	Net Direct Expenditures	Assessment Income	Assessment Expenditures
Arts and Humanities	$ 0	$ 0	$ 3,836,142
Physical and Math Sci	0	0	8,297,964
Social & Behavrl Sci	0	0	7,647,516
Dentistry	0	0	1,136,666
Medicine	0	0	5,394,788
Nursing	0	0	1,528,641
Optometry	0	0	680,451
Business	0	0	4,496,637
Education	0	0	2,892,682
Engineering & Tech	0	0	1,997,785
Law	0	0	537,333
Music	0	0	2,619,690
Physical Education	0	0	1,582,597
Public Affairs	0	0	1,232,108
SUBTOTAL: ACADEMIC	$ 0	$ 0	$ 43,881,000
Libraries	15,306,000	15,647,120	341,120
Academic Computing	7,484,000	7,525,055	41,055
Academic Affairs	4,494,000	4,747,362	253,362
Student Services	9,758,000	10,484,105	726,105
Physical Facilities	1,518,000	1,940,247	422,247
Central Administratn	5,321,000	5,413,425	92,425
SUBTOTAL: SUPPORT	$ 43,881,000	$ 45,757,314	$ 1,876,314
TOTAL	$ 43,881,000	$ 45,757,314	$ 45,757,314

support centers before rounding to the nearest thousand dollars.) Net direct expenditures for academic units appear as zero because at this point in the process they have not been determined. The zero elements are required, however, to complete the column vector, [K].

To determine next year's assessment income and allocations, the inverse of the *updated* allocation coefficient matrix is multiplied by the column vector of net direct expenditures appearing in Table 9.10 to produce total net cost. Applying the support centers' total net costs to their respective updated allocation parameters found in Table 9.6 produces the schedule of assessment income and expenditures appearing in the second and third columns of Table 9.10. Assessment income for the support centers appears in the second column. Assessment expenditures for all centers appear in the third column. One of the two requirements for building next year's operating budget now has been determined.

Appropriation Allocations

For academic centers, next year's total income/expenditure levels are yet to be determined. Earned income will have been estimated. Appropriation allocations are needed to complete the picture and provide school deans with estimates of their total income. Determining appropriation allocations among schools is central administration's responsibility. The big moment has arrived. However, other parties play a role.

The expectations of three groups legitimately influence appropriation allocations: state government, schools and any other primary mission units directly receiving state support, and central administration. State funds are appropriated to the university's campuses as a lump sum. But they are not provided without some understanding as to how the money will be spent. In requesting additional support, universities indicate how they intend to use the funds. In recommending and approving state appropriations, the legislative and executive branches of state government indicate to the universities what higher education objectives they feel should be addressed. Although usually understandings are informal and not made explicit in appropriation acts, they are nonetheless binding and cannot be ignored. Indeed, their status as agreements among ladies and gentlemen tends to assure careful attention to the spirit (since there is no letter) of the terms under which funding is made available.

The largest single source of revenue to the general fund is state appropriation. Although the proportion of state support varies among schools, it is a major source of revenue for all of them. Appropriation allocations among schools and other primary mission centers have to be reasonably stable in the short run and predictable in broad outline over the long run for deans and center heads to operate and plan efficiently.

Two uncertainties beset a school's appropriation allocation: (a) funding level provided by state government and (b) central administration's allocation decisions. The state's funding level is determined largely by forces external to the university, but its fluctuations—usually upward but not always—can be anticipated and predicted within tolerably narrow limits. Higher education's share of state general fund revenue is fairly stable, and state revenue closely follows economic conditions. If state economic performance indicators are projected to increase at 6 percent annually, an increase in a public university's appropriation of around 6 percent is a reasonably safe bet.

Despite constraints imposed by mutual understandings between state government and the universities, central administration possesses considerable flexibility in allocating appropriated funds among centers—from the standpoint of the school deans, possibly too much. A possibility of large and unpredictable swings in school revenue resulting from appropriation allocations introduces an element of instability that can undermine confidence in the responsibility center budgeting approach.

To provide deans and other center managers with prospects of a reasonably stable resource base upon which commitments can be made and long range plans developed, central administration must adopt self imposed constraints on the flexibility with which it allocates appropriation. The rules for distribution must be compatible with the state's expectations as to how appropriated funds will be used and yet allow for central administration direction of institutional priorities.

State Funding in Indiana

Whatever rules are adopted have to be tailored to the way state funding is negotiated and received and to each institution's peculiar circumstances. However, the Indiana experience placed in the context of our illustration may provide a useful guide.

Four factors essentially determine the additional appropriation public institutions of higher education receive from the State of Indiana.

    inflation allowances

    enrollment change

    expansion of physical facilities

    program development

Allowances for price inflation constitute the most significant factor in quantitative terms—at least it has been the most significant for the past several decades. Because of its overwhelming importance, state support to institutions has been distributed largely on a base plus basis. Other factors pale by comparison, and in times of financial stress one of them—program development—virtually disappears.

For the past three biennia, enrollment change funding has been based on a standard formula recognizing enrollment change that has occurred over the preceding two years. (That's right, funding for enrollment change is retroactive.) Enrollment increases are funded at one half the average level of appropriation per full time equivalent student. One half the average appropriation per full time equivalent student is taken to be an acceptable approximation to the marginal cost of enrollment additions. (A fall in enrollment results in an appropriation reduction equal to one sixth the average appropriation in deference to the sophism that cost cuts are more difficult to achieve.)

Operating and maintenance costs for new or acquired facilities used for academic purposes are funded through additional state funds. The amounts usually are negotiated and agreed upon with state reviewing agencies before construction or acquisition is authorized and have first claim on whatever increments in state support are available.

Program development funding usually has last claim on additional state dollars. Items placed in the category include support to attract and retain faculty, equipment replacement, early intervention, recruitment, and reten-tion of minority students, graduate student fellowships, library automation and acquisitions, computing equipment and support, replacing part time teachers with regular faculty, and offering new degree programs. The lacklus-ter list of inputs goes on and on. Occasionally, something from the smorgas-bord of wants is funded.

Accounting for the Use of State Funds

Under traditional budgeting techniques, demonstrating how state funds are used can be difficult. Appropriations are poured into a common trough that includes student fees, indirect cost recovery on grants and contracts, and other forms of general fund earned income. From the trough, resources are ladled out to operating units. In the process, state funds lose their identity.

With responsibility center budgeting, income is attributed to centers as it is earned or allocated. A structure is in place to track the use of appropriated funds—an accounting of interest not only to state elected and appointed officials but also to deans and managers of responsibility centers. It behooves central administration, therefore, to adopt the factors employed in the state's funding decisions and adapt them for internal use as devices for allocating appropriation among centers.

Given the need for leveraged institutional leadership, one additional factor in distributing funds among centers is appropriate: a discretionary allowance for central administration to allocate in accordance with institutional priorities and plans. The amount is arbitrary, but the Indianapolis chancellor, Jerry Bepko, appears to have hit on the right amount by defining it as one half of one percent of the campus expenditure base. Each year, out of additional state funds, about $1 million is allocated to centers by central administration to respond both to short run perturbations and to longer run institutional objec-tives for quality enhancement. The rest of the state dollars are distributed to reflect enrollment changes, plant expansion, program development, and inflation allowances.

Enrollment Change Funding

A school's student fee income rises or falls when credit hour enrollment in the courses it teaches increases or decreases. Fee income changes occur immediately, in the same semester that enrollment fluctuates. Such changes are of two types: anticipated and unanticipated. If anticipated, expenditure levels have been budgeted to accommodate to the change in the level of teaching activity. If unanticipated, a school may increase its expenditure level to handle additional enrollments and has to curb expenditures in the event of a fall to avoid a deficit.

Enrollment change funding occurs retroactively—a year after enrollment change has occurred. The difference between last year's total annual credit hour enrollment and the preceding year's defines enrollment change. A dean knows her/his school's enrollment change and the funding associated with it in September before the fiscal year in which the appropriation allocation is adjusted. Recruitment plans during the current year can reflect next year's anticipated funding change. If they were up, commitments to hire additional faculty for next year can be made; if they are slipping, recruitment can be limited. Further refinement in recruitment activity can occur as the current year's enrollment performance unfolds. If a rise in enrollments continues, recruitment can proceed enthusiastically; if a drop follows a rise, recruitment can be constrained.

Since at least a year elapses before appropriation allocations reflect enrollment changes, downward and upward funding adjustments are equal. Deans are expected to manage their schools' resources in a manner that preserves expenditure flexibility as enrollments fluctuate.

The equality of upward and downward funding allocations for enrollment change is but one of the differences between the state's practice and the institution's. State appropriations are determined for a biennium. Every other year, the state legislature considers the budget. For the university, enrollment change funding is addressed annually.

A second difference is the magnitude of the funding adjustment. For the state, each full time equivalent student increase is funded at one half the average appropriation per student. The institution's allowance depends on whether or not the adjusted budget base includes allocation parameter updates. If the resource active option has been selected, and the adjusted budget

TABLE 9.11 ENROLLMENT CHANGE FUNDING

	Prior Year Credit Hour Enrollments	Last Year's Credit Hour Enrollments	Enrollment Change	Enrollment Change Funding*
Arts and Humanities	107,112	110,989	3,877	$ 294,652
Physical and Math Sci	148,878	159,443	10,565	802,940
Social & Behavrl Sci	181,542	189,198	7,656	581,856
Dentistry	8,880	6,635	(2,245)	(170,620)
Medicine	57,240	56,670	(570)	(43,320)
Nursing	23,028	23,348	320	24,320
Optometry	11,550	12,033	483	36,708
Business	109,704	109,585	(119)	(9,044)
Education	43,884	47,542	3,658	278,008
Engineering & Tech	39,204	37,892	(1,312)	(99,712)
Law	17,940	19,028	1,088	82,688
Music	45,330	46,115	785	59,660
Physical Education	39,102	39,833	731	55,556
Public Affairs	24,048	24,853	805	61,180
TOTAL	857,442	883,164	25,722	$ 1,954,872

* Enrollment change funding rate, $76 per credit hour, equals one half prior year's appropriation, $130,175,787, divided by prior year's total credit hour enrollment, 857,442.

base does not incorporate allocation parameter updates, funding for enrollment change at one half the average appropriation per credit hour may be a reasonable allowance. With the resource neutral option and an adjusted budget base reflecting allocation parameter updates, such an allowance may reward or penalize enrollment changes excessively.

Despite differences, institutional practice with respect to enrollment change funding is compatible with the state's intentions. Variances between funding an entire campus and schools within a campus should be expected and acceptable.

Table 9.11 contains an illustration of the calculations for enrollment change funding. Differences in actual annual credit hour enrollments between last year and the year preceding it are multiplied by a constant dollar amount. In this illustration, the dollar amount is one half the average appropriation per credit hour. "Credit hour enrollment for which year is divided into appropriation for which year?" you may ask. Take your pick.

For all schools, credit hour enrollment rose from 857,442 to 883,164, an increase of 25,722 (nearly 3 percent). Not all schools participated in the growth, however. Enrollment losses are posted for dentistry, medicine, business, and engineering and technology. The School of Physical and Mathematical Sciences experienced the largest absolute increase, 10,565 credit hours. The School of Education shows the largest relative increase, over 8 percent.

Increases and decreases in enrollment are funded or unfunded at $76 per credit hour. It's the same for all schools, although their average cost of instruction varies substantially. We're dealing with marginal cost, and absent additional information the level of marginal cost cannot be inferred from the level of average cost. Relative to current operations, enrollment increments or decrements usually are small. Distortions resulting from continuous enrollment increases and decreases over a prolonged period of time can be addressed through the discretionary portion of the appropriation allocation. That's what it's for.

In the aggregate, nearly $2.0 million is allocated for enrollment change funding. Over $800,000 (41 percent) goes to the School of Physical and Mathematical Sciences. Allocations to just four schools—Physical and Mathematical Sciences, Arts and Humanities, Social and Behavioral Sciences, and Education—approximate $2.0 million. For the other schools, gains and losses are offsetting.

Compared with past practice, the magnitudes of the enrollment change funding amounts appear a bit startling. Nevertheless, they seem appropriate. Without an explicit mechanism to recognize financially changes in teaching activity, allocations are liable to be too small.

Table 9.12 continues the buildup of the appropriation allocation among schools. The first column displays the distribution of enrollment change funding and is identical to the third column of Table 9.11. The remaining columns show the other components that constitute each school's appropriation allocation.

Expansion of Physical Facilities

With adoption of charging rather than assessing centers for the space they occupy, the state's component of appropriation buildup for physical facilities expansion is passed on directly to the schools. For support centers, their assessment income is increased by the amount of the funding for operations and maintenance cost, and schools' appropriation allocations are increased by the amount their assessment expense increases. Differences between actual and funded operating and maintenance costs of new or acquired facilities are absorbed by the centers occupying the space.

In our illustration, we assume plant expansion funding of $888,000 for a new

TABLE 9.12 COMPONENTS OF NEXT YEAR'S
APPROPRIATION ALLOCATION

	Enrollment Change Funding	Physicl Faciltes Expnsion		Program Development	
		Schools	Acdmc Cmptng	Schools	Library
Arts and Humanities	$ 294,652		49,241	158,000	43,125
Physical and Math Sci	802,940		232,132	227,000	79,875
Social & Behavrl Sci	581,856		116,316	269,000	97,275
Dentistry	(170,620)		14,929		9,645
Medicine	(43,320)		101,182		26,725
Nursing	24,320		18,787		21,598
Optometry	36,708		5,488		13,538
Business	(9,044)	724,000	71,031		58,670
Education	278,008		31,300		48,170
Engineering & Tech	(99,712)		65,385	432,000	19,055
Law	82,688		10,942		5,050
Music	59,660		20,401		44,123
Physical Education	55,556		16,447		19,573
Public Affairs	61,180	164,000	23,419		13,578
SUBTOTAL: ACADEMIC	$1,954,872	888,000	777,000	1,086,000	500,000
Libraries					
Academic Computing					
Academic Affairs					
Student Services					
Physical Facilities					
Central Administratn					
SUBTOTAL: SUPPORT	$ 0	0	0	0	0
TOTAL	$1,954,872	888,000	777,000	1,086,000	500,000

facility housing the Schools of Business and of Public and Environmental Affairs. The amounts are distributed to the two schools in proportion to the assignable square feet each of them occupies in the new building. Additional state funding of $777,000 to cover the operating and maintenance costs of a new computing facility is distributed among the schools in accordance with increases in their assessment expenditures for academic computing.

Program Development

Program development funding related directly to the activities of one or more schools is allocated to the schools. As illustrated in Table 9.12, a new

Discretionary Allocation					
Schools	Stdnt Svcs	Inflation Allowance	Total Change	Base Appropriatn	Next Year's Appropriatn
200,000	44,100	111,016	$ 900,134	4,315,017	$ 5,215,151
300,000	58,800	420,286	2,121,033	16,335,845	18,456,878
300,000	70,500	317,096	1,752,043	12,325,018	14,077,061
	2,100	287,680	143,734	11,181,659	11,325,393
	8,700	1,270,713	1,364,000	49,390,565	50,754,565
	7,500	256,611	328,816	9,974,040	10,302,856
	1,800	46,529	104,063	1,808,502	1,912,565
	38,100	147,098	1,029,855	5,717,482	6,747,337
	14,100	165,105	536,683	6,417,351	6,954,034
	14,400	148,572	579,700	5,774,762	6,354,462
	1,800	48,748	149,228	1,894,771	2,043,999
	15,000	218,537	357,721	8,494,165	8,851,886
	14,400	66,912	172,888	2,600,756	2,773,644
	8,700	78,680	349,557	3,058,157	3,407,714
800,000	300,000	3,583,583	$ 9,889,455	139,288,090	$149,177,545
0	0	0	$ 0	0	$ 0
800,000	300,000	3,583,583	$ 9,889,455	139,288,090	$149,177,545

degree program in reverse engineering, funded at $432,000, is assigned to the School of Engineering and Technology. Funding in the amount of $654,000 to replace part-time teachers with regular faculty in the general academic courses for undergraduates is distributed among the Schools of Liberal Arts, Mathematical and Physical Sciences, and Social and Behavioral Sciences. For support units—e.g., libraries, academic computing—assessment income is increased by the amount of the infusion of state appropriation; the additional appropriation is distributed among schools in accordance with the resulting increases in their assessment expenditure.

The example shown in Table 9.12 assumes that $500,000 in additional appropriations have been provided to augment library acquisitions. Further, the additional $500,000 is assumed to be budgeted with the library and

TABLE 9.13 NEXT YEAR'S FUND INCOME AND
EXPENDITURE BY RESPONSIBILITY CENTER
USING CURRENT ALLOCATION PARAMETERS

	Student Fee Income	Indirect Cost Recovery	Income Other Earned Income	Subtotal
Arts and Humanities	$ 11,673,000	$ 298,000	$ 1,000	$ 11,972,000
Physical and Math Sci	16,502,000	2,212,000	412,000	19,126,000
Social & Behavrl Sci	20,066,000	974,000	429,000	21,469,000
Dentistry	2,399,000	285,000	1,543,000	4,227,000
Medicine	6,425,000	3,937,000	12,208,000	22,570,000
Nursing	2,055,000	47,000	0	2,102,000
Optometry	1,561,000	93,000	783,000	2,437,000
Business	15,399,000	27,000	19,000	15,445,000
Education	6,912,000	234,000	50,000	7,196,000
Engineering & Tech	2,474,000	33,000	0	2,507,000
Law	4,022,000	2,000	28,000	4,052,000
Music	7,659,000	1,000	19,000	7,679,000
Physical Education	5,037,000	170,000	144,000	5,351,000
Public Affairs	3,877,000	331,000	3,000	4,211,000
SUBTOTAL: ACADEMIC	106,061,000	8,644,000	15,639,000	130,344,000
Libraries	0	32,000	177,000	209,000
Academic Computing	0	0	0	0
Academic Affairs	938,000	245,000	77,000	1,260,000
Student Services	284,000	37,000	792,000	1,113,000
Physical Facilities	0	0	27,334,000	27,334,000
Central Administratn	72,000	0	3,190,000	3,262,000
SUBTOTAL: SUPPORT	$ 1,294,000	$ 314,000	$ 31,570,000	$ 33,178,000
TOTAL	$ 107,355,000	$ 8,958,000	$ 47,209,000	$ 163,522,000

covered through increased assessments to the schools. Alternatively, the $500,000 in increased state support could have been allocated directly to the schools, and they could have paid the library to purchase books on their behalf. The latter approach would test the alleged demand for more library books since the school deans could weigh the academic contribution of increased acquisitions against other program needs. But it might drive librarians berserk.

How are increases in assessment expenditures among schools for a support center's plant expansion and program development determined? Answer: by multiplying the matrix inverse of updated allocation coefficients by a column vector containing the support center's assessment income increase and with zeros in all other elements.

Appropriatn Allocation	Assessment Income	Total Income/ Expenditure	Expenditure Direct Expenditures	Assessment Expenditures
$ 5,215,151	$ 0	$ 17,187,151	$ 13,214,543	$ 3,972,608
18,456,878	0	37,582,878	28,914,107	8,668,771
14,077,061	0	35,546,061	27,614,454	7,931,607
11,325,393	0	15,552,393	14,389,053	1,163,340
50,754,565	0	73,324,565	67,793,170	5,531,395
10,302,856	0	12,404,856	10,828,330	1,576,526
1,912,565	0	4,349,565	3,648,288	701,277
6,747,337	0	22,192,337	17,527,899	4,664,438
6,954,034	0	14,150,034	11,163,782	2,986,252
6,354,462	0	8,861,462	6,764,837	2,096,625
2,043,999	0	6,095,999	5,540,874	555,125
8,851,886	0	16,530,886	13,831,672	2,699,214
2,773,644	0	8,124,644	6,491,627	1,633,017
3,407,714	0	7,618,714	6,340,909	1,277,805
149,177,545	0	279,521,545	234,063,545	45,458,000,
0	16,147,223	16,356,223	16,015,000	341,223
0	8,302,055	8,302,055	8,261,000	41,055
0	4,750,698	6,010,698	5,754,000	256,698
0	10,485,068	11,598,068	10,871,000	727,068
0	2,240,429	29,574,429	29,152,000	422,429
0	5,415,762	8,677,762	8,583,000	94,762
$ 0	$ 47,341,235	$ 80,519,235	$ 78,636,000	$ 1,883,235
$ 149,177,545	$ 47,341,235	$ 360,040,780	$ 312,699,545	$ 47,341,235

Discretionary Allocation

Central administration's discretionary appropriation allocation is distributed according to institutional priorities and objectives. For schools, the allocation is direct. For support centers, it is provided indirectly by allowing an increase in the favored center's assessment income and covering it through an offsetting appropriation allocation to schools.

In Table 9.12, illustrative discretionary allocations to three schools—Arts and Humanities, Social and Behavioral Sciences, and Law—total $800,000. An additional $300,000 distributed among schools offsets assessment expenditure increases augmenting student services activities.

Inflation Allowance

Allowances for inflation are distributed to schools in proportion to their adjusted appropriation base. The aggregate allowance is determined as a residual—the difference between the total increase in appropriation less enrollment change funding, physical facilities expansion, program development, and the discretionary allocation.

In terms of our illustration, the total appropriation increase amounts to $9,889,455. The other components account for $6,305,872, leaving a residual of $3,583,583. With an appropriation base of $139.3 million, the inflation allowance provides about 2.6 percent for next year's compensation and general price increases.

Next Year's Budget

Determination of the schools' appropriation allocations completes the steps required before preparation of next year's operating budget can begin. At this stage, a summary of general fund income and expenditure by responsibility center can be presented for next year.

Table 9.13 displays an illustrative budget incorporating the foregoing examples. As readers may have surmised from our enrollment change funding example, the adjusted base budget developed under the resource active option, Table 9.8b, was used to construct the table.

Next year's estimates of student fee income, indirect cost recovery, and other earned income occupy the first three columns and are totaled in the fourth. The appropriation allocations to the schools are taken from Table 9.12. Assessment income of $47,341,235 is $1,583,921 more than the amount shown in Table 9.10. Allocations to academic computing, libraries, and student services account for $1,577,000. The difference, $6,921, is accounted for by assessments among support centers generated by the $1,577,000 increase.

For example, look at libraries. Assessment income in Table 9.10 is $15,647,120; in Table 9.13, it is $500,103 more. The program development allocation in Table 9.12 accounts for $500,000. The remaining $103 is the libraries' share of the $777,000 increase in academic computing's assessment income.

The sum of earned income, appropriation allocations, and assessment income equals total income/expenditure. For schools, assessment expenditures are given; direct expenditure is determined as the difference between total income/expenditure and assessment expenditure. For support centers, assessment expenditures *and* direct expenditures are given. That they sum to total income and expenditure demonstrates a low level of entropy in the little high-energy world of responsibility center budgeting.

As in the case of assessment income, libraries provide a good example of the derivation of direct expenditure. Table 9.10 shows next year's net direct expenditures for libraries to be $15,306,000. Adding to that number earned income of $209,000 and the $500,000 shown in Table 9.12 for program development produces $16,015,000.

Comparisons of the current year's budget and next year's budget in the format of Table 9.13 can provide a useful vehicle for describing and explaining the budget to a wide variety of audiences. Accompanied by variations of the other schedules appearing in this chapter and a narrative describing special issues addressed, problems confronted, and objectives emphasized, the tables constitute a complete information package for deans, faculty and staff, elected and appointed state officials, and the general public.

Every other year, the major features of a similar table can be prepared well in advance of the budget construction process. The Indiana legislature meets from January to the end of April in odd numbered years to consider appropriating funds for a biennium. In those years, the university and schools do not know what the appropriation will be until about two months before the first year of a biennium begins. For the second year of the biennium, however, with the exception of central administration's discretionary allocation, the appropriation allocations to schools can be determined eight or nine months in advance—a great aid to long range planning.

10. Outcomes and Opportunities

It is good to be zealously affected always in a
good thing.

Galatians 4:18

"This is terrific! I understood responsibility center budgeting intellectually,
but you have to experience it to really take it to heart. This is terrific!" a
delighted Indianapolis dean exclaimed at his first first quarter fiscal performance review.

His school's student fee income was estimated at more than $100,000 over
budget. Jerry Bepko had just explained to him that the additional fee income
belonged to the school, no strings attached. The dean had come to the meeting
planning to plead for additional resources to fund a new faculty position.
More importantly than being told, he now understood that the school already
had earned the money it needed.

"Terrific" literally means causing great fear, terrifying. The dean's exclama-
tion was evidence of enthusiasm, not terror. However, there was an element
of awe in his reaction, and in that regard he was not alone.

Commenting on how his situation had changed under responsibility center
budgeting, the dean observed, "Power. I have never had such power. I've been
in charge of large federal agencies and served as dean at other schools, but this
kind of discretion has not been available to me. It's almost scary."

Academic Choice

His faculty wanted their school to contract its enrollment "to improve
quality." However, he was enjoying a surplus because the entering class of the
school's professional program had not been effectively constrained. Enrollment had increased, not decreased. The outcome was an increase in fee
income. The dean was under pressure to add a faculty member; now he had
the resources to do it—if enrollments were maintained at their current level.

"The system really pits a dean against his faculty," he complained wryly.
The system pits objectives against reality.

Some persons (nosy and noisy) may be horrified at the prospect of a school's
dean having to grapple with the resource consequences of alternative courses

of action affecting program quality. But who is better able to make a judgment about the academic consequences of alternatives than those who know their program best? Assessing income consequences is easy. Plenty of bean counters are available to make that estimate. But only a school's dean—the person in charge—can weigh the easily measured income result against the imponderables associated with reduced enrollments versus an additional colleague.

Why would deans want to lose control over the income their schools generate and leave such delicate decisions up to outsiders? Situations in which such opportunities for authority and responsibility are abdicated are typical in traditional budgeting arrangments and are accepted for lack of a better alternative. However, in a healthy institutional setting, responsibility center budgeting provides an environment in which deans can bring to bear their incomparable expertise in making choices about their programs.

Such decisions admittedly are not easy to make. But they are not easily made either by a school or by central administration. So why not have them made by the schools, where the likelihood of an optimum decision is greatest?

Coping with Shortfalls in Enrollment

Not every school enjoyed an excess of student fee income over budget. At the end of the first quarter, expenditure was forecast to exceed income for the School of Business. The reason: student fee income in summer sessions offered in July and August had not lived up to expectations. The dean, R. Thomas Lenz, admitted that the overly optimistic estimate of fee income was a result of their error. They had failed to anticipate that a professor offering a popular business law course was going to be on leave. Rather than find an instructor to replace him, the course was dropped from the summer session's schedule of classes.

"Before responsibility center budgeting, we would not have noticed," Tom acknowledged. Without complaint, he recognized that under the new regime he would have to make up the lost income or cut expenditures. He preferred the former course of action and outlined a plan to correct the problem. In the spring semester, additional sections of Introduction to Business, a course popular with freshmen, would be offered. They could be taught by advanced graduate students, so the additional cost would be exceeded by the additional income they generated. During the May and June summer sessions, graduate courses in business administration would be made available. In the past, when the sections filled up, they were closed. Now more students would be served.

No one had to tell the dean to take those actions which satisfied the fiscal requirements of the school. He figured them out for himself. Moreover, the principles of responsibility center budgeting—although only in place for less than six months—were not questioned. No special dispensation was sought. The responsibilities attending responsibility center budgeting were accepted without complaint. At the same time, when coping with an adverse situation, academic standards were not compromised.

What would have happened in the absence of responsibility center budgeting? Not only would the dean not have noticed the shortfall in student fee income; no one would have noticed. The business school's shortfall would have been offset by other schools' better than budget performance. And an opportunity to garner additional revenue and serve additional students would have been missed. If all schools had experienced a fee income shortfall, the problem would have been viewed as one for central administration to address. Most probably, an edict would have been issued to cut expenditures. Now income as well as expenditure can be managed.

Academic Program Trade-Offs

Not everyone at Indianapolis was initially and automatically enthusiastic about the discipline and opportunities responsibility center budgeting imposes and presents. At the second quarter fiscal performance review, William Voos, dean of Herron School of Art, commented, "Responsibility center budgeting on some occasions does cause the academic program to be budget driven." He cited art appreciation courses as an example. "Although studio courses are a much better personal experience, we lose money on them. We make money on art appreciation courses, but as an art educator I consider them to be a less creative form of instruction. We've had to add art appreciation courses to generate a surplus. . . ." As his discourse on the subject proceeded, I got the impression that he came to realize that the "less creative" surplus from art appreciation courses could be used constructively to finance additional studio courses. After a healthy exchange of views, he concluded, "It's a trade-off and not a major problem."

Not a problem, indeed! In fact, from the perspective of one who is not an art educator, responsibility center budgeting is a solution. More students are being served both in art appreciation courses and in studio courses. They're being served at the school's initiative. No administrative hierarchy is needed to issue edicts to the dean to teach more students. He and his faculty quickly figured out the new rules to the budget game. No one was needed to point out the built-in incentives. An appropriate response followed, as it does when dedicated and able people are involved.

A New View of Support Services

"Before I pay the additional cost, I want to know what the school will be getting," commented R. Bruce Renda, the dean for the School of Engineering and Technology, when told of the aspirations of the computing center for an expanded operation. "Sure, we are going to need more computing resources, but as work stations become more powerful I expect that our demands on main frame computing will decline. Why should I have to pay more?"

Suddenly, frenzied claims for huge increases in computing support began to sound a bit hollow. Who did the computing center serve if not the schools? Alleged cravings of faculty and students for ever higher high technology would have to be placed in a context of the academic plans and programs of those who have operational responsibility for them.

Responsibility center budgeting was subjecting support units to a test. Those who ultimately paid for support centers now had something to say about the quantity, quality, and kind of service they were to receive. No one said support center heads ought to be responsive to their constituencies. To survive, the system made them do it.

User Charges

Norman Lefstein, dean of the School of Law–Indianapolis, was off to a national meeting of the American Bar Association. In addition to the usual agenda of faculty recruitment and attending meetings, he carried with him data on the operating and maintenance cost of the law school's building and the amount of space in it occupied by the Association's national office of the Consultant on Legal Education. He wanted the Association to reimburse the school for its operation and maintenance costs. It did! "Before responsibility center budgeting was implemented, asking for a reimbursement would not have occurred to me," Norm admitted. "Space was free."

Space is one of a number of items that appeared free to users before implementation of responsibility center budgeting. Who does not need more of something useful and free? Who cannot afford to be generous?

However, none of those items was without cost to the university. But who is concerned with the university's cost? The notion that people neglect the public welfare is not new; it was noted by Pericles as he addressed his fellow Athenians about 2,500 years ago: "They take the lesser part of their time to debate the common business, and the greater to dispatch their own private affairs. And everyone supposes, that his own neglect of the common estate can do little hurt, and that it will be the case of somebody else to look to that for his own good: not observing how by these thoughts of every one in several, the common business is jointly ruined."[1] Responsibility center budgeting helps make those who use the university's centrally provided services aware of their costs. When the common business appears to be individuals' business, it becomes everyone's concern.

Fresh Air into the Faculty Governance Vacuum

Indiana University is blessed with eight Faculty Councils—representative groups of faculty members—one for each campus and one for the entire university system. Those forums for academe's politicians ensure that university and campus administrators do not suffer from lack of advice. Much of that advice takes the form of proposals designed to please and accommodate selected constituencies without regard to their fiscal consequences. In years past, such brilliant ideas as medical insurance for graduate student employees, salary minima for faculty and graduate students, and fee courtesy for faculty and staff dependents have been brought forth by valiant faculty council members to an apparently unimaginative and hesitant administration.

At the time of the second quarter budget conferences, another recommendation of the same genre was wending its way through the faculty council process: a proposal to pay full fringe benefits to faculty members engaged in summer session teaching. The deans did not seem much concerned with the prospect of that development until Jerry Bepko pointed out to them that the money for summer session fringe benefits would have to be found in their budgets. Suddenly, for the deans, the faculty council chatter became more meaningful, even threatening. What formerly had been a central administration problem was being shared.

Responsibility center budgeting offered the prospect of a likely scenario: concerned deans meeting with their respective faculty and explaining the consequences; concerned faculty expressing their views about the latest proposal to their faculty council representatives. In the future, faculty council members may find that voting their conscience and representing their constituents do not always correspond.

---

1. Thucydides, *The History of the Peloponnesian War*, Book I, trans. Thomas Hobbes, ed. Richard Schlatter (New Brunswick, New Jersey: Rutgers University Press, 1975), p. 107.

Research Activity

Indirect cost recovery of the School of Medicine was $250,000 behind first quarter budget estimates. It was also lagging behind for the School of Dentistry. The disquieting prospect of an income shortfall at year end launched an exacting inquiry into its cause. Several key researchers, it turned out, had taken vacations during the month of August. Their laboratories cut back on activity. When the flow of direct expenditures slowed so also did receipts of indirect cost recovery income.

The implications of the relationship between contract research activity and the rate of recovery of indirect costs had been lost until responsibility center budgeting made the connection a matter of interest to the schools' management. In the future, greater attention would be paid to the vacation schedules of key researchers. Moreover, the pace of research activity would be monitored since future indirect cost recovery estimates will rely on assumptions about how quickly research contracts will be completed.

Longer Term Prospects

Although implementation of responsibility center budgeting appears to be producing beneficial responses and results, realization of its full potential will require further change and careful monitoring. Four areas of concern can be identified: achieving balance in the organizational structure, developing financial information for management purposes, thwarting attempts to beat the system, and avoiding external interference. Other institutions moving toward responsibility center budget probably will encounter the same problems.

Structural Balance

Concerns about organizational structure beset responsibility center budgeting from the beginning. In the short run, organizational structure clearly dominates identification of responsibility centers. However, wide variations in the size and complexity of the existing structure's units are inconsistent with the principle that centers should be about the same size. On the Indianapolis campus, for example, the largest center, the School of Medicine, is 160 times larger than the smallest, the School of Journalism. Moreover, the School of Medicine accounts for over 30 percent of total campus income/expenditure.

Whatever reasons formerly influenced organizational structure, responsibility center budgeting introduces new considerations. Can a center be too small to survive in an environment which presumes financial viability? For large units, large numbers of random events can offset wide swings in enrollment, income, and expenditure. Will sufficient stability characterize small units? We'll have to see.

If one accepts the axiom that the effectiveness of decision making improves as the point of decision approximates the point of implementation, much of the benefit of responsibility center budgeting is suspended by the persistence of large centers characterized by centralized management. As with the university or campuses, individuals operating in such a large enterprise are liable neither to recognize the full consequences nor to appreciate the full benefits of their actions. Decentralization of management within a large center can obviate the need for structural change, or the issue of approximate equality in the size of decision making units has to be addressed to realize the full potential of responsibility center budgeting in the long run.

Management Information

Many colleges and universities report their financial information in accordance with standards set by the National Association of College and University Business Officers or some approximation thereof.[2] However, adherence to such accounting conventions does not assure accurate, timely, and useful financial information for internal management purposes.

Responsibility center budgeting places a premium on financial management information. While organizing data according to the fund groupings required by extant reporting standards will have to be maintained, an internal accounting system that recognizes the interaction between operating and capital decisions and explicitly recognizes allowances for depreciation on plant and equipment is required. Decision makers have to be able to appreciate from easily retrievable and consistently presented information long and short term trade-offs between current operations and investment in plant and equipment.

Perversion of Principles

Decentralized decision making does not mean that centers are independent or autonomous. University policies with respect to accounting, budget control, purchasing, personnel recruitment, hiring, evaluation, promotion and

---

2. National Association of College and University Business Officers, *College and University Business Administration*, 4th ed., 1982.

termination, payroll, physical facilities construction, acquisition, maintenance, and operations still apply. If those policies are objectionable or inappropriate, they should be changed. But such problems should be addressed whether or not responsibility center budgeting is adopted. Many will invoke responsibility center budgeting as a rationale for sweeping aside ineffective and troublesome (as well as effective and necessary) policies. They have to be resisted.

Another tendency to be resisted when a new system is put in place is establishing policies to correct for problems that can be imagined but do not exist. I have observed that the need for unnecessary policies limiting managers' discretion is produced by their creation. For that reason, responsibility center budgeting was implemented on the Indianapolis campus without establishing an intercenter bank arrangement that characterizes the University of Pennsylvania and University of Southern California systems. We took our cue from the state of Indiana which places no special restrictions on universities' level and use of fund balances and relied instead on existing university policies that charge interest to auxiliary enterprises and other self supporting units which incur a deficit.

External Interference

For Indiana University, the story of the long term impact of responsibility center budgeting on state relations has not yet been told. Short run reactions, however, are encouraging. H. Kent Weldon, the associate commissioner for financial affairs at the Indiana Commission for Higher Education, seems to approve of our efforts. Presenting financial information for the Indianapolis campus in a responsibility center budgeting format has aided his understanding and that of his colleagues. The format may prove useful in developing the university's request for state funding and showing how the funds have been employed.

Attending the possibilities is a risk that appropriations to campuses or the university would be detailed by responsibility center. As the illustration of budget construction in the preceding chapter demonstrates, such a development would severely constrain the flexibility of responsibility center budgeting and introduce dislocations into the allocation of assessment income and expenditure. Continuation of the mutual respect and understanding between universities and their state government sponsors probably will have more to do with the outcome than the mechanics of responsibility center budgeting. If responsibility center budgeting makes communication and accountability easier, fewer rather than more constraints should result.

Responsibility Center Budgeting and Higher Education

Indiana University is in the process of joining seven other institutions of higher education in adopting responsibility center budgeting or one of its variations (Cornell University, Harvard University, Johns Hopkins University, University of Miami, University of Pennsylvania, University of Southern California, and Washington University).[3] What about the other 2,000 institutions?[4] Are they candidates?

If size is a factor determining the usefulness of responsibility center budgeting for a college or university, some institutions are better candidates than others. To get an idea of the number of candidates, a look at enrollments by institution may be instructive. The enrollments of the institutions currently adopting responsibility center budgeting range from about 6,700 to over 89,000 if we count Indiana University (and why not?)[5] Since only one of the universities has an enrollment of less than 10,000, a conservative lower bound is 10,000 students. The number of four year colleges and universities with enrollments greater than 10,000 is 233. Although they account for only 12 percent of the number of institutions, they account for 56 percent of total enrollment in four year college and university enrollment of 7.7 million students. Clearly, widespread adoption of responsibility center budgeting by those institutions whose scale of operation merit such a system would have a significant impact on higher education.

Is such a move needed?

Assessment of Higher Education's Performance

The professional literature and the popular press are replete with criticisms of higher education's performance. One, a widely circulated article that caught the attention of Indiana University's trustees, appeared in the January 27, 1987, edition of the *Wall Street Journal*. Its author, Robert V. Iosue, president of York College of Pennsylvania, observes, "The single biggest reason the cost of college is so high is declining and insufficient productivity as defined by the

---

3. Gilbert Fuchsberg, "Several Big Universities Give Fiscal Autonomy to Divisions, but the System Has Its Risks, as Johns Hopkins Case Shows," *Chronicle of Higher Education* (January 25, 1989), pp. A25-A27.

4. U.S. Department of Education, Office of Educational Research and Improvement, National Center for Education Statistics, *Digest of Education Statistics 1988*, Thomas D. Snyder, project director (Washington, D.C.: U.S. Government Printing Office. 1988), p. 184.

5. *HEP. 1990 Higher Education Directory*, Constance Healey Torregrosa, editor (Falls Church, Virginia: Higher Education Publications, Inc., 1990).

number of students taught by the faculty and serviced by the administration."[6]
He cites and dismisses a series of myths offered by college administrators and
faculty in response to criticisms of rising costs:

> The high cost of college is due to expensive equipment, buildings, computers
> and other items peripheral to education. Wrong. The single biggest reason for
> the high cost of college, public institutions as well as private ones, is staff. The
> average college spends more than 80% of its budget on salaries and fringe
> benefits.
> The average professor is overpaid. Wrong. The average professor is under-
> worked. There are more than 450,000 full-time professors teaching in this
> country's 3,300 colleges, earning an average salary of $31,000 for nine months of
> work plus numerous breaks. . . .
> A few decades ago professors taught 15 credits a semester (about one-half the
> teaching load of a high school teacher today) and were expected to engage in
> research. Today, some teach 12 credits, but nine credits is the norm at many
> colleges.
> All those college administrators are necessary for the operation of the college.
> Wrong. They may be working hard, but there is a lot of bumping into one another.
> Colleges, especially public ones whose costs are subsidized by high taxes, excel
> in building bureaucracies.

A more recent criticism of higher education's performance is described in
ProfScam: Professors and the Demise of Higher Education. The author, Charles J.
Sykes, charges that domination by the American university professor results
in

> a modern university distinguished by costs that are zooming out of control;
> curriculums that look like they were designed by a game show host; nonexistent
> advising programs; lectures of droning, mind-numbing dullness often to 1,000
> or more semi-anonymous undergraduates herded into dilapidated, ill-lighted
> lecture halls; teaching assistants who can't speak understandable English; and
> the product of all this, a generation of expensively credentialed college graduates
> who might not be able to locate England on a map.[7]

Getting access to *ProfScam* proved to be unexpectedly instructive. To obtain
a copy of the book, Barbara L. Pogoni, in the University Budget Office, went
to the Indiana University's main library in Bloomington. The library's collection of books and bound journals numbers over 4.8 million volumes. In size,
it ranks eighteenth among research libraries in the United States and sixth
among Big Ten institutions. However, a copy of Sykes's book was not among

---

6. Robert V. Iosue, "How Colleges Can Cut Costs," *Wall Street Journal* (January 27, 1987), p. 34.

7. Charles J. Sykes, *ProfScam: Professors and the Demise of Higher Education,* Washington, D.C.:
Regnery Gateway, 1988), p. 4.

the millions. Moreover, Barbara could only find two reviews of *ProfScam*. It hardly seemed to exist.

She then went to the Monroe County Public Library. They had four copies! The helpful librarian there told her she was lucky to have one available. Most of the time, all four volumes are checked out!

How strange that a research library—and, as evidenced by the dearth of reviews, the larger academic community—would ignore a book—right or wrong, just or unjust—influencing the thoughts of many about higher education. Is higher education's attempt to ignore the charges a manifestation of their confirmation? It is said that dying persons pass through stages: denial, pseudodenial, anger, bargaining, depression, and finally acceptance or resignation.[8] Higher education may be yet in the early stages of coping with bad news.

According to Thomas Short, "though Sykes's charges are not always entirely on the mark, he is basically right about the 'scam' that allows scholars to remove themselves from teaching, that overloads academic circuits with inferior work, that raises the cost of education without improving the state of our knowledge, and that results not only in larger classes but in classes taught by underprepared and overworked junior faculty or graduate teaching assistants."[9] Not all of higher education's ills can be placed at the doorstep of professors, however. In his review of ProfScam, Short states, "Readily available statistics, which Sykes does not cite, show the enormous increase that has already taken place in the number of university and college administrators and in their share of academic budgets. From 1976 to 1986, while instructional costs for all U.S. colleges (including library purchases, etc.) went up 21 percent, administrative costs rose at double that rate, or 42 percent."

The dreary recitation of higher education's many problems goes on and on. It extends back to the indefinite past and undoubtedly will continue into the future. Most of the problem finders tend to be problem solvers. For every problem discovered, a solution is suggested.

To correct the ills of higher education that he identifies, Sykes looks to trustees, legislators, Congress, foundations and research grantors, students, parents, and—last but not least—professors. Involvement of all the other groups becomes unnecessary and the probability of a satisfactory outcome is vastly increased if the intellect, creativity, and energy of the faculty can be unleashed and directed to the improvement of higher education.

---

8. Elisabeth Kubler-Ross, *Coping with Death and Dying*, sound recording (New York: Psychology Today, 1973).

9. Thomas Short, "Higher Education?" (review of *ProfScam: Professors and the Demise of Higher Education*), *Commentary* 88:1 (July 1989), pp. 68–70.

A Solution?

Can responsibility center budgeting correct higher education's shortcomings? Of course not. To suggest that it can would be folly. Can a hammer drive a nail? Not without a carpenter. Responsibility center budgeting is a tool, an instrument that, placed in the hands of able academic leadership, can—and at Indiana University does—assist in the process of managing a complex university. Responsibility center budgeting is a useful concept that can help create an environment that mobilizes and focuses the human resources of the academic community toward an institution's fundamental and overall objectives. But leadership is required to make it work.

11. Care and Feeding of the Monster

Whoever fights monsters should see to it that in
the process he does not become a monster.

Friedrich Wilhelm Nietzsche,
Beyond Good and Evil

Responsibility center budgeting has many advantages. It also poses some hazards. Among its advantages is a rational structure. Not only do people understand the way it operates within their institution but you can also explain the system to outsiders. For large and complicated institutions of higher education, a centralized approach to budgeting is liable to result in a Byzantine structure that defies description or analysis. Such systems, intended to obfuscate instead of elucidate, may be congenial to some. But they are unnecessary in institutions with a clear academic agenda and a forthright leadership that encourages active participation of those charged with management responsibilities.

Businessmen readily associate responsibility center budgeting with "full cost" accounting or with "profit center" management. Responsibility center budgeting is neither of those. No responsibility center is a profit center. Every one of them is on the dole. The academic units performing primary mission activities receive an appropriation allocation that reflects university wide objectives and priorities. Support units receive guaranteed income in the form of assessments for the services they provide. Since they tend to spend everything they receive, "full cost" is "full income."

More importantly, responsibility center budgeting is more than a mechanism to determine an underlying economic reality, a production function, underlying teaching, research, and service activities. It provides a structure for allocating resources in a way that manifests a university's objectives.

But what about the disadvantages? Well, yes, responsibility center budgeting does pose certain hazards. If not directed carefully, it can result in dissension, discord, distortion, dissonance, disaster, *and* doom. My compatriots seem to feel that truth in advertising (but what about advocacy?) requires that the downside be mentioned. Caveat emptor!

Proceeding from basic principles, responsibility center budgeting establishes a set of rules with respect to organization, income attribution, and expense allocation. Those rules—as understood by the participants—elicit certain responses. If those responses result in behavior that automatically serves not only the purposes of a local unit but also the objectives and priorities of the entire institution, we have a good set of rules. However, if the resulting behavior serves poorly either local or university interests (or worse, serves neither local nor university interests), we have a bad set of rules.

As you can see, the possibilities for bad rules exceed the possibilities for good rules three to one. Only when both local and university interests are served well simultaneously do we have good rules.

Good rules are hard to find. When found, they are subject to another hazard. They are not always observed. Failure to enforce them undermines the entire system—which ultimately is based on trust of the participants. Each exception is like a Hydra's head; it begets others. Strong leadership with involvement of deans and other participants to produce a sense of ownership and community is required to assure adherence to rules designed to promote unit and university objectives.

At the outset, the situation is an unstable one. Unless responsibility center budgeting's underlying principles are accepted by the participants, the participants themselves, without vigilant leadership, are liable to engage in a series of exception swapping that accommodates parochial interests at the expense of the entire enterprise. Initially, the probability of an Abilene paradox outcome is very high.

The types of problems that can occur can be classified in various ways. I have chosen to group them in three categories: Organization, issues that relate to identification of responsibility centers; Income Attribution, which concerns how earned income is distributed to units; and Cost Allocation, how indirect costs are distributed to units.

Organization

Academic units—schools—are fairly easily identified. Support units constitute the area where games to protect local interests are liable to be played.

The Summer Session Case

Summer session courses provide an example. Remember the criteria for defining responsibility centers? Clear definition of management responsibility? Remember the functionality principle, coupling responsibility and authority? Whose courses are taught during the summer? Answer: the schools'. Whose faculty will teach those summer courses? Answer: the schools'. What deans will determine what courses are taught and who will teach them.

Answer: the schools'. Wrong! The dean of faculty or the dean for summer school. Not on all campuses at Indiana University, but on some, changes to the existing hierarchy and loss of the possibility of central meddling in intraschool affairs was too much to bear. The thought of transforming a major administrative operation into a modest service unit facilitating summer session programs directed by school deans was too novel. Needless to write, that aberration spawned further complications in income attribution and cost allocation. Similar scenarios occurred in the area of continuing education and outreach efforts organized to offer off-campus instruction.

Differences in Size

With a clearly established structure, academic units presented less of an initial problem when defining responsibility centers. However, their disparate size presents a long run problem. Among the criteria for defining responsibility centers, remember approximate parity among units in terms of size and complexity? If a unit is too small, the cost of participating in responsibility center budgeting outweighs the benefit. If a unit is too large, potential benefits from placing decision making close to the point of execution are lost.

Just as budgeting arrangements should not drive resource allocation decisions, so also the existing organizational structure should not inhibit optimum use of those resources. An institution's objectives and priorities should be served by both budgeting arrangements and organizational structure.

Income Attribution

Remember the principle of performance recognition, in which managers receive and incur the full benefits and full costs of their unit's actions? And motivation, in which each center receives the income (and bears the cost) that its operation produces? No sooner was responsibility center budgeting announced than speculation began on how crafty deans could pervert the system to their own selfish ends.

Battles over Service Courses

One of the first concerns was that professional schools would begin offering service courses to capture additional student fee income. Imagine the School of Engineering and Technology offering art appreciation courses! Or the School of Social Work, advanced calculus! Or the School of Business, introductory courses in ethics! Pretty scary! Awful!

Your reaction depends on that to which you have become accustomed. Isn't the problem of juniors and seniors trying unsuccessfully after two and three years to enroll in service courses required for their degree scary? Awful? Semester after semester, offerings of basic courses required for a degree are not sufficient to meet student demand for them. Wouldn't it be scary and awful if students were served well by a system of incentives that made meeting their educational needs for introductory courses worthwhile to school deans. Or is providing an excellent undergraduate education really what we're about?

Clearly, anarchy in course offerings among schools is not desirable. But the possibility that schools will have an incentive under responsibility center budgeting to offer a sufficient number of service courses to meet students' needs is not bad news. Uncommon common sense suggests that the ways in which schools compete to attract student fee income will have to be monitored to strike a happy balance between responsiveness and orderliness. For those who have wondered what deans of faculty do, here's a possible assignment. Central administration is not exactly helpless against ruthlessly competitive deans. Don't forget that everyone's on the dole, and central administration determines who gets the appropriation allocation. Responsibility center budgeting is not a substitute for strong, courageous central leadership; indeed, the system requires it.

Central leadership is not alone in the struggle to contain the unbridled ambition of unruly deans. If deans and other unit managers are involved in responsibility center management—if they participate in the rule development process—such aberrant behavior will be checked by peer pressure (especially if the units are approximately equal in size and complexity, and no "super" dean of a big school can bully the others). Accreditation agencies also can limit such tendencies.

Other tendencies toward academic bankruptcy to achieve fiscal solvency require surveillance. Excessive use of part-time instructors and graduate students to teach courses (which goes on now), courses notorious for lack of content and for inflated grades (ditto), and a school padding degree requirements with courses it offers have to be watched—and limited through fine tuning the reward (i.e., appropriation allocation) system.

Indirect Cost Recovery

No income attribution rule is neutral with respect to incentives. The statement is extreme, but the emphasis is intended because occasionally the relationship is forgotten or ignored. Attributing income from indirect cost recovery on grants and contracts to the center of the principal investigator seems rather straightforward and unequivocal. However, it was challenged from an expected quarter. Indirect costs are not recovered equally on all grants and contracts. The state of Indiana, for example, pays no indirect costs on grants and contracts awarded to public universities. State grants and contracts constitute a significant portion of the total awards of the School of Education.

Guess who proposed that indirect cost recovery income be prorated to centers according to the direct costs of grants and contracts? The assurance was not sufficient that indirect costs incurred on state grants and contracts were to be recognized through compensating adjustments in appropriation allocations. Folks wanted to tinker with the rules in a way that clouds where income really is earned and where costs really are incurred. A far more constructive approach would have been to argue for a greater share of appropriation allocations as state grants and contracts increase. And to the extent that those state-sponsored activities complement institutional priorities and objectives, such an argument should be recognized. Such discussions among deans and support center managers are precisely what is needed to guide the formulation of responsibility center budgeting.

A Continuing Struggle

Jockeying for position through the rules is something that goes on forever. During our first visit to the University of Southern California I was struck by the fact that a change in the way student fee income was attributed to schools was under active consideration. Certain deans were advocating a move from attributing fee income based on course enrollments to one based on number of majors. Such a change would have reduced fee income attributed to to the College of Letters, Arts, and Sciences and increased it for the professional schools. Had the change been adopted, the shifts in income would have been offset by compensating shifts in subvention, but perceptions about relative subvention would have been altered.

Continuing review of the existing rules and proposals for their alteration are part of a process of keeping center heads involved in the development of responsibility center budgeting. Such review is constructive inasmuch as it renews understanding of why the rules have been adopted and how they influence behavior.

Income Grabbing and Gouging

School deans do not have a monopoly on craftiness and willingness to pervert the rules for their particular purposes. Support units were quick to demonstrate their income grabbing and income gouging proclivities. Academic computing and the student health center hastened to come forward with proposals for a "technology" fee and a "student health service" fee that all students would be required to pay, thus assuring a dedicated income stream linked to enrollment and not level of service or institutional priorities. Tendencies to preserve the illusion of "free" public goods on the part of administrators of many support units can be very strong.

Evidence of similar tendencies elsewhere prompted a university-wide policy on student fee structure. Without a vision of how the institution wants to present its fees to students and the public, responsibility center budgeting is liable to unleash a chaotic fee structure as units attempt to grab income.

Income gouging is another ploy for support units. Support unit income can take two forms: assessments and charges. Assessments are intended to cover the public goods aspects of support services; charges, the marketable portion of support services.

Initially, all income for support units took the form of assessments. Shortly after implementation of responsibility center budgeting, however, support units began to invoke charges for the marketable portion of their services. So far, so good. But they also wanted to keep the assessments at their original level. Double plus ungood. That's income gouging! "Ouch!" said the deans. For a given level of service, charges replace, do not supplement, assessments.

A surveillance and approval mechanism is required to prevent income gouging. First, in order to be legitimate, charges have to be budgeted to the support units levying them as income and to the centers incurring them as an expense. That requirement uses an existing management device, the budget, to (a) insure that both parties to the transaction—those being paid as well as those paying—are informed, (b) allow compensating adjustments in assessments to offset the charges, and (c) confine invoking of new charges to the beginning of a fiscal year. Second, if a support unit initiates charges, a decision is required about whether users can seek alternative sources. If the support unit retains a monopoly, the price has to be controlled. If alternative sources are permitted, price control is less of a consideration. Who makes those decisions? A representative group of producers and consumers. Initially, direct involvement of school deans and support unit managers is desirable so that the principal players are fully informed about the process. As precedents are established and decisions become routine, responsibility for such decisions can be delegated.

If a center manager desires additional services from a support unit, she or he can arrange to pay for them. For example, if the dean of the School of Business needs additional computing capacity for the school, he can reimburse academic computing for the cost of installing equipment operated and maintained for his program. Among consenting heads of responsibility centers, anything can happen.

Cost Allocations

Maintaining simplicity is a major challenge of cost allocation routines. Support units often prefer rather complicated approaches to allocating their costs to using responsibility centers. While refinement may lead to some satisfaction that costs are distributed among responsibility centers realistically, the tediousness of a sophisticated approach inhibits understanding. How will the behavior of center managers be influenced by cost allocation methodology? That is the appropriate question that should guide the procedures that are adopted. For those support services that fall into the public goods sector and whose costs are basically fixed, the answer to the question, How will the behavior of center managers be influenced by cost allocation methodology? is: Not much.

Responsibility center budgeting is not a route for the fainthearted, wimps, or daisy killers. Not every institution of higher education has a clear vision of its objectives and a commitment to an academic agenda designed to achieve those objectives. Not every institution possesses strong leadership characterized by a willingness to communicate and participatory management. Even with those ingredients in place, success is not assured. But can we afford not to take a chance?

Appendix
Determining Total Costs

All hope abandon, ye who enter here!

Dante Alighieri, *The Divine Comedy, Inferno*, Canto III, line 9

Welcome, fearless reader, to our discourse on a simultaneous equation approach to allocating indirect costs and determining total costs for all of the responsibility centers. Although you are now entering the netherworld of an appendix, I hope you will not find the journey difficult. The mathematics is less important than the way the data should be structured.

To brace ourselves for the mathematical notation to follow and represent the responsibility centers succinctly and generally, let's number them from one to n. In preceding chapters, we have been dealing with twenty responsibility centers, so

$n = 20$.

The first responsibility center is the School of Arts and Humanities; the nth center (or in our illustration, the 20th), Central Administration.

Since distinguishing between academic and support responsibility centers is necessary, let's represent generally academic centers with a range from 1 to h and support centers with a range from k to n. In our illustration the first fourteen centers are academic responsibility centers; the last six are support centers. Thus,

$h = 14$

and stands for the School of Public Affairs; and

$k = 15$

and stands for libraries.

A responsibility center's total cost is equal to its direct costs plus allocated indirect costs of support centers that provide services to it. If T_i represents total cost of the ith responsibility center; D_i, its direct costs; and A_{ik}, the allocated cost of the kth responsibility center provide service to center i, then

$$T_i = D_i + \sum_{j=k}^{n} A_{ij}$$

To determine net total cost net of earned income we have to subtract each center's earned income from its total cost. If N_i represents total net costs and E_i is earned income,

$$N_i = T_i - E_i = D_i - E_i + \sum_{j=k}^{n} A_{ij}$$

Letting K_i stand for a center's direct cost net of earned income produces

$$K_i = D_i - E_i$$

and

$$N_i = K_i + \sum_{j=k}^{n} A_{ij}$$

As now stated, a responsibility center's total net cost is equal to its net direct costs plus the allocated costs of the support centers serving it.

What are those allocated costs? As already indicated, they are equal to a percentage of a support center's net direct costs. In terms of our notation,

$$A_{ij} = c_{ij} \cdot N_j$$

where c_{ij} represents the percentage of support center j's net direct cost assigned to responsibility center i. As readers may recall from the preceding chapter, a support center's percentage assigned to itself is zero; that is, c_{jj} is zero.

A responsibility center's total net cost now can be stated

$$N_i = K_i + \sum_{j=k}^{n} c_{ij} \cdot N_j$$

One of those equations can be produced for each responsibility center, and together they define a system of n equations. For each equation, we already have determined K_i and c_{ij}; we don't know N_i and N_j. Fortunately, under conditions we are likely to encounter, the system of equations can be expected to provide a unique solution for all N_i.

If we have n responsibility centers, we must have n equations. With appropriate ellipses, the system of equations can be expressed

$$N_1 = K_1 + c_{1k}N_k + \ldots + c_{1m}N_m + c_{1n}N_n$$
$$N_2 = K_2 + c_{2k}N_k + \ldots + c_{2m}N_m + c_{2n}N_n$$

.

.

.

$$N_m = K_m + c_{mk}N_k + \ldots + c_{mm}N_m + c_{mn}N_n$$
$$N_n = K_n + c_{nk}N_k + \ldots + c_{nm}N_m + c_{nn}N_n$$

Total net costs, the N_i, appear on both sides of the equation. That arrangement is not handy.

If we arrange them in the form of solutions for net direct costs, the system of equations becomes

$$K_1 = N_1 - c_{1k}N_k - \ldots - c_{1m}N_m - c_{1n}N_n$$
$$K_2 = N_2 - c_{2k}N_k - \ldots - c_{2m}N_m - c_{2n}N_n$$

$$\cdot$$
$$\cdot$$
$$\cdot$$

$$K_m = N_m - c_{mk}N_k - \ldots - c_{mm}N_m - c_{1mn}N_n$$
$$K_n = N_n - c_{nk}N_k - \ldots - c_{nm}N_m - c_{nn}N_n$$

Under that transformation, the signs before the coefficients have become negative. Note that N_m and N_n appear twice on the right hand side of the last two equations. Recall that c_{mm} and c_{nn} are both equal to zero. Eliminating the superfluous terms and arranging according to the sequence of subscripts produces

$$K_1 = N_1 \qquad\qquad - c_{1k}N_k - \ldots - c_{1m}N_m - c_{1n}N_n$$
$$K_2 = \qquad N_2 \qquad - c_{2k}N_k - \ldots - c_{2m}N_m - c_{2n}N_n$$

$$\cdot$$
$$\cdot$$
$$\cdot$$

$$K_m = \qquad\qquad\qquad - c_{mk}N_k - \ldots + \quad N_m - c_{mn}N_n$$
$$K_n = \qquad\qquad\qquad - c_{nk}N_k - \ldots - c_{nm}N_m + N_n$$

Now the equations can be expressed in matrix form[1]

$$\begin{bmatrix} K_1 \\ K_2 \\ \cdot \\ \cdot \\ \cdot \\ K_m \\ K_n \end{bmatrix} = \begin{bmatrix} 1 & 0 & \ldots & -c_{1k} & \ldots & -c_{1m} & -c_{1n} \\ 0 & 1 & \ldots & -c_{2k} & \ldots & -c_{2m} & -c_{2n} \\ \cdot & \cdot & & \cdot & & \cdot & \cdot \\ \cdot & \cdot & & & & \cdot & \cdot \\ \cdot & \cdot & & & & \cdot & \cdot \\ 0 & 0 & \ldots & -c_{mk} & \ldots & 1 & -c_{mn} \\ 0 & 0 & \ldots & -c_{nk} & \ldots & -c_{nm} & 1 \end{bmatrix} = \begin{bmatrix} N_1 \\ N_2 \\ \cdot \\ \cdot \\ \cdot \\ N_m \\ N_n \end{bmatrix}$$

or to be really succinct

$$[K] = [c]\,[N]$$

---

1. A complete presentation of matrix operations is contained in G. Hadley, *Linear Algebra*, Reading, Mass. Addison-Wesley Publishing Company, Inc., 1961.

We know the values for the elements of [K] and [c]. We want to determine the values for the elements of [N].

If we multiply both sides of the equation by the inverse of the matrix of coefficients, $[c]^{-1}$ and transpose the right and left sides of the equation, we have

$$[N] = [c]^{-1} [K]$$

and the system of equations is in a form to solve for net direct costs.

Of course, inverting a matrix is easier said than done. Until the advent of electronic computing, this approach had little practical significance. Now the calculations can be performed easily at one's desk (if a microcomputer sits on it). Using the data accumulated in the preceding chapters, we will proceed to demonstrate the process.

Net Direct Costs

As already stated, responsibility center's net direct expenditure is defined as

$$K_i = D_i - E_i$$

where D_i is its direct general fund expenditure and E_i is its earned income. The equation causes the common sense notion that net direct expenditure is the difference between its direct expenditure and earned income to look less familiar than the terms already are. In Table 3.7, we displayed an illustration of general fund direct expenditures for all responsibility centers in the chapter concerned with defining responsibility centers. In Table 4.8, earned income for all responsibility centers was displayed.

The relevant columns of numbers in Tables 3.7 and 4.8 are brought forward and presented in Table A.1. The difference between general fund direct expenditures and general fund earned income appears as the third column in Table A.1, net direct expenditures.

The sum of direct expenditures, $269 million, represents the total general fund budget. Total earned income provides an offset of nearly $130 million. The residual, net direct expenditures, amounts to about $139 million. What income source makes up the difference between direct expenditures and earned income? State appropriation. However, as we shall see, it is not distributed among responsibility centers according to their net direct expenditures.

In terms of our notation, K_1, the first element in the [K] vector, corresponds to $465,971, net direct expenditures for the School of Arts and Humanities. In our illustration, we have twenty responsibility centers. Net direct expenditure for central administration, $4,468,000, corresponds to K_{20}, the last element in

TABLE A.1 GENERAL FUND NET DIRECT EXPENDITURES

	General Fund Direct Expenditures [D]	*General Fund Earned Income* [E]	*Net Direct Expenditures* [K]
Arts and Humanities	$ 11,862,000	$ 11,396,029	$ 465,971
Physical and Math Sci	22,860,000	18,083,145	4,776,855
Social & Behavrl Sci	25,108,000	20,437,282	4,670,718
Dentistry	12,599,000	4,049,322	8,549,678
Medicine	59,540,000	21,650,469	37,889,531
Nursing	9,696,000	2,001,602	7,694,398
Optometry	3,291,000	2,332,679	958,321
Business	15,535,000	14,709,356	825,644
Education	10,215,000	6,850,525	3,364,475
Engineering & Tech	5,808,000	2,487,166	3,320,834
Law	4,850,000	3,859,859	990,141
Music	12,335,000	7,313,664	5,021,336
Physical Education	5,384,000	5,094,906	289,094
Public Affairs	5,687,000	4,005,200	1,681,800
SUBTOTAL: ACADEMIC	$204,770,000	$124,271,204	$ 80,498,796
Libraries	$ 12,574,000	$ 201,731	$ 12,372,269
Academic Computing	6,630,000	0	6,630,000
Academic Affairs	4,777,000	1,196,611	3,580,389
Student Services	4,867,000	1,073,662	3,793,338
Physical Facilities	27,983,000	37,700	27,945,300
Central Administratn	7,634,000	3,166,000	4,468,000
SUBTOTAL: SUPPORT	$ 64,465,000	$ 5,675,704	$ 58,789,296
TOTAL	$269,235,000	$129,946,908	$139,288,092

the [K] vector. In other words, net direct expenditures shown in the third column of the table are represented by [K] in the system of equations expressed in matrix form.

Matrix of Allocation Coefficients

Allocation coefficient is a fancy name for the proportion of a support center's cost that is allocated to the center receiving its services. In our mathematical formula, it is represented as

TABLE A.2 MATRIX OF ALLOCATION COEFFICIENTS

	Arts & Human ities	Physcl & Math Sci	Socl & Behvrl Sci	Den tis try	Medi cine	Nurs ing	Optom etry	Busi ness	Educa tion
Arts and Humanities	1.000	0.000	0.000	0.000	0.000	0.000	0.000	0.000	0.000
Physical and Math Sci	0.000	1.000	0.000	0.000	0.000	0.000	0.000	0.000	0.000
Social & Behavrl Sci	0.000	0.000	1.000	0.000	0.000	0.000	0.000	0.000	0.000
Dentistry	0.000	0.000	0.000	1.000	0.000	0.000	0.000	0.000	0.000
Medicine	0.000	0.000	0.000	0.000	1.000	0.000	0.000	0.000	0.000
Nursing	0.000	0.000	0.000	0.000	0.000	1.000	0.000	0.000	0.000
Optometry	0.000	0.000	0.000	0.000	0.000	0.000	1.000	0.000	0.000
Business	0.000	0.000	0.000	0.000	0.000	0.000	0.000	1.000	0.000
Education	0.000	0.000	0.000	0.000	0.000	0.000	0.000	0.000	1.000
Engineering & Tech	0.000	0.000	0.000	0.000	0.000	0.000	0.000	0.000	0.000
Law	0.000	0.000	0.000	0.000	0.000	0.000	0.000	0.000	0.000
Music	0.000	0.000	0.000	0.000	0.000	0.000	0.000	0.000	0.000
Physical Education	0.000	0.000	0.000	0.000	0.000	0.000	0.000	0.000	0.000
Public Affairs	0.000	0.000	0.000	0.000	0.000	0.000	0.000	0.000	0.000
Libraries	0.000	0.000	0.000	0.000	0.000	0.000	0.000	0.000	0.000
Academic Computing	0.000	0.000	0.000	0.000	0.000	0.000	0.000	0.000	0.000
Academic Affairs	0.000	0.000	0.000	0.000	0.000	0.000	0.000	0.000	0.000
Student Services	0.000	0.000	0.000	0.000	0.000	0.000	0.000	0.000	0.000
Physical Facilities	0.000	0.000	0.000	0.000	0.000	0.000	0.000	0.000	0.000
Central Administratn	0.000	0.000	0.000	0.000	0.000	0.000	0.000	0.000	0.000

c_{ij}

where c is the proportion of support center j's cost allocated to center i.

How do we construct a matrix of those little devils? Each responsibility center is assigned a row and a column. In terms of our illustration, the coefficient in the 8th row and 18th column represents the portion of the cost of the student services support center to be allocated to the School of Business.

The first row and the first column, proceeding from the upper left hand corner, has the same responsibility center. In the case of our example, it is the School of Arts and Humanities. The last row and the last column—the row at the bottom and the column on the right hand side—have the same responsibility center. For us, it is Central Administration. In between appear the other responsibility centers ordered by column in the same sequence as the row order.

The allocation coefficients whose row represents the same responsibility center as its column fall in a diagonal running from the upper left hand corner to the lower right hand corner of the matrix. Those coefficients represent the portion of a center's cost that is allocated to itself. All of a center's cost is allocated to itself, so the value of those coefficients is one.

What about the values of the other $n^2 - n$ coefficients? If none of a center's cost is allocated to another, the coefficient takes a value of zero. In our

Engi neer ing & Tech	Law	Music	Phys ical Educa tion	Pub lic Af fairs	Li brar ies	Aca demic Comput ting	Aca demic Af fairs	Stu dent Ser vices	Phys ical Facil ities	Cen tral Admin strtn
0.000	0.000	0.000	0.000	0.000	-0.088	-0.062	-0.049	-0.140	-0.011	-0.039
0.000	0.000	0.000	0.000	0.000	-0.153	-0.290	-0.144	-0.191	-0.145	-0.096
0.000	0.000	0.000	0.000	0.000	-0.190	-0.147	-0.109	-0.231	-0.023	-0.084
0.000	0.000	0.000	0.000	0.000	-0.009	-0.019	-0.058	-0.007	-0.063	-0.043
0.000	0.000	0.000	0.000	0.000	-0.053	-0.136	-0.299	-0.030	-0.239	-0.271
0.000	0.000	0.000	0.000	0.000	-0.044	-0.024	-0.039	-0.028	-0.032	-0.031
0.000	0.000	0.000	0.000	0.000	-0.028	-0.007	-0.015	-0.006	-0.006	-0.011
0.000	0.000	0.000	0.000	0.000	-0.131	-0.092	-0.069	-0.133	-0.015	-0.055
0.000	0.000	0.000	0.000	0.000	-0.094	-0.039	-0.067	-0.046	-0.016	-0.044
1.000	0.000	0.000	0.000	0.000	-0.040	-0.087	-0.023	-0.052	-0.028	-0.018
0.000	1.000	0.000	0.000	0.000	-0.010	-0.014	-0.020	-0.006	-0.016	-0.016
0.000	0.000	1.000	0.000	0.000	-0.088	-0.027	-0.049	-0.051	-0.039	-0.040
0.000	0.000	0.000	1.000	0.000	-0.040	-0.021	-0.029	-0.049	-0.028	-0.022
0.000	0.000	0.000	0.000	1.000	-0.028	-0.030	-0.030	-0.030	-0.007	-0.022
0.000	0.000	0.000	0.000	0.000	1.000	0.000	0.000	0.000	-0.068	-0.040
0.000	0.000	0.000	0.000	0.000	0.000	1.000	0.000	0.000	-0.010	-0.004
0.000	0.000	0.000	0.000	0.000	-0.004	-0.001	1.000	0.000	-0.025	-0.022
0.000	0.000	0.000	0.000	0.000	0.000	-0.001	0.000	1.000	-0.192	-0.065
0.000	0.000	0.000	0.000	0.000	0.000	0.000	0.000	0.000	1.000	-0.077
0.000	0.000	0.000	0.000	0.000	0.000	-0.003	0.000	0.000	-0.037	1.000

illustration, the schools are found to be engaged only in the delivery of teaching, research, and service; they do not provide services to other centers. As a result, with the exception of the coefficient in the diagonal, all the coefficients in the columns representing the schools are zero. Our support centers are viewed as providing only services to other centers. As a consequence, in the columns representing support centers, many of the coefficients outside the diagonal are not zero and reflect a value indicating the portion of their cost allocable to other centers.

Table A.2 displays a matrix of allocation coefficients for all the responsibility centers in our illustration. As expected, the values of the coefficients in the diagonal running from the upper left hand corner to the lower right are equal to one. The other coefficients in the columns for the School of Arts and Humanities and the School of Public Affairs and all the schools in between are zero. Many of the coefficients in the columns for Libraries through Central Administration appear as negative numbers, less than zero but greater than -1.0. Why are they negative and where did they come from?

The matrix of allocation coefficients appearing in Table A.2 is represented as the matrix [c] in the system of equations defining net direct costs

$$[K] = [c][N].$$

TABLE A.3 INVERTED MATRIX OF ALLOCATION COEFFICIENTS

	Arts & Human ities	Physcl & Math Sci	Socl & Behvrl Sci	Den tis try	Medi cine	Nurs ing	Optom etry	Busi ness	Educa tion
Arts and Humanities	1.000	0.000	0.000	0.000	0.000	0.000	0.000	0.000	0.000
Physical and Math Sci	0.000	1.000	0.000	0.000	0.000	0.000	0.000	0.000	0.000
Social & Behavrl Sci	0.000	0.000	1.000	0.000	0.000	0.000	0.000	0.000	0.000
Dentistry	0.000	0.000	0.000	1.000	0.000	0.000	0.000	0.000	0.000
Medicine	0.000	0.000	0.000	0.000	1.000	0.000	0.000	0.000	0.000
Nursing	0.000	0.000	0.000	0.000	0.000	1.000	0.000	0.000	0.000
Optometry	0.000	0.000	0.000	0.000	0.000	0.000	1.000	0.000	0.000
Business	0.000	0.000	0.000	0.000	0.000	0.000	0.000	1.000	0.000
Education	0.000	0.000	0.000	0.000	0.000	0.000	0.000	0.000	1.000
Engineering & Tech	0.000	0.000	0.000	0.000	0.000	0.000	0.000	0.000	0.000
Law	0.000	0.000	0.000	0.000	0.000	0.000	0.000	0.000	0.000
Music	0.000	0.000	0.000	0.000	0.000	0.000	0.000	0.000	0.000
Physical Education	0.000	0.000	0.000	0.000	0.000	0.000	0.000	0.000	0.000
Public Affairs	0.000	0.000	0.000	0.000	0.000	0.000	0.000	0.000	0.000
Libraries	0.000	0.000	0.000	0.000	0.000	0.000	0.000	0.000	0.000
Academic Computing	0.000	0.000	0.000	0.000	0.000	0.000	0.000	0.000	0.000
Academic Affairs	0.000	0.000	0.000	0.000	0.000	0.000	0.000	0.000	0.000
Student Services	0.000	0.000	0.000	0.000	0.000	0.000	0.000	0.000	0.000
Physical Facilities	0.000	0.000	0.000	0.000	0.000	0.000	0.000	0.000	0.000
Central Administratn	0.000	0.000	0.000	0.000	0.000	0.000	0.000	0.000	0.000

Remember? Net direct costs for all centers is defined as total net cost *minus* allocated costs. The allocating coefficients in the matrix are negative to recognize that deduction.

Where did they come from? Alert readers will note that the values for the negative coefficients in matrix correspond to the values appearing in Table 5.12. Were you one of them? In Table 5.12, they are shown as the percentages of support center costs to be allocated to other centers—the same function they perform here where they are presented as proportions.

Observe what happens if the values of each column of allocation coefficient matrix of Table A.2 are summed. (The totals are not shown, since the exercise is straightforward and within the capabilities of most students of responsibility center budgeting.) For the schools, the sums of their columns obviously are 1.000. Not so obvious, the sums for the support centers are zero. Since the support centers are exclusively service units, all of their total net cost is allocated to other centers. That the sums for the schools' columns are one indicates that none of their total net costs are allocated to other centers. As will be demonstrated, their total net costs are funded through state support.

That the academic centers' columns sum to one and support centers' to zero is an accident of the illustration. In general, this approach to structuring

Engi neer ing & Tech	Law	Music	Phys ical Educa tion	Pub lic Af fairs	Li brar ies	Aca demic Comput ing	Aca demic Af fairs	Stu dent Ser vices	Phys ical Facil ities	Cen tral Admin strtn
0.000	0.000	0.000	0.000	0.000	0.088	0.062	0.049	0.140	0.048	0.057
0.000	0.000	0.000	0.000	0.000	0.154	0.291	0.144	0.191	0.204	0.135
0.000	0.000	0.000	0.000	0.000	0.190	0.148	0.109	0.231	0.089	0.116
0.000	0.000	0.000	0.000	0.000	0.009	0.019	0.058	0.007	0.068	0.050
0.000	0.000	0.000	0.000	0.000	0.054	0.137	0.299	0.030	0.269	0.303
0.000	0.000	0.000	0.000	0.000	0.044	0.024	0.039	0.028	0.043	0.039
0.000	0.000	0.000	0.000	0.000	0.028	0.007	0.015	0.006	0.010	0.014
0.000	0.000	0.000	0.000	0.000	0.131	0.092	0.069	0.133	0.055	0.075
0.000	0.000	0.000	0.000	0.000	0.094	0.039	0.067	0.046	0.035	0.055
1.000	0.000	0.000	0.000	0.000	0.040	0.087	0.023	0.052	0.043	0.027
0.000	1.000	0.000	0.000	0.000	0.010	0.014	0.020	0.006	0.019	0.019
0.000	0.000	1.000	0.000	0.000	0.088	0.027	0.049	0.051	0.058	0.053
0.000	0.000	0.000	1.000	0.000	0.040	0.021	0.029	0.049	0.042	0.031
0.000	0.000	0.000	0.000	1.000	0.028	0.030	0.030	0.030	0.017	0.027
0.000	0.000	0.000	0.000	0.000	1.000	0.000	0.000	0.000	0.070	0.045
0.000	0.000	0.000	0.000	0.000	0.000	1.000	0.000	0.000	0.010	0.005
0.000	0.000	0.000	0.000	0.000	0.004	0.001	1.000	0.000	0.026	0.024
0.000	0.000	0.000	0.000	0.000	0.000	0.001	0.000	1.000	0.195	0.080
0.000	0.000	0.000	0.000	0.000	0.000	0.000	0.000	0.000	1.003	0.077
0.000	0.000	0.000	0.000	0.000	0.000	0.003	0.000	0.000	0.037	1.003

responsibility center budgeting does not impose a constraint that academic centers provide no services to other centers and that support centers engage in no teaching, research, or public service activities.

The School of Physical and Mathematical Sciences, for example, could be responsible for academic computing, whose costs would be allocable to other academic and support centers. Under that circumstance, negative allocation coefficients would appear in the column of the school. However, the column would not sum to zero but rather to a value between zero and one reflecting the portion of the School's total cost attributable to academic computing services. If, say, academic computing accounted for 20 percent of the School's cost, its column of coefficients would sum to 0.80.

Inverted Matrix of Allocation Coefficients

Now we have values for centers' net direct cost (Table A.1) and their allocation coefficients (Table A.2). In the equation

$$[K] = [c][N]$$

the values for [K] and [c] have been determined. We don't know [N], total net

TABLE A.4 DERIVATION OF TOTAL NET EXPENDITURE
BY RESPONSIBILITY CENTER

	Total Net Expenditure [N]	Earned Income [E]	Total Expenditure [T]
Arts and Humanities	$ 4,266,544	$ 11,396,029	$ 15,662,573
Physical and Math Sci	16,135,587	18,083,145	34,218,732
Social & Behavrl Sci	12,274,783	20,437,282	32,712,065
Dentistry	11,164,641	4,049,322	15,213,963
Medicine	49,511,058	21,650,469	71,161,527
Nursing	10,023,067	2,001,602	12,024,669
Optometry	1,769,468	2,332,679	4,102,147
Business	5,683,168	14,709,356	20,392,524
Education	6,439,672	6,850,525	13,290,197
Engineering & Tech	6,001,841	2,487,166	8,489,007
Law	1,922,217	3,859,859	5,782,076
Music	8,524,020	7,313,664	15,837,684
Physical Education	2,532,524	5,094,906	7,627,430
Public Affairs	3,039,500	4,005,200	7,044,700
SUBTOTAL: ACADEMIC	$139,288,092	$124,271,204	$263,559,296
Libraries	14,523,092	201,731	14,724,823
Academic Computing	6,935,872	0	6,935,872
Academic Affairs	4,476,560	1,196,611	5,673,171
Student Services	9,607,660	1,073,662	10,681,322
Physical Facilities	28,371,769	37,700	28,409,469
Central Administratn	5,538,563	3,166,000	8,704,563
SUBTOTAL: SUPPORT	$ 69,453,516	$ 5,675,704	$ 75,129,220
TOTAL	$208,741,608	$129,946,908	$338,688,516

cost. As already indicated, total net cost can be determined by multiplying both sides of the equation by the inverse of the matrix of allocation coefficients, $[c]^{-1}$,

$$[c]^{-1} [K] = [c]^{-1} [c] [N]$$

The product of a matrix and its inverse becomes an identity matrix—essentially they cancel—so the equation becomes upon exchanging the left and right sides

$$[N] = [c]^{-1} [K]$$

To solve the equation for total net costs for all centers, our next step is to invert the matrix of allocation coefficients.

Inverting a matrix is easier said than done. We're dealing with a matrix of 20 rows and columns. Formerly, its inversion was a major undertaking. With electronic computing, the task is routine and can be done in an instant. The inverse of matrix of allocation coefficients appearing in Table A.2 is presented in Table A.3. A number of software programs are marketed to perform the necessary calculations. The results in Table A.3 were calculated on a micro-computer using Lotus 1-2-3.

At first glance, a comparison of Table A.2 and Table A.3 suggests that not very much has happened. The negative coefficients have become positive, because now we are solving for total net cost, which equals net direct cost plus allocated costs. Although many of allocation coefficients appear unchanged, the excitement is occurring in rounding levels beyond the fourth decimal place. They have been adjusted to reflect the fact that allocated cost is being calculated as a portion of net direct cost rather than as a portion of total net cost.

Total Net Cost and Total Cost

In the equation,

$$[N] = [c]^{-1}[K]$$

the inverted matrix $[c]^{-1}$ is presented in the columns and rows of numbers of Table A.3. Net direct costs, the vector $[K]$, appear in the right hand column of numbers in Table A.1. Multiplying the matrix by the vector produces total net costs for each center, the vector $[N]$, which is shown in the left hand column of Table A.4. That is our solution!

At least, it's the solution to our system of equations. Ultimately, we are interested in determining each center's total cost. That objective can be achieved by employing the equation

$$T_i = N_i + E_i$$

where T_i represents total cost, N_i, its total net cost, and E_i, its earned income. Each center's earned income appears as the second column in Table A.4. The sum of each center's total net cost and its general fund earned income is its total cost, which is presented in the third column. We have achieved our objective!

An Alternative Definition of Total Cost

While a center's total cost can be defined as its total net cost plus its earned income, an alternative definition is more informative. We began our discus-

TABLE A.5 TOTAL COST BY RESPONSIBILITY CENTER
FROM ALLOCATED AND DIRECT COSTS

| | | | *Allocated Costs* | |
| | | *Academic* | *Academic* | *Student* |
	Libraries	*Computing*	*Affairs*	*Services*
Arts and Humanities	$ 1,278,032	$ 430,024	$ 219,351	$ 1,345,072
Physical and Math Sci	2,222,033	2,011,403	644,625	1,835,063
Social & Behavrl Sci	2,759,387	1,019,573	487,945	2,219,370
Dentistry	130,708	131,782	259,640	67,254
Medicine	769,724	943,279	1,338,491	288,230
Nursing	639,016	166,461	174,586	269,014
Optometry	406,647	48,551	67,148	57,646
Business	1,902,525	638,100	308,883	1,277,819
Education	1,365,171	270,499	299,930	441,952
Engineering & Tech	580,924	603,421	102,961	499,598
Law	145,231	97,102	89,531	57,646
Music	1,278,032	187,269	219,351	489,991
Physical Education	580,924	145,653	129,820	470,775
Public Affairs	406,647	208,076	134,297	288,230
SUBTOTAL: ACADEMIC	$ 14,464,999	$ 6,901,193	$ 4,476,560	$ 9,607,660
Libraries	0	0	0	0
Academic Computing	0	0	0	0
Academic Affairs	58,092	6,936	0	0
Student Services	0	6,936	0	0
Physical Facilities	0	0	0	0
Central Administratn	0	20,808	0	0
SUBTOTAL: SUPPORT	$ 58,092	$ 34,679	$ 0	$ 0
TOTAL	$ 14,523,092	$ 6,935,872	$ 4,476,560	$ 9,607,660

sion, you will remember, by defining a responsibility center's total cost to be equal to its direct costs plus allocated indirect costs of the support centers which provide services to it. Our very first equation in this series was

$$T_i = D_i + \sum_{j=k}^{n} A_{ij}$$

where D_i is the direct costs of responsibility center i; and A_{ij}, the allocated cost of responsibility center j assigned to center i. Now that we have established values for the total net costs for all the responsibility centers—and for the support centers in particular—we can employ this more informative approach to determining each center's total cost.

	Physical Facilities		Central Administratn	Total Allocated Costs	General Fund Direct Expenditures		Total Cost
$	312,089	$	216,004	$ 3,800,573	$ 11,862,000	$	15,662,573
	4,113,907		531,702	11,358,732	22,860,000		34,218,732
	652,551		465,239	7,604,065	25,108,000		32,712,065
	1,787,421		238,158	2,614,963	12,599,000		15,213,963
	6,780,853		1,500,951	11,621,527	59,540,000		71,161,527
	907,897		171,695	2,328,669	9,696,000		12,024,669
	170,231		60,924	811,147	3,291,000		4,102,147
	425,577		304,621	4,857,524	15,535,000		20,392,524
	453,948		243,697	3,075,197	10,215,000		13,290,197
	794,410		99,694	2,681,007	5,808,000		8,489,007
	453,948		88,617	932,076	4,850,000		5,782,076
	1,106,499		221,543	3,502,684	12,335,000		15,837,684
	794,410		121,848	2,243,430	5,384,000		7,627,430
	198,602		121,848	1,357,700	5,687,000		7,044,700
$	18,952,342	$	4,386,542	$ 58,789,296	$ 204,770,000	$	263,559,296
	1,929,280		221,543	2,150,823	12,574,000		14,724,823
	283,718		22,154	305,872	6,630,000		6,935,872
	709,294		121,848	896,171	4,777,000		5,673,171
	5,447,380		360,007	5,814,322	4,867,000		10,681,322
	0		426,469	426,469	27,983,000		28,409,469
	1,049,755		0	1,070,563	7,634,000		8,704,563
$	9,419,427	$	1,152,021	$ 10,664,220	$ 64,465,000	$	75,129,220
$	28,371,769	$	5,538,563	$ 69,453,516	$ 269,235,000	$	338,688,516

As has already been indicated, A_{ij}, is equal to the product of the percentage of support center's j's cost allocated to center i multiplied by center j's allocable cost

$$A_{ij} = c_{ij} \cdot N_j$$

The percentages appear in Table 5.12. From Table 5.12, we can see that 8.8 percent of library costs is allocated to the School of Arts and Humanities. From Table A.4, we see that total net cost of the libraries is $14,523,092. The product of the two numbers produces $1,278,032, which is the value for $A_{1,15}$. Similarly, 6.2 percent of academic computing's total net cost of $6,935,872 is allocable to the School of Arts and Humanities; the product, 430,024, is the value for $A_{1,16}$. Continuing the process for Academic Affairs, Student Services, Physical Facilities, and Central Administration produces all the allocated costs for the School of Arts and Humanities.

The result of that process for the School of Arts and Humanities is shown in the first row of Table A.5. The sum of all of the allocated costs appears in the 7th column, $3,800,573. When added to its direct costs, $11,862,000—found in Table A.1—we arrive at the school's total costs, $15,662,573. Happily, the the figure is equal to the one appearing in Table A.4.

Employing the same process for the other centers produces their total costs. Each row of the table shows the components of each responsibility center's allocated costs as well as its direct expenditures. For support centers, a two-way table results. Each support center's column shows what it will receive from other centers; the sum of its column is equal to its total net cost.

Congratulations! You made it.

Afterword

The USC Experience with Revenue Center Management by John R. Curry

The plan was laid in September 1981. Reality set in on July 1, 1982: that's the day revenue center management (RCM)[*] went live at the University of Southern California (USC). Reality has continued to set in for the last eight years. How does it compare with the promise? That is the subject of this afterword.

Redundancy with earlier chapters notwithstanding, I shall repeat here the essential features of USC's approach to decentralized budgeting and planning:[1]

- The system defines the traditional colleges and schools of the university as academic revenue and cost centers. Revenues such as tuition, recovery of indirect costs, gifts and endowment income are allocated to each center; indirect costs such as operations and maintenance, library acquisitions, and general administration are allocated as well.

- The deans and faculties of the colleges and schools are vested with fiscal responsibility commensurate with their academic authority (over courses, curriculum, degree requirements, research thrusts, quality control). More specifically, they have the responsibility to develop feasible revenue and expenditure budgets for upcoming years and to manage the attendant budget *performance* to meet their bottom line targets for those years.

- Once annual budgets are established, schools which exceed their bottom line targets carry surpluses forward (with interest) to support future years' academic plans; conversely, budget deficits become internal loans whose repayments (with interest) are obligations of future years' budgets.

- The academic revenue centers are guaranteed 80 percent of their attributable revenues to cover direct program expenditures as well as full indirect costs. Thus 80 percent of incremental reserves are available to

---

[*] Responsibility center budgeting and revenue center management are different names for essentially the same approach.—ELW

1. John R. Curry, "Focused Decentralization: Planning at USC," *University of Southern California Financial Report*, 1985, p. 12.

enhance programs, while 80 percent of revenue decrements must be met with program scalebacks.

The remaining 20 percent of school-specific revenues (called *participation*) plus unrestricted investment income and gifts fund a central pool from which block grants—*subventions*—are allocated back to the schools as a function of university priorities and school-specific unit costs.

These primary characteristics derive from a set of management principles which evolved back in 1981, and have served since as diagnostics when things appeared to be going wrong. I list them here because they infuse subsequent assessments of what has worked and what has not:

P1   Responsibility should be commensurate with authority, and vice versa.

P2   Decentralization should be proportional to organizational size and complexity.

P3   Locally optimal decisions are not always globally optimal: central leverage is required to implement corporate (global) priorities.

P4   Outcome measures are preferable to process controls.

P5   Accountability is only as good as the tools which measure it.

P6   Quantitative measures of performance tend to drive out qualitative measures (a variant of Gresham's Law).

P7   Outcomes should matter: plans which work should lead to rewards, plans which fail should lead to sanctions.

P8   Resource-expanding incentives are preferable to resource-dividing ones.

P9   People play better games when they own the rules.

I shall illustrate these principles in action by addressing the questions most commonly asked (and pathologies discovered) about revenue center management, with examples drawn both from our experience at USC and from other universities experimenting with decentralization.

Q1. Does giving deans authority over and responsibility for revenues unleash academic entrepreneurship? Do resources expand?

Yes, if the dean is entrepreneurial! Several deans at USC have either built significant programs from modest beginnings (such as Urban and Regional Planning), or turned obsolescing programs around by redefining missions and tapping new markets (such as Pharmacy). Other deans have steadily developed strong programs and attendant revenue streams. A few deans, however, appear to have spent more time shopping for subvention (that money's already here, let's try to get a bigger share), or explaining why their programs deserve support in spite of declining revenues, than strategically positioning their programs for comparative advantage in the enrollment, research, or philanthropic markets. The former deans have an external perspective: they look outward to bring resources into the university. The latter have an inward orientation: they want more of what others have acquired.

In the early days of revenue center management, the inward entrepreneurs outnumbered the outward ones, and I sense that would be the state at many universities today. Over time, an inversion has occurred as new deans are recruited for their demonstrated, or at least potential, entrepreneurial prowess. Revenue incentives don't automatically beget resource expansion. But they unleash entrepreneurship among entrepreneurs. People, and the criteria for selecting them, matter. *Relevant principle:* P8.

Q2. Can (will) deans of colleges and schools within a university really take responsibility for budgeted revenues and expenditures?

Yes, if they take ownership of their revenues and expenditures. Let me illustrate with an example from another university. Let's call it AU.

AU had implemented a version of RCM and lived through the first budget developed accordingly. Several academic units delivered year-end deficits due to tuition revenue shortfalls. Their deans did not even try to reduce costs, let alone reduce them commensurate with the shortfalls, during the year. And the deans were refusing to pay back the deficits.

Asked to troubleshoot AU's new system, I interviewed the budget director at length. "Describe the process by which you and the deans developed last year's budget (the budget that failed)," I said. Listening to the blow-by-blow account, I suddenly heard, "and then in March we gave the deans their tuition incomes for the upcoming year." "But I thought the deans were to give you *their* tuition revenues according to RCM," I queried. "Oh no, we couldn't trust the deans with budgeting tuition," he came back.

I had the last word: "If you won't trust them to develop their own tuition revenues," I said, "then you can't expect them to respond to variances. If the revenue budget is yours, then so is the responsibility for the consequences." Participation and ownership are prerequisites to responsibility. After a one-year respite, centralized budgeting returned to AU. *Relevant principles:* P1, P9.

Here is another related example, one where revenues are implicitly owned but responsibility for delivering them is not. A couple of years ago, I was talking with the budget director of a centralized university in the east. He was lamenting a looming year-end deficit, the consequence of a tuition revenue shortfall. His explanation: the School of Engineering had decided, without telling him, to reduce from historical levels the number of students admitted to the school. He viewed this as perfectly normal faculty behavior. And he should have, since in his university, faculty have authority over enrollments, but the central administration has responsibility for balancing the budget! *Relevant principles:* P1, P3.

How responsible have deans been at USC? Let's look at the corrective measures of those schools, from a total of twenty, which generated revenue shortfalls during recent fiscal years. The following table compares the sum of revenue shortfalls from budget (that is, actual minus budgeted revenues) with bottom line deficits or surpluses—that is, total actual revenues *minus* total actual expenditures. Note that all *budgeted* bottom lines are zero.

CENTERS WITH REVENUE SHORTFALLS:
MEASURES OF MID-YEAR CORRECTIONS
(in $ millions)

	1985	1986	1987	1988	1989
(a) Sum of revenue shortfalls	(2.2)	(3.1)	(8.8)	(5.7)	(3.3)
(b) Sum of bottom-line variances	(1.3)	(0.5)	(2.5)	(0)	(0.6)
(c) % of revenue shortfall corrected*	41%	84%	72%	100%	82%

* $c = [(a-b)/a] \times 100\%$

When these bottom-line variances were added to those from revenue centers with positive revenue variances, the university delivered overall surpluses in each of the above five years. Worthy of note may be the fact that on average, eleven of the twenty academic centers experienced revenue shortfalls during this five-year period. This suggests rather aggressive revenue budgeting, but the table also suggests extraordinary flexibility in meeting revenue shortfalls with expenditure cutbacks. Now I can't argue that RCM is responsible for a string of five consecutive surpluses. Indeed, USC has never run a deficit. But I can contrast the style with which surpluses were achieved before and after 1982-83.

Before 1982-83, if a given budget unit had a revenue shortfall or expense overrun, the whole university had a problem. (Usually we didn't know which unit had a revenue shortfall since there were only a few school-specific revenue accounts.) Consequently, whole-university solutions were announced: hiring freezes—and hiring review committees; travel freezes—and travel review committees; equipment purchase freezes—and . . . We froze everyone and everything. Then only the most politically powerful or tear-jerking special pleaders benefited from the ultimate central dispensation: the dispensation to thaw.

Contrast this approach with what happened in 1989-90. USC experienced a $5.8 million unrestricted revenue shortfall among its twenty colleges and schools: the shortfalls summed to $7.4 million occurring in thirteen centers;

overrealized revenues ("longfalls") summed to $1.6 million in seven centers. Through local management intervention, seven of the first thirteen succeeded in producing small surpluses by year end; the other six delivered deficits vastly less than their revenue shortfalls; and the seven centers with revenue longfalls agreed not to spend their surpluses during the year (since they would get them back later with interest). The university delivered a $188,000 unrestricted surplus without a single all-points bulletin announcing a problem!

Very responsible indeed. But I should hasten to add that responsibility has increased over time as the credibility of rewards and sanctions has grown through consistent enforcement. And the enforcer is the provost. At USC, the provost has required that deficits be repaid and that withdrawals be scrupulously honored. Moreover, the fiscal (budgetary) performance record of each dean is part of his or her annual individual performance evaluation dossier used by the provost. The integrity of the Intercenter Bank, in which surpluses are deposited and through which loans to cover deficits are made at USC, has been established.

I can't resist going back to AU for a final example.[2] Remember those deans who didn't own their revenues and wouldn't repay their deficits? Well another of their decanal colleagues delivered a surplus. When he wanted to use part of it, he was told by the AU provost that he couldn't because the other deans wouldn't pay (the AU bank was not capitalized). Guess what he did when another surplus began to loom? Or, worse, when he began to generate a deficit during a subsequent fiscal year? *Relevant principles:* P5, P7.

Q3. What happens when a school consistently delivers year-end deficits? Or, are there academic equivalents of the savings and loans in 1990—and the Resolution Trust Corporation?

It depends! Sometimes a school simply finds itself in a down market or loses its market draw and there isn't much anyone can do about it. In the 1970s, USC's School of Library Science witnessed enrollment freefall. If RCM had been in place, consecutive deficits would surely have ensued. For even if upcoming years' budgeted revenues reflected the most recent shortfalls from budget, we would always have been behind: the downward revenue slope got steeper each year. When we fully grasped the condition of the school in the early 1980s, it was not clear that at private university tuition USC could regain its lost market, even with a revamped program. The school was closed in 1986.

We have seen other circumstances, however, when we were convinced that school leadership was at fault and that new leadership could effect a turnaround. It takes time to determine whether deans or the market environ-

---

2. *Note:* AU, introduced earlier, is a pseudonym and *not* the initials of the university in the examples.

ment—or both—are responsible for declining revenues and consequent deficits. We all know that when times are good, leaders take and get the credit for their organizations' successes. When times are bad, it is hard to tell whether a leader is worthy of continuing confidence.

The performance of one school at USC has been especially vexing. It has delivered deficits in seven of eight years since the advent of RCM, and has accumulated loans from the Intercenter Bank in excess of $2 million. Repaying the debt, required by policy to be 20 percent per year, has threatened the viability of the program. The dean says the school feels like the victim of a leveraged buyout laboring under a killer debt load. Should the debt be restructured, allowing for a longer payout period? Should the university, following the Resolution Trust Corporation's lead with respect to the savings and loan industry, pay off the school's liability (with taxpayers'—i.e., other schools'—money), and seek a reorganization plan? Does the school have assets it can sell to pay down the debt? Can a new dean be recruited if the debt is not forgiven?

Are these questions unseemly in the context of the academy? Or are we finally getting our management act together? We restructured the debt, paying half the interest with additional subvention for two years, and with the 1990-91 budget performance appear at least momentarily to have restabilized. *Relevant principle:* P7.

Q4. Do presidents and provosts have the courage to hold individual deans accountable for academic and fiscal outcome?

Some do and some don't. But only academic officers can. At USC, the president and provost have held deans accountable (recall the Intercenter Bank discussion earlier). At another university that flirted with RCM, the chief financial officer was appointed the enforcer, and the provost became the apologist for those deans who ran deficits. Since deans don't report to CFOs, it's not hard to infer the fate of the incentive system in this example. Performance driven systems are not for the fainthearted.

Successful maintenance of RCM requires extraordinary cooperation between provost and CFO. I have just noted that the provost ensures integrity of the incentive system by rewarding positive performances and sanctioning negative ones. The CFO/comptroller *monitors* performance, and coordinates projections of year-end with center-specific financial personnel. The CFO/comptroller then reports potential problem performances to the provost who, if necessary, can intervene to reinforce the need for corrective action and the consequences of delivering an unacceptable deficit. Such a sequence of events repeats monthly at USC, starting in October and ending in June. (The fiscal year is July 1 through June 30.) Budgeting, comptrolling, and financial reporting are so coordinated that the sum of positive and negative performances across all centers (revenue and service) equals the change in the current unrestricted fund balance at year end.

Successful RCM obviates the oft-heard lament of university comptrollers that the faculty and deans just spend money and that only the comptrollers' efforts to stop them (by delaying purchases, invoking freezes of some kind after scaring the president with a large potential deficit) prevent ultimate insolvency. But then these comptrollers live in worlds where authority and responsibility coexist out of wedlock. *Relevant principles:* P1, P4, P7.

Q5. Will a president or provost cede authority to the deans sufficient for them to run their schools?
Some will and some won't. When our provost, Cornelius Pings, met with the chancellor and deans of the Indianapolis campus of Indiana University as they were about to adopt RCM, he opened his remarks by saying, "I predict your experiment will fail. The chancellor will not be willing to give up his authority to micromanage the schools' budgets. The deans will not accept responsibility to keep them in balance." This warning was not entirely facetious.

For RCM to be in equilibrium, chief academic officers have to change style: from managing the detailed inputs to budgets of the schools (individual faculty appointments, new staff appointments, levels of cost rise on materials and supplies, . . .) to setting *academic* performance expectations within reasonable resource constraints, and then holding deans accountable for academic and fiscal outcomes.

Let me give an example of an input-controlling provost, again drawn from AU. Recall that AU implemented a version of RCM. In troubleshooting what went wrong, I spied a two-page single-spaced list on AU's budget director's desk. It was called something like "unreconciled requests." Items on the list were:

- one FTE assistant professor position, Department of English
- one-half FTE administrative assistant, deans office in Engineering
- six PCs with CAD software, School of Architecture
- laboratory renovation funds, Department of Physics,
- etc.

These were unfunded items in the budget that failed. But, the budget director averred, if revenues exceeded budget, the provost would decide mid year whether to fund some of these requests.

Here's how budgets were being built at AU: deans requested incremental expenditure authority from the provost by listing line items like those which wound up unfunded on the above "unreconciled requests" list; the deans were *handed* their revenues and indirect expenses by AU's financial officer, and some (or none) of their requested direct expenditure additions by the provost; subvention was added to balance the schools' budgets. The central administration had managed *all* the inputs at the detail level. How could the central administration, therefore, expect to hold deans accountable for *any* outcomes? *Relevant principles:* P1, P2, P4, P9.

Q6. Do fiscal tails wag academic dogs when the fiscal stakes are clear and performance accurately measured? What's required to make the dog wag the tail?

Revenue center management has a name: it's *the system*. When people want to blame the system, they'll often blame RCM and claim that the financial folks are in charge. If they perceive themselves or their programs as underfunded, or as low priorities within their schools, they will rarely blame their deans (or themselves), they'll blame the system. They will even allege that budgets are influencing academic decisions!

Well, my answer to that last allegation is, "You bet they are, and they should!" But in the following sense: academic decisions have financial consequences, and one needs to understand them in advance. Understanding them, in turn, often alters the decision: the cost of a contemplated decision forces consideration of opportunity costs when resources are limited. And that's the beginning of determining academic priorities: which is to say, budgetary winners and losers.

Talk, indeed ferment, about academic priorities—mission, uniqueness, distinction, comparative advantage, strategic excellence—will put RCM in its place: as a means to an end, not an end in itself. For then, budget trade-offs serve to implement the highest academic priorities; and budget performance (the over- or under-realization of revenues) may signal the need for a revised *academic* plan. Hence, RCM serves the faculty, the deans, and the provost and president as an implementation instrument as well as an outcome measure. But precisely because RCM has a name, is clearly defined, and has strong accountability measures, it demands strong academic leadership lest "the system" appear to overshadow the true character and mission of the university. RCM and its incentives are fun and easy to talk about. They will consume all the conversation time available if the academic agenda is empty.

I should also emphasize that measures of academic performance are required to keep issues of fiscal performance in perspective. A few years ago, one of our deans negotiated a five-year academic plan with the provost. The dean would reduce undergraduate enrollments, increase enrollments in the Ph.D. program, and replace part-time faculty with tenure track faculty; the provost would increase subvention each year to replace the lost undergraduate revenues and recognize the increased costs of enriching the full-time/part-time faculty mix. That was the plan.

During this five-year period, the school delivered surplus bottom lines every year: fiscally the school looked fine. But, undergraduate enrollment *increased*, Ph.D. enrollment *declined*, and the ratio of tenure-track to total faculty *decreased*! No wonder bottom lines were positive! But the dean failed by academic accountability measures, and the subvention growth supplied by the provost would have generated better academic returns elsewhere. The academic opportunity costs were high.

When the dean was questioned about his performance, he pointed to the bottom line, asking what else the provost wanted. This dean had let one quantitative measure drive out the relevant qualitative measures; he let the tail wag the dog. *Relevant principles:* P4, P5, P6, P7.

Q7. Can deans of schools with undergraduate programs be responsible for tuition revenues when a central admissions office has authority over recruiting the freshmen and transfer classes?

One of the little-heralded consequences of allocating indirect costs, such as the costs of operating an admissions office, is the increased pressure on administrative units (whose budgets constitute the indirect costs) to perform. Not only are they expected to perform to the expectations of their bosses (president, provost, CFO . . .), they are also expected to perform for the clients/customers who (indirectly) pay the bills: the deans of the colleges and schools. The deans want to know what they're getting for their money.

In the case of admissions at USC, this question has led deans to work closely with the admissions office to specify the number of entering majors each school needs or would like. When these "local" expectations are summed, however, the total is over 3,500, about 500 to 700 more than the infrastructure of housing, dining, student services, and freshmen writing sections can accommodate. Moreover, in the increasingly competitive marketplace for freshmen in the 1990s, especially among the large private universities, it is not clear that with constant academic standards the university could deliver such a large class. Again, the sum of locally optimal decisions appears globally suboptimal. But when our deans learn of the indirect costs (including the necessary diversion of capital) which attend their ambitions, they are able to recognize that there is no free lunch, and rarely free marginal revenue.

At USC, our provost and I have worked with the deans of the schools and the dean of admissions to reach appropriate goals for the incoming class, numbers which are both desirable and feasible. Sometimes it is not feasible, however, given applicant interests, to achieve the desired *distribution* among majors.

Over time our deans have assumed some of the authority for recruitment by hiring specialized admissions counselors of their own to complement the central admissions staff. This reveals an inherent characteristic of RCM: if deans have responsibility for tuition revenues, they will tend to assume as much authority as they can get to deliver the class. Redundancy of administrative roles—and too many administrators—will result unless the central office is managed to meet the deans' enrollment plans.

The occasional dissonance at USC between authority over recruitment and responsibility for tuition revenues has been obviated at one pioneer of RCM, the University of Pennsylvania. There, the applicant pool is deep enough and enrollment stable enough that the central administration predicts overall undergraduate enrollment for the upcoming year; each school's share of expected tuition revenues is calculated as a ten-year average of annual shares weighted toward the most recent year's experience. Then budgeted undergraduate tuition revenues are *guaranteed:* for purposes of determining bottom-line performance, actual tuition revenues are set equal to budgeted revenues for each school. Hence, a time lag and a smoothing rule are introduced into revenue budgeting. Also, authority and responsibility are both assumed centrally for undergraduate tuition revenues.

At USC, undergraduate tuition revenues have remained "live," and our deans have done a remarkable job of responsibly responding to periodic shortfalls due either to unpredicted course-taking patterns (enrollment redistribution) or fewer than expected entering students. But the feedback to our admissions office during such occasions has been powerful, and the role of our dean of admissions in working with the deans of the schools is very demanding. *Relevant principles:* P1, P3, P6.

Let's turn to the more general question:

Q8. What is the interaction between schools and administrative units when the schools pay indirect costs?

RCM is a strong accountability system. If revenue centers are to be held accountable for academic and fiscal performance, then administrative (or service) centers have to be held accountable for delivering the requisite services at an acceptable price. Our council of deans has a costs and services committee which works from time to time with heads of service centers to understand the nature and costs of their activities better, and to reach informed recommendations with respect to their "price-worthiness." Directors of administrative centers benefit from the necessity of justifying costs and quality to new audiences.

Deans of schools are not the only receivers of services, however, and their perspectives on service are very school-specific. There are other clients/customers with different perspectives: faculty, students and staff. The central administration needs to worry about them, too.

Consider the library, for instance. Deans may not recommend or appear readily willing to pay for (through their indirect cost allocations) any initiatives in the library. Deans are rewarded by their faculty mostly for competitive compensation, opportunities to hire new colleagues, quality facilities, PCs on every desk and the like. If the library is not serving the faculty (or the students), they'll blame the library, not their deans.

Consequently, special and central attention to the needs and quality of service of the library is required in a decentralized system. One can make similar observations about other administrative services, such as academic computing. Central administration has to have a very compelling case, however, for funding central services at levels which deans experience as crowding out their opportunities for academic program development. The debates can be exhilarating.

One final note on life under RCM in administrative centers.

Our associate vice president for student affairs, who is responsible for budgeting a revenue center (the student health center) and a large service center (student affairs), has pointed out an apparent double standard in RCM. Because deans constantly press us to keep indirect costs down, we annually urge our administrative units to improve service, while sustaining as much as 3 percent real decreases in expenditures. It's the Bauhaus challenge: do more with less. We challenge our managers to manage! However, as long as the market will bear annual increases in the student health fee, and the health center balances its budget (direct revenues equal total expense), we rarely subject this center to the Bauhaus challenge. No fair, says our student affairs colleague. Ability to produce revenues may seem to be *prima facie* evidence of efficient management. But it is far from conclusive proof.

And she is right. The Bauhaus challenge is a prod to achieve productivity gains. And we should think about applying it everywhere, even in academic units. It's the only way we will constrain tuition price increases and achieve quality gains at the same time, assuming constant enrollment. *Relevant principles:* P1, P2, P6.

Q9. Are major diseconomies of scale inherent in decentralization? If so, what are the antidotes?

In answering question Q7, I gave an example of how RCM can cause administrative growth (additional admissions counselors) in the schools. Analogs can be found with respect to other administrative services as well. Development (fundraising) is an example. There is a natural tendency for such growth as deans attempt to gain increasing authority over those activities for which they feel accountable, such as financial performance. Central administration needs to monitor such local administrative growth with periodic body counts and evaluate the reasons.

Such growth may be appropriate given needs for specificity of service (which is inverse to economies of scale) within a school. Such growth may also be a leading indicator of inadequate or deteriorating service from a central administrative unit. If the latter is the case, then improving the central service, either through adding resources or replacing management, is the antidote. And then the "local" staff growth should be undone, so that a new service equilibrium is established. I should mention that undoing "local" staff growth is not easy. Deans remember why they created the positions, and they often value staff as much as faculty. And unless you can produce compelling proof that the central service is now up to snuff, you'll look like a micromanager. However, under RCM, deans who give up redundant staff retain the compensation budgets (and the office space!) to reallocate.

There are other possible diseconomies. When the basic unit of organization is the traditional college or school under RCM, then some units may be so small that having the required financial management staff may make them top heavy, requiring more revenues than they can generate to be solvent. They may try to get by on the cheap by hiring clerks to do serious financial management, and that tends to make matters worse. We are experimenting currently at USC with sharing our quality financial managers. We now have one top-notch senior business officer (SBO is our language at USC) serving two schools, thus cutting the compensation costs of both while providing them with more talent than they could afford individually. We'll have to see how this works out.

What is the "right" size for a revenue center? A couple of years ago, I was asked this question by a faculty member of USC's Budget Advisory Committee. I cited the example above of a center too small to carry out its implied responsibilities. Satisfied that I had addressed his question, I was about to go to another topic when he stopped me. "Oh no, you've missed the point," he said. "I'd kill to belong to a small revenue center so I could be part of the action."

Here was a faculty member—among our most distinguished—from a very large revenue center which had not moved responsibility and authority beyond the dean's office. He, and it turns out many of his colleagues, felt uninformed, disenfranchised, not to mention disaffected. Faculty governance and RCM rang dissonant to them.

There may have been economies of scale in this centralized revenue center, but if one believes that decision quality is inversely proportional to "organizational distance" from the point of implementation, those economies may have been negated by poor decisions. *Relevant principles:* P1, P2, P3, P9.

Q10. When the dollar and the square foot are fungible, does more efficient space utilization result?

An interesting measure of space utilization is average number of offices per tenure-track faculty member. I have heard of one university where that number is 4.2. We're getting the number down almost to 1 at USC.

The answer to this question (Q10) is *yes.* Let me give some examples. A few years ago our Gerontology School experienced a period of decline in federally sponsored research and was struggling to balance its budgets within the subvention allocation from the provost: research revenues, including indirect cost recovery, were declining; subvention was constant; indirect costs were increasing slightly; hence a squeeze play on the direct expenditure budget of the program. The school had laid off personnel totally supported by research sponsors, and thus had office and laboratory space available. The dean realized that the squeeze could be eased if another school could use the space. He put it on the market. It so happened that Engineering, just next door, was experiencing a surge in research and needed offices and labs. The two deans struck a deal, with Gerontology leasing the space to Engineering until Engineering could raise the money needed for a new building. Engineering has since moved into new quarters and Gerontology, in another growth period, has moved back into its old digs.

There are potential pathologies, however. One dean became so enthralled with renting "his" space that he allocated increasing portions of his and his staff's time to negotiating lease agreements. I came across one of these and was astounded: there were words like "lessee," "leasor," "thereunto pertaining." There were penalties for premature evacuation. Our legal office was even involved. In the meantime, the dean was neglecting the primary *academic* business of the school; consequently revenues were in jeopardy.

This was a classic case of resource dividing (rather than resource expanding) run amuck. The dean's successor is getting on with the primary mission of the school. Moral: We have to monitor the effects of the incentives we create. *Relevant principles:* P3, P5, P6, P8.

Q11. When full income and cost data are public within a university, do civil wars break out between apparent "subsidizors" and "subsidizees"?

Information is power. Some people interpret this as, "I have it, you don't, so I have power over you." Others see the world differently: "We share the information, and that enables us to reach deeper understandings and make better decisions." An example will illuminate this distinction.

In the 1970s, the USC financial administration did an annual profit and loss statement for colleges and schools. After the fiscal year closed, an elaborate study was conducted to attribute all revenues and all costs (indirects, too) to the colleges, schools, and auxiliaries. Then the differences between revenues and expenses were observed. These P & L statements were held in the most extreme confidence. Deans were dimly aware of their existence, yet all proclaimed that they were subsidizing everyone else—disaffected altruists to a person! Every so often, however, a dean who got out of hand in high places learned, to his chagrin, of his lowly status as a subsidizee.

In the late 1970s, we learned that these P & L statements could be enlightening and motivating when shared and explored with some of our deans. We did so with the School of Dentistry, and when we did, RCM had a trial run at USC. The school finally understood that it was generating $1 million less in revenue than it needed to cover costs, and that the administration could no longer tolerate the subsidy. The accounting and incentives of RCM were put in place and a new dean recruited to improve revenues. He did, and the success was so resounding that it contributed to our total changeover in 1981.

Why is all this relevant to the question at hand, Q11? Well, when we mocked up all schools' and auxiliaries' budgets in RCM format, we decided to share the information broadly—for example with the university-wide budget advisory committee and with all our deans and directors. And the questions and proclamations began to fly. A couple of examples will illustrate that reality can be as edifying as lore is brutal.

In 1982-83, the unrestricted budgets of the Schools of Business and Performing Arts looked approximately like this:

Illustration of Revenue Redistribution among Schools
(in $ millions)

	Business	*Performing Arts*
Direct Revenue	25.0	11.0
Participation	(5.0)	(2.2)
Subvention	2.0	5.2
TOTAL INCOME	22.0	14.0
Direct Expense	15.0	9.5
Indirect Expense	7.0	4.5
TOTAL EXPENSE	22.0	14.0

When the dean of Business saw his profile, he said, with triumph and disdain, "I told you this university was riding on the back of the business school." (Note that in our version of RCM, the difference between the participation tax and subvention is a measure of who might be subsidizing whom.) Now, the dean of Performing Arts, who had calculated his tuition revenues on the backs of envelopes for years and knew that his direct revenues exceeded his direct expenses—hence his prior claim to altruism—was momentarily taken aback by the facts. But he recovered quickly, pronouncing that the uniqueness and quality of his program surely warranted more subvention than he was receiving. After the posturing died down, the real questions could be dealt with: Is it reasonable or understandable that there should be internal transfers like those between Business and Performing Arts?

In the example at hand, we came to understand that the transfers were more in the nature of things than a consequence of perverse priorities of the past. The cost of educating a music major is extravagant, especially in a conservatory-like program. The dominant mode of instruction is one-on-one: a master pianist and pupil on the same bench. Business is a higher paradigm course of study: accounting and finance can be taught well to classes of twenty-five to fifty. Yet, we charge both music and education students the same tuition. Common price, but most uncommon "unit" costs!

Should we charge differential tuition? No, we decided. We wanted students to be able to shop around among the schools to determine their undergraduate majors without price considerations at every turn.

By revealing information, we learned something: the relative costs of education among our schools, and a rationale for common tuition prices among our undergraduate schools. Other contexts might lead to different understandings, but all understandings are preferable to lore. Understandings bond. Lore divides, feeding paranoia, breeding feelings of oppression, and leading to misrepresentations—and sometimes misanthropy.

Let's look at another example, where understanding led to closing a program. Our College of Continuing Education had a revenue center profile almost identical to that of Performing Arts above. We asked whether the $3 million subsidy was understandable and warranted. It was quickly understandable: our tuition for extension courses had to be equal to or less than that of a public cross-town rival to generate enrollments. But the public rival's prices were heavily subsidized by state taxpayers. Our market could not bear higher prices.

Was the subsidy warranted? This led to antecedent questions: What was the priority of continuing education at USC? It was lower than all the traditional degree-granting programs. Was there a community service obligation? No, not necessarily, especially when the public institutions in town were providing that service anyway. What were the opportunity costs of this investment in a continuing education college? A reduced ability to invest in the College of Letters, Arts, and Sciences for one. The expense of constructing buildings for expanding high priority programs for another. What would happen to the best of our professional executive programs if the school closed? They were already being managed primarily by the deans' staffs in Business, Law, Engineering, and Medicine anyway, and could continue under their aegis.

The decision: ask the professional schools to assume full responsibility for the programs they deem beneficial, and close the College of Continuing Education. Knowing what programs cost leads to knowing their opportunity costs leads to priorities and strategic reallocations.

Public knowledge of inter-school transfers and central priorities often invites simple-minded interpretations. But those interpretations were there in the form of lore before RCM, and were even more simple-minded. With information, those interpretations can be countered and the debates can lead to deeper understandings. And sometimes those simple-minded interpretations turn out to be legitimate, and to lead to gradual changes in subvention priorities. Is it a surprise that information facilitates learning in an academic institution?

One final note on this subject. Subventions implicitly reveal over time the president's and provost's academic priorities. The faculty, the deans, and the students will ask for revelation, clarification, and justification of these priorities if they don't know them in advance. RCM works best when priorities have been worked through appropriate advisory groups and stakeholders, then made explicit, and consequently lead budget development, rather than being inferred from budget outcomes.

While appearing to be a decentralized system, RCM requires strong academic leadership from presidents and provosts. The budgetary black box is turned inside out under RCM, and everything is up for *explicit* consideration. An open information system is not for the duplicitous.

Q12. Do clearer fiscal boundaries around schools reinforce the "Balkanization of the disciplines"? Or, what is the fate of multidisciplinary or cooperative ventures among schools under RCM?

Multidisciplinary programs require unnatural acts. Students of higher education know of the long-standing and chronic lament over the paucity of multidisciplinary courses, or courses-of-study. In the old days, the disciplines were to blame—and for understandable reasons.[3] At USC, RCM is to blame.

---

3. See for example Lewis B. Mayhew and Patrick J. Ford, *Changing the Curriculum* (London: Jossey-Bass, Inc., 1971), pp. 106–107.

Remember? It's *the system*. If people are looking for another reason not to do multidisciplinary programs, RCM gives them one.

My office has made a standing offer to help anyone do the necessary revenue and expense accounting attending prospective joint ventures. No one has taken us up on that offer. We are considering taking out a one-page ad each semester in the *Daily Trojan*, our student newspaper.

Some enlightened deans have negotiated interschool arrangements on their own that work quite well. In addition, strong central leadership can initiate multidisciplinary programs. At USC, we launched a multidisciplinary program in neurosciences, recruiting faculty into several schools (some with joint appointments) and raising money for a new laboratory and office facility. It can be done. But it is a common view among our faculty that RCM stands in the way. Perceptions are as powerful as facts, and we need to develop and advertise better incentives for good multidisciplinary program development. One might, for example, earmark $100,000 of subvention to be awarded to those schools which propose the best joint initiatives.

Another common view, unsubstantiated by the facts, is that RCM leads to duplication of service courses (calculus in every corner) and, worse, to generation of "gut" courses to attract revenues. In my experience, both phenomena predate decentralization, and tendencies toward both exist in any system which bases resource allocations on credit hours generated or teaching loads—which is to say, most universities! The antidote is quality control: for example, curricula review committees which assess academic quality and can certify or decertify service or general education courses.

We have used revenue incentives at USC, however, to encourage our professional schools to participate in the general education program for undergraduates—to share the faculty wealth more broadly. Letters, Arts, and Sciences students, for example, can fulfill parts of their general education requirements with courses offered by faculty members in Law, Cinema, Urban and Regional Planning, Architecture, Music, Fine Arts, and Accounting. That's the upside of revenue incentives, even those which lead to some internal redistribution of tuition revenues. *Relevant principles:* P3, P6, P8.

Q13. Other than a common accounting (or heating) system, what integrates a decentralized university into *one* university?
Clark Kerr attributes the description of a modern university as a "series of separate schools and departments held together by a central heating system" to John Maynard Hutchins. Kerr goes on to say, "In an area where heating is less important and the automobile more, I have sometimes thought of [the modern university] as a series of individual faculty entrepreneurs held to-

gether by a common grievance over parking."[4] At USC, at least, a further contribution to integration is: the common need for subvention (and the chronic lament over its insufficiency).

Decentralization can contribute to increased parochialism within the schools. One can promote a more global perspective by making subvention growth proportional to the contribution of a school's academic plan to implementation of university-wide goals. Thus the competition for subvention can be waged, in part, over which schools most advance the university's cause rather than just their own. To make this work, the participation rate needs to be high enough that every school needs some of its "tax" back as subvention.

Warning: incentive systems cannot supplant the kinds of vision and leadership that also integrate a collection of schools and disciplines into *one* coherent (if not cohesive) institution. They can only supplement. *Relevant principle:* P3.

Q14. How do the president and provost implement corporate goals when revenues are allocated to the schools? And when deans are expected to be local entrepreneurs.

Through multiyear subvention commitments.

In a decentralized university, planning proceeds on two fronts simultaneously: locally, from a school-specific perspective; and globally, from a university-wide perspective. The sum of local perspectives does not always equal the global one! Nor should it. The trick is to keep the system loosely coupled enough to sustain faculty and decanal entrepreneurship and survive in a complex world, yet tightly coupled enough to create a sense of the whole, a sense of bonding commonality, of one university. Corporate priorities don't necessarily conflict with school-specific ones, they just don't arise out of any one school's academic plan. Sometimes they are inferred from the intimations or suggestions of several plans taken together, or they may be centrally promulgated by president or provost. Implementation of university-wide goals may take the form of:

- reallocation of subventions among schools;
- funding multidisciplinary programs directly through subvention, or combinations of earmarked subventions in the schools; and
- increasing administrative (indirect) costs to fund central initiatives (say, in the library or in the student financial aid budget), thereby claiming additional amounts of school-specific direct revenues and subventions.

Whatever the central priorities are, whatever the "financial form" of their

---

4. Clark Kerr, *The Uses of the University with a Postscript—1972* (Cambridge, Mass.: Harvard University Press, 1972), p. 20.

implementation, they are the better for extensive consultation with the deans of the schools and appropriate representative committees of the university.

A priority at USC during the last several years, for example, has been development of key disciplines in the College of Letters, Arts, and Sciences (LAS). That continuing priority has been funded, in part, through reallocation of subvention from the health sciences schools to LAS. Some years ago, the health sciences at USC required $5 million more in subvention than they contributed in participation; LAS was approximately the reverse. Through rapid growth in sponsored research and faculty practice, the health sciences replaced $5 million in subvention with $5 million (and more!) in direct revenues. LAS saw a commensurate change in their relative subvention status.

I should inject an important note about planning here. Changes in academic programs require long lead times because the recruitment of quality faculty is time-intensive and the inevitable remodeling of laboratory and office space is time- and dollar-intensive. Consequently, subvention commitments, to matter, need to be made for several years at a time. We use a five-year cycle at USC.

Deans need to know these commitments, as well, to develop their school-specific plans. Indeed, since five-year budget plans are required to be balanced to feasible revenue projections, deans could not do good planning if a key revenue component (*viz.*, subvention) were missing! Recall that planners rarely strategize or prioritize if they imagine that resources are unlimited.

A final observation about the value of multiyear subvention commitments. Deans often suspect that if they generate a surplus, the provost or president (but certainly not the budget director) will infer that their schools don't need as much subvention. Hence, the system is perverse: the better you do on your own, the more you stay even. It's sort of a Newton's Law applied to budgeting: for every overrealized dollar of direct revenues (action), there is an equal and opposite reduction of subvention (reaction). (I should note that one sometimes suspects that some deans hope that a symmetric version of this law will apply: that deficits become proofs of the need for more subvention!) Multiyear subvention commitments obviate this potential problem; they decouple performance from priorities and keep performance incentives credible. *Relevant principles:* P3, P7.

Q15. Can administrative information systems support the accountability RCM demands of individual budget units?

They can. USC's systems do, as do systems at several other universities. The systems need to be designed with local responsibility in mind, however. A few guides to the "right" systems are useful. The systems should:

1. be on-line and instantly responsive to account-status queries;
2. be centrally developed and maintained, and be "owned" by the users (those who are held accountable for their units' fiscal performances) in the sense that they helped design the systems and continually participate in improvements;
3. produce regular (monthly) projections of year-end performance for each center;
4. provide for easy download of management information to facilitate unique unit-specific analyses and reports;
5. be easily adapted to changes—RCM is a dynamic, evolving system;
6. be the database of record: the only accounting data by which every revenue and administrative center's fiscal performance is measured.

People cannot be held accountable for fiscal performance if they don't have the tools to help them detect variances from budget early, and if the data by which their fiscal management is judged lack integrity. *Relevant principles:* P1, P4, P5, P9.

I shall close with two observations, the first about maintenance of decentralized management systems—that is, more on the care and feeding of the monster. Once decentralization is established, there will be constant pressure to recentralize, either to bring more decision making to the center of the organization or to increase the degree of regulation of the individual budget units. The pressure will come from faculty, staff, or students who believe their agendas have a better chance with the president than with the deans of their schools. The pressure will come from those who detect genuine abuses of local authority—apparently unchecked by responsibility to university accountability standards. The pressure will come from statists who believe that individual (or school-specific) entrepreneurship will allow the rich to get richer at the expense of the poor. The pressure will come from some central administrators who resent local empowerment. All arguments need to be aired; many may be valid; and a few should lead to either improved accountability or additional regulations. On the other hand, most centralized systems I know are now tending toward decentralization, with proponents for change arguing that there are no incentives to perform when one is not rewarded for generating incremental revenues, or achieving expense reductions.

When a system like RCM is explicit, it is easily attacked. It is equally easily defended. And arguments about what's really so can lead to continuous and successful adaptations toward a more stable central/local equilibrium. One is always managing the equilibrium, however. Too much regulation kills entrepreneurship and endangers the enterprise: large research universities are too complex to be run like monoliths. Anyway, monoliths rarely survive changing environments. Too little quality control or accountability can sometimes lead to programs developed to deliver the quick buck. These do not endure and tarnish academic reputations.

Which leads to my second observation, this one directed at the current environment in the higher education industry. Private universities are facing increasing price sensitivity, and are no longer able to fund enhancements of programs through extra points on the tuition rate increase. Moreover, their financial aid budgets are consuming increasing fractions of tuition revenues. Public colleges and universities are feeling similar pressures as state budget deficits, fueled by recession, lead to reduced appropriations for higher education. Some observers, for example William F. Massy and Robert Zemsky,[5] believe the transition from the eighties to the nineties brought a sea-change in higher education which will require new directions and new riggings. They argue that quality gains will have to come through reallocation from low- to new-priority activities; that growth will occur through substitution rather than addition; and that client/customer service will emerge as a management issue.

Most presidents, provosts, and CFOs understand the revenue constraints clamping down on their universities. Yet fundamental and enduring change will occur, if it does, through faculty action, not through top-down edicts. There is a conundrum here: the changes that may be necessary and the language characterizing them—productivity, reallocation, client/customer service—are staples of for-profit corporations whose management structure and style seem virtually antithetical to the character and traditions of faculty governance. Can a new management culture be imposed upon or cultivated within universities?

I believe that RCM can (does) aid and abet change, but not through imposition so much as through enhanced awareness. The reality or credibility of constraints is inversely proportional to the actor's distance from them. Deans who do not know their schools' revenues will not "own" the budgetary consequences of a university revenue decline. They may not even believe the decline is real, but even if they do, the likely response is to blame the provost or president for the expenditure squeeze, hunker down around across-the-board cuts, and hope for a better day or more enlightened university leaders. Faculty members uninformed by their deans about their schools' revenue constraints will have similar responses.

But when the revenues belong to the dean and are shared with members of

5. See for example, William F. Massy, "Gaining Productivity," (*Policy Perspectives*, The Higher Education Research Program sponsored by the Pew Charitable Trusts, September 1989) p. 4. Other issues of *Policy Perspectives* are germane, as well.

the faculty, they become more real: the revenues have the school's name on them; they are monitored monthly by the school to manage performance; they are forecast annually by the school to develop upcoming budgets; they and their vagaries are in the language. There is no one to blame if they decline. Hoping for a better day is replaced by getting on with making a better day.

Reality and ownership of resource constraints (revenues in our language) are surely prerequisites to grappling fundamentally with quality enhancement through productivity gains or reallocation. We might expect that departments and schools, under such *real* constraints, would begin doing serious strategic planning, working toward comparative advantage or academic complementarity rather than imitation via-à-vis their competitors.

RCM has one other productivity enhancing feature: it substitutes outcome measures for process controls wherever possible. And with respect to one of the USC Trustees' most stringent rules—budgets will be balanced and so will performance—we have proved that outcome measures work. Along the way we have eliminated sixty-five FTE positions whose primary functions were to stop the paper flow and second guess our deans' intended expenditures.

RCM is not for every university and not for every taste. There may be several systems consistent with principles P1 through P9. When a system is not, however, one can change the current system toward greater consistency, reject one or more of these principles with reason, or develop other (better) principles and create new management worlds accordingly.

Whatever budget and management systems we administrators attempt to develop, however, we should always remember: the faculty are our entrepreneurs. They do the research and write the proposals for external funding. They teach the courses and develop the curricula. Ultimately their work and personal quality attract students, colleagues, research support, and philanthropic donations. They must be involved.

References

Association of Research Libraries. *Association of Research Libraries Statistics, 1987–88: A Compilation of Statistics from the 119 Members of the ARL.* Washington, D.C.: ARL, 1989.

Gilbert Fuchsberg. "Several Big Universities Give Fiscal Autonomy to Divisions, but the System Has Its Risks, as John Hopkins Case Shows." *Chronicle of Higher Education* (January 25, 1989), pp. A25-A27.

G. Hadley. *Linear Algebra.* Reading, Massachusetts: Addison-Wesley Publishing Company, Inc., 1961.

HEP. 1990 Higher Education Directory. Constance Healey Torregrosa, editor. Falls Church, Virginia: Higher Education Publications, Inc., 1990.

Robert V. Iosue. "How Colleges Can Cut Costs." *Wall Street Journal* (January 27, 1987), p. 34.

Charles T. Horngren. *Cost Accounting: A Managerial Emphasis.* 5th edition. Englewood Cliffs, New Jersey: Prentice Hall, Inc., 1982,pp. 475–489.

Elisabeth Kubler-Ross. *Coping with Death and Dying* (sound recording). New York: Psychology Today, 1973.

National Association of College and University Business Officers. *College and University Business Administration.* 4th edition. 1982.

National Center for Education Management Systems. *Program Classification Structure.* 1st edition. Technical Report 27. Boulder, Colorado: 1972.

Thomas Short. "Higher Education?" (review of *ProfScam: Professors and the Demise of Higher Education*). *Commentary* 88:1 (July 1989), pp. 68–70.

Charles J. Sykes. *ProfScam: Professors and the Demise of Higher Education.* Washington, D.C.: Regnery Gateway, 1988.

Thucydides. *The History of the Peloponnesian War.* Translated by Thomas Hobbes. Edited by Richard Schlatter. New Brunswick, New Jersey: Rutgers University Press, 1975.

U.S. Department of Education, Office of Educational Research and Improvement, National Center for Education Statistics. *Digest of Education Statistics, 1987.* Thomas D. Snyder, project director. Washington, D.C.: U.S. Government Printing Office, 1988.

University of Southern California. *Financial Report,* 1982, pp. 7–23.

University of Southern California. *Financial Report,* 1984, pp. 12–34.

University of Southern California. *Financial Report,* 1985, pp. 10–20.

Index

EDWARD L. WHALEN is an economist who has spent most of his career in university administration. Until 1990, he was Assistant Vice President, University Director of Budgeting, and Associate Professor of Economics at Indiana University. He is currently Vice Chancellor for Administration and Finance at the University of Houston System.